2019 ICW Cruising Guide By Bob423 Charts Updated March 2020

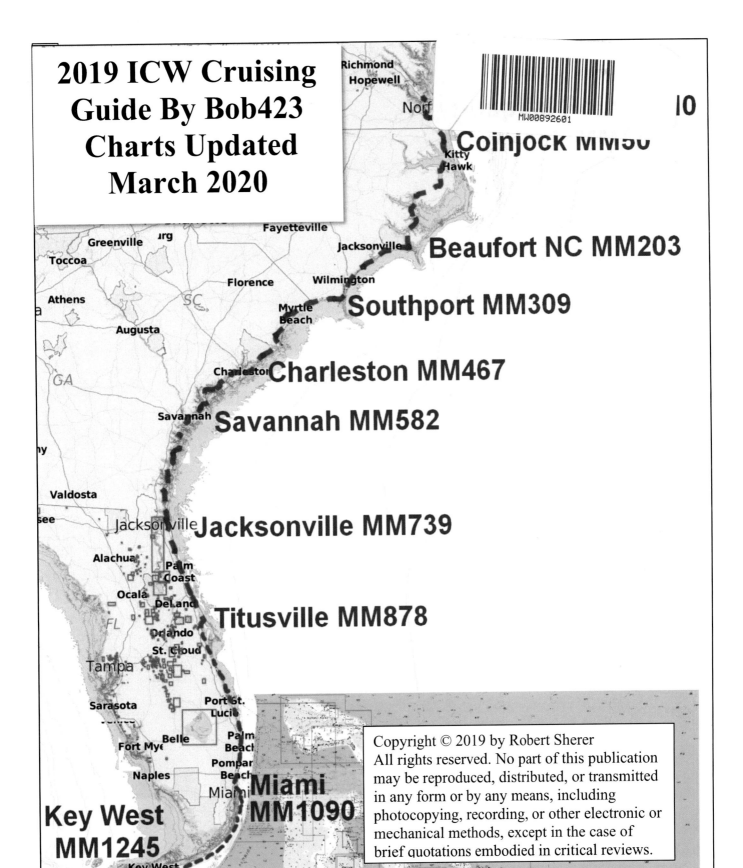

Coinjock MM50

Beaufort NC MM203

Southport MM309

Charleston MM467

Savannah MM582

Jacksonville MM739

Titusville MM878

Miami MM1090

Key West MM1245

Table of Contents

Introduction to the 2019 Edition (with updated charts as of March 2020)

We are all getting along in years. When I had this photo taken by my daughter in law, I asked Ann if she liked the photo and she said it was the best that could be done with the subject matter. Oh well. It will have to do.

I'm trying to ease the way south so you don't have to repeat all the mistakes I've already made in my eight trips from New York to Key West. I've learned that most mishaps are avoidable and if so, why repeat them? It's really not fun to run aground and wait for rescue from BoatUS or SeaTow, there's no need. After nine years on the ICW, you learn what allows you to have more time to enjoy the sunsets. Why not? A cruise ought to be fun, so looking over what we discovered the hard way sounds like a better strategy, and that leads us to the guide.

The guide is organized into two parts:
- Chapters 1 – 7: Covers what we've learned while cruising the ICW that you may find helpful. It covers getting your house and boat ready for the trip south and your affairs in order for a long stay away from home along with an overview of basic ICW knowledge needed for the trip south and additional topics in the ICW University chapter.
- Chapter 8: Provides charts of shoaling areas by mile marker and how to avoid going aground. Also included are the anchorages and marinas we've found conveniently spaced for traveling south. Not every marina or every anchorage is covered since there are many other books for that, most notably, the Waterway Guide series. I wanted to focus on the places I found the most convenient and in the case of anchorages, those that have shore access for pet relief and are spaced at convenient stopping points.

So, what's new for the 2019 edition? Of course, all the hazards have been updated per my passage through them October 2019 and January 2020. The charts now include the USACE survey of the shallow areas as displayed in Aqua Map Master where available. It has been a great year for the new guy on the block, Aqua Map. Including the USACE survey charts has given the mariner an increased level of confidence in navigating the shallows of the ICW. Your first investment should be to purchase Aqua Map Master if you haven't already done so. It's a bargain that can't be beaten. Examples of what you can see with Aqua Map Master will be apparent when you flip through the hazard guidance in Chapter 8. I'll have more to say on the app in the body of the guide.

It has also been a great year for dredging! The list of sites dredged since last year is impressive and includes Ponce de Leon, Jekyll Creek, Sawpit Creek, Ashepoo-Coosaw Cutoff, Fenwick Cut, Watts Cut, Dawho River, Johns Island, Isle of Palms, parts of McClellanville, Shallotte, Lockwoods Folly, and Browns Inlet. Other sites due to be dredged this summer include Fields Cut, Hell Gate, and parts of Butterfield Sound. All of this activity will be covered in the guide. One may ask, with all the dredging, why do you even need a guide? Well, it turns out that even though Ashepoo-Coosaw Cutoff was dredged to 11 feet, it is already shoaling in spots. It's good to know where the shallows are.

The Call of the ICW and the Cruising Lifestyle

Yesterday is but a memory,
Tomorrow is yet to be
Only Today is real...

As you travel the ICW, you are immersed in the present. You're looking at the charts, the boats coming towards you, the next shallow spot, that barge over there, that something in the water ahead (a log?). Time passes quickly. How far to the anchorage or marina? Can I make it in time before the storm comes? Will I make the bridge opening on top of the hour? There are lots of things to consider while underway on the ICW. The experience will anchor you in the present like almost nothing else. I find it exhilarating, perhaps you will too.

Ask yourself, why delay? You will never remember 10 years from now the reasons you didn't start your ICW adventure this very year. A trip down the ICW is an experience of a lifetime. It's challenging, it's exciting, it'll test your mettle, and you'll see new things and meet new people. You will experience at least

one heart-stopping moment a day! You will get more opportunities for such "excitement" spending nine months a year on a boat, especially cruising the shallows of the ICW. There is nothing like resting in a peaceful anchorage at the end of a long day, wine in hand, and watching a sunset like the one above in a secluded anchorage – immersed in the present.

So, relax, sit back, and plan ahead but first let's get acquainted. Ann is an artist. She paints in watercolors and in pastels. Most recently, she paints scenes from our ICW travels and while we're in Key West. Her pastel at left is a scene from the Merritt Island Wildlife Refuge. Her paintings can be seen at <u>Pastels by Ann</u>.

As for myself, I worked 38 years for IBM as a senior engineering manager before retiring in 2002 when we bought our third boat, Fleetwing, a 42 ft Beneteau 423 sailboat. I post regularly on Waterway Guide with the handle Bob423. I like to have all the latest stuff in electronics and computers, which I'll go through later in the guide. I am also the Forum Owner of the Beneteau 423 Yahoo Group site with over a thousand members worldwide. You can join that group too but you must have a Yahoo account.

 In 2018, I joined the staff of Waterway Guide as an On-The-Water Cruising Editor where I periodically write articles for publication and update the Waterway Guide Alerts for the areas where I cruise, which includes the ICW from New York to Key West and Long Island Sound.

More recently, I started a Facebook group, ICW Cruising Guide by Bob423, devoted exclusively to the Atlantic ICW which currently has 5700 members who post their real-time experiences as they proceed along. I'll post updates as they become available from many sources. It has become the go-to place for the latest Atlantic ICW status. I also maintain all the Waterway Guide alerts for each of the shallow areas and they will have the current guidance on passing through them without incident. Be sure to join the Facebook group, just google the name underlined above.

Thank you for buying the guide. If you chose the hardcopy version then the eBook version is free on Amazon.com. It's the one with all the links, which will be active on the Kindle, the Kindle on PC, or the iPad Kindle app. I will also post the links ordered by page number in the Cruising Tips section of my blog at fleetwing.blogspot.com so you don't have to google anything if you just have the book version. For that reason, I've left the links in blue and underlined so you can find them.

Please leave a review on Amazon.com. All reviews are helpful to other boaters considering a trip down the ICW. Hoolie needs a few more friends along the way. We can't wait to start enjoying those ICW sunsets again, why don't you come along too?

Look for us as you cruise the ICW and stop by when you can. Hoolie will greet you and I'll pour the wine. We can talk of our adventures and of things to come.

"IN THE END… We only regret the chances we didn't take, the relationships we were afraid to have, and the decisions we waited too long to make."
— Lewis Carroll
3/2020 Update

Chapter 1: How to Prepare Your House for an Extended Absence

This may sound like a dull subject - but it's not dull if you're stuck with a problem that requires your presence at a house 1000 miles away! So, in no particular order, here's what we've learned, in most cases the hard way.

Home Security System

This depends on your level of comfort in leaving your home unoccupied for nine months at a time. I wanted a security system for peace of mind with a temperature alarm if the house temperature dropped below 50 F since we live in the cold northeast with occasional power outages. It's monitored 24/7, and the security company has instructions on how to enter the house if the system needs repairing which has happened twice in the last nine years. The neighbors do not like a house alarm going off in the middle of the night! My system was professionally installed but there are some do-it-yourself kits out there.

Webcams for the Home

When away from home, I like to check in to see how things are at home (is the driveway plowed so the fuel truck can get in, any packages delivered in error to our home address, any trees down, etc.). Nothing beats having a few webcams scattered around the house with views of the driveway, backyard, back porch, and a few inside the house. The IP webcams are relatively inexpensive and only require a WiFi connection. They do not require a PC to be running but do require an active router. I can view the webcams in real-time or access my website to see if any of the webcams uploaded photos after detecting motion in their field of view. The real-time or stored webcam photos can be viewed with an iPad, iPhone, or laptop with an internet connection which I have at all times through my cellular provider, Verizon. For outside use, I just position the webcam to look through a window.

On one occasion I received a call from my home security service saying the temperature in the house was below 50 F. I accessed my webcam pointed at the furnace and discovered it had not turned on even though it had power. I called my furnace service with my story and they asked how I knew it wasn't a false alarm (it was the weekend and at night, they were not eager to come out). I replied that I was looking at my furnace in real-time from Florida and it was off! "Oh, then we'll come out."

The webcams I use are from Trendnet, which has many models. The basic one is fine for home use, the TV-IP110WN. They can also take a snapshot whenever motion is detected in their field of view and upload it to a website of your choosing. Caution, these things are NOT simple to set up, doable but not simple, I published a camera setup guide, which can be downloaded via the link provided. The camera model has been updated to TV-IP314PI and the price has increased but still not all that expensive. There are other manufacturers too such as the 2GC5804 - D-Link DCS-932L for $39.99 but I have no experience with the model. If you shop for other models be sure to check that it can send pictures without the need for the PC to be on. Such models can communicate directly with the router, no PC needed. However, remember that the setup is not easy and best done by someone with computer experience, although my camera setup guide ought to be helpful.

Antifreeze Your Furnace

I know of two instances where friends of ours have come home to a flooded basement and water all over their house after a power outage in the winter. They had baseboard water heating and the pipes burst when the house temperature dropped below freezing during a power outage in a winter storm. When power returned and the furnace turned back on, the baseboard heating water just poured out of the burst pipe. What a mess! I had antifreeze put in my heating system by my local oil dealer, no more worries about burst heating pipes.

Turn Off House Water

Having antifreeze in your water heating lines won't prevent burst pipes in your hot and cold-water lines unless you turn off your water and drain the lines. So, I had valves installed to turn off the water and I also turn off the well pump when we leave so even if the pipes from the well burst the basement won't fill up with well water.

But, as the ads say, there's more! You also have to turn off the supply water separately to your dishwasher, washing machine, and refrigerator (also turn off the ice maker, usually a separate switch inside the freezer). These three appliances usually have one-way solenoid valves. That means they open via a solenoid but depend upon external water pressure to close. If the water pressure drops below 20 psi (typically), the valve will open and allow any water in the pipes higher than the valves to flood into the appliance if the water was not completely drained from the second floor. This is a common insurance claim I'm told for dishwashers which have a small capacity for excess water.

Set Up Automatic Forwarding

You can have all your first-class mail forwarded automatically to another address (e.g., son or daughter) for six months, renewable for another six months if needed. There is no charge for this service from the USPS as long as you don't sign up for their premium forwarding service, which I don't recommend. You should buy a supply of prepaid Forever Priority Mailers so your son or daughter can send your mail to a marina of your choice in advance of your arrival. We haven't been at a marina yet that wouldn't accept mail for transients. If the contents weigh more than 13 oz then it has to be taken to the nearest post office for acceptance instead of just leaving them in your mailbox. This rule started after 9/11. There is still no charge for any weight up to 70 lbs and it comes with free tracking from USPS.

Have a Yard Keeper

You still need your yard mowed and driveway shoveled even when you're down south enjoying the sun. You don't want your house to look unoccupied but I do it so it looks nice. I've heard that there's snow in the wintertime (haven't seen it for nine years...) so arrangements have to be made so oil can be delivered for your furnace. This also requires shoveling out the inlet pipe manually; the oil delivery person usually won't do that.

Make Arrangements for House Entry

Sometimes a repairman or someone you know needs to enter the house to fix something. You need to make arrangements for a key somewhere. You can always give the security system code over the phone, although my security system and oil furnace company already have the code. Twice we've needed the furnace repaired and twice the security system needed a sensor replaced. Besides, I get lots of photos of their work over my internal webcams.

Turn Off All House Services

We turn off the newspaper delivery and trash pickup while away. I cancel the cable but keep the internet service so I can view my home webcams from the ICW, although I do downgrade the internet speed tier to save money.

Get Rid of All Food

It's amazing what can be done with leftover boxes of organic matter no matter how well sealed given nine months of work by hungry little critters. If there is something you must keep, put it in the refrigerator, which I leave plugged in. The oven and dishwasher are other choices for storage. We put all the dry goods we don't take along in coolers, tightly sealed. This past year, I forgot my own advice and left a 20 lb bag of dog food in the garage, unopened. Upon returning in the spring, I lifted the bag and found it weighed a lot less than I expected. I checked the top and it was still sealed but then I noticed a small hole in one corner – uh oh. The mice had a grand time converting the contents into new mice. Live and learn.

Turn Down the Heat
I set the house at 60 F, which is probably too high but it's what I choose. Much lower than that and the refrigerator has a problem according to the manual. I also put the boiler temperature on the furnace to the lowest setting recommended by the manufacturer.

Notify the Sheriff
Most localities will offer to check your house while you're away. We've seen them check our house on our webcams so we know they come by.

Leave Contact Info with a Friendly Neighbor
Someone who's near your house all the time can keep an eye out for anything unusual and give you a call.

Chapter 2: How to Prepare Yourself for an Extended Absence

Now that the house is taken care of, how about yourself? You want to enjoy the trip, not be burdened with things to worry about.

Automate Your Bills

We have our mail forwarded to my son who will periodically send them along to one of our stops at a marina, but it's easier to just have the bills automatically paid. You can arrange to have companies (electric, phone, internet, fuel oil, etc.) automatically deduct the payment from either your checking account or charge your credit card automatically. Furthermore, be sure to set up a bill pay account with your local bank where you can enter a bill and get a check sent for payment with no check writing required and no first-class stamp needed for those cases where automatic payments don't work. I prefer a direct deduction from my checking account vs using an automatic charge to a credit card. If you ever have a credit card canceled (remember Home Depot and stolen card numbers) then it's a pain to go over all your automatic charges and update the card number and expiration date.

Use Quicken for Financial Records

Quicken will communicate with all your financial institutions (banks, brokerage, credit cards, etc.) and download the data to your laptop, all with one tap on the Update button. They now have Quicken for the iPad that allows access to all the accounts you've set up on your laptop or home computer. It will automatically download all the latest banking data to your iPad so you'll know the current amounts in all your accounts and therefore know if there's any unwarranted use of your credit cards. I found such a problem after dining at a restaurant in Fernandina where I found charges on my card the next day from a company in California. The credit card company reversed the charges but it pays to watch your accounts. Recently, there are more options since most banks will now allow you to enter accounts from other banks and track them just like Quicken – for free.

Enroll in TaxAudit

So, you're in a remote anchorage somewhere down the ICW and in the course of conversation with your son you hear that a letter from the IRS arrived a few days ago. From past experience, I know that the reply is time-limited, usually to two weeks, so you arrange for a mail drop but by now you are already late. You need all your tax records (softcopies from tax software, TurboTax in my case) and have to decide how to respond, but that's the easy part. If you want to dispute the audit you will be in a communication loop via mail, difficult while going down the ICW, to say the least.

With a tax service such as TaxAudit, you never communicate directly with the IRS. The service handles all communications and will work with you via e-mail and phone and answers all the mail questions sent by the IRS. I've had two tax audits. In the first case, I made a mistake, which the IRS thought resulted in my owing them money. During the tax audit, it came out that the error was in my favor and the IRS owed me money! It took two years (!!) for me to collect from the IRS, they wanted their money in two weeks! There were multiple court appearances and one court letter written to the IRS by TaxAudit to complain about harassment. I even received a letter of apology from the IRS, which I had framed! Through all of this, I was never involved directly with the IRS - the audit service did all the work - and all the communication was via email with TaxAudit. In the second case, the IRS claimed the deduction for interest on my boat loan was not valid as a second home. I just emailed documentation off to the audit service and they handled all the communication with IRS and I won the case. The audit service coverage is the best money I've ever spent, $35 at the time but it's gone up to $50 now.

Scan All Medical Records and More

Make a habit of scanning all important documents and storing them in a file that syncs automatically to your laptop, iPad, and iPhone or equivalent. The all-in-one printers include a scanner that works fine such as the Epson XP-6000 for $69.99 on sale pictured at left. Later on, I will recommend a file syncing system that syncs everything to keep all copies on all computers, laptops, iPads, and iPhones you own current. If you have a medical problem on the ICW, it's valuable having all your medical information already downloaded and stored on a readily accessible device such as an iPad. You can review such information directly with the doctor if you have to see one on the ICW using your iPad.

Spend a day and scan in everything you keep in your desk files and wallet. For example, I have softcopy, meaning a PDF file or jpeg image of:

- Immunizations and license for your dog, usually provided by your vet.
- Passports, just in case.
- Drivers Licenses.
- Marriage Certificate. In a hospital, wife unconscious, "Who are you?"
- Living Will and Health Proxy for yourself and wife. Hospitals will ask for them.
- Social Security cards.
- House Insurance contract and coverage details. Your insurer will usually provide a PDF file for your use.
- Boat Insurance and coverage details. Most marinas will ask to see your insurance coverage if you stay a month or more.
- Car Registrations. Some companies use car IDs as a second way of certifying it's really you over the phone and not a pretender.
- Taxes submitted, all years. TurboTax 1040s are very useful for tax audits!
- House purchase papers in case you're challenged on a tax deduction.
- Boat purchase papers. One year when in Maine I had to prove I paid NY state sales tax or else Maine wanted me to pay them!
- Boat registration and documentation for Coast Guard checks and for some marinas.
- Dinghy license. Florida Wildlife Commission was checking one year for stolen dinghies.

Of course, I have a hard copy of my Passports, driver's licenses, social security cards, boat insurance, boat registration, and documentation. However, if the boat was to sink, I would still have everything I need since the files are not only stored on the laptop, iPad, and iPhone that are probably at the bottom of the ICW, but also in the cloud in my free 15 GB Google Drive, which auto-syncs between all devices I own.

I've been stopped by the Coast Guard twice in nine years. They were only interested in the boat documentation and whether we had any firearms on board. Oh yes, they asked if the dog was friendly! I don't recall them checking anything else.

Chapter 3: Outfitting a Boat for Cruising the ICW

I'm sure your boat came fully instrumented so I'll only cover some additional items that could make life easier or more enjoyable while cruising the ICW that you may want to add.

Full Enclosure for the Cockpit

A full enclosure is number one on the list for a sailboat traveling down the ICW in the fall. There are some cold days as fronts come barreling down from the north. A full enclosure for a sailboat allows cruising in comfort and adds considerably to the living space. It is conducive for watching sunsets in comfort with a drink in hand. In the fall, we often pass fishermen on the ICW wrapped up in layers (ski jackets!) while we're in shirtsleeves in our cockpit.

Genset

We wanted all the comforts of home so 120v AC was a requirement. We wanted coffee from a drip coffee maker along with hot water and battery recharging, not to mention an occasional running of the A/C for cooling or warming up. I had a 4.7 kW Panda installed in 2004 but it died multiple times, and thousands of dollars later I had a Kohler 6 kW installed (more thousands of dollars!) which has run perfectly; it better for the cost! By the way, there is really no way to do a cost/benefit analysis vs just staying in marinas. I just wanted 120v when at anchor, though purists would frown. Others favor wind generators and/or solar cells, which are good choices and much less expensive. It just depends on your power needs.

Air Conditioning

We desired the ability to cool or heat the cabin. The A/C is really a heat pump for cooling or heating. We have two, one for the main cabin and one for the aft cabin. It's used more as a heat pump for warming the cabin in the fall and spring than as an air conditioner.

Large Freezer

We wanted the freedom of not having to visit a supermarket every week so we looked for a large freezer for food storage. Fleetwing's freezer is 2.9 cubic feet; it's as big as the freezer in my 25-ft3 GE refrigerator at home.

Windlass for Hoisting the Anchor

The Ericson did not have a windlass and weighing the anchor was a good exercise for the back (not!). We have a windlass on Fleetwing with a washdown pump.

Full Control of the VHF at the Helm

It's not enough to have a Standard GX1600 VHF down below; where you want it is at the helm and not a puny handheld. I want a full 25 watts (can be reduced for talking to nearby boats) with the antenna on top of the mast for maximum distance. We have a remote mike that doubles as a speaker and it's capable of changing the VHF channel, the volume, squelch, and everything else you can do at the main station.

Autopilot

You do not want to travel the ICW without an autopilot. We don't have it wired into the chartplotter with stored routes because that can get a little dangerous. I like the helmsman to make course corrections manually and the autopilot allows the helmsman to pay more attention to the surroundings.

An Anchor That Never Fails (Ha! Well almost)

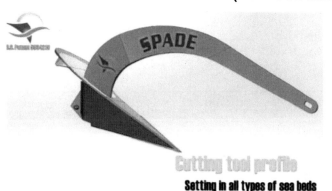

Cutting tool profile

Setting in all types of sea beds

Let the anchor wars commence! We anchor in mud and sand with the occasional covering of grass and weeds. We needed an anchor to perform well in all those conditions along with surviving current reversals without pulling out or slipping! Anchor design has evolved over the past 15 years to a cupped shape with the major players being the Spade, Rocna, and the Manson Supreme anchors. They cup the bottom and stop, not plow along the bottom and all three are good.

I looked at Practical Sailor's Anchor Test in 2004 and simply chose the one that came out on top in holding power, setting ability, and holding after a pull direction change. Practical Sailor ran another series of tests in 2013 and once again the Spade anchor came out on top against the Rocna and Supreme, so why go with second best?

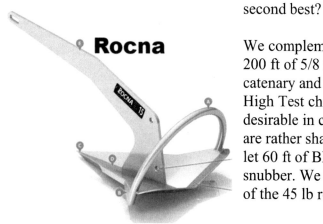

We complemented our anchor with 60 ft of 3/8 inch BBB chain and 200 ft of 5/8 inch nylon rode. The 3/8-inch BBB provides a better catenary and a more nearly horizontal pull on the anchor than 5/16" High Test chain for better holding, or the same angle at less scope, desirable in crowded ICW anchorages. Since most ICW anchorages are rather shallow, rarely more than 15 ft and mostly 8 to 10 ft, I just let 60 ft of BBB and the rest nylon (10 - 20 ft) so I have an automatic snubber. We did go with an oversized anchor, a 66 lb Spade instead of the 45 lb recommended for our size boat.

Since 2004, the Rocna and the Manson Supreme came out but I like the weighted point on the Spade that pivots well in current changes, Here's a quote from the Practical Sailor 2013 anchor tests, "The Rocna and Supreme exhibited the worst resetting characteristics in the sand/clay seabed of any anchor tested, except

the CQR" so I stayed with the Spade anchor since I often anchor in reversing currents near inlets. Rocna has since come out with a Spade knock-off, the Vulcan, advertising "enormous holding power." They were always a competitor and critic of the Spade design but I guess they've joined the fold now. According to Rocna, it's for boaters that cannot fit their regular design on the bow but still want a Rocna. Why not just get a Spade?

If you're looking for a less expensive anchor that has earned a more recent reputation, look into a Manta. They are from a company that has long made earth anchors for use on land and to anchor pipes underwater.

Propeller for Efficient Forward, Good Reverse, and Little Drag Under Sail

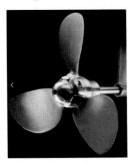

Now it's the propeller wars! We chose the Flex-O-Fold that can back out of our slip at PYC with ease against a 2 kt current and folds up under sail. The prop shaft exits directly to the propeller on our Fleetwing, doesn't require a separate strut, and so bypasses all the chances for vibration and misalignment of an extended shaft. It has required zero maintenance in the last 15 years, no oil, no grease, nothing. It just works. If you're in the market for a new prop, be sure to read the Yachting Monthly test of props.

AIS: Automatic Identification of Ships (AIS)

While AIS is a boon to coastal cruisers, in transiting NY Harbor it's a godsend. There are over a dozen very large ships close to you and knowing which direction they are headed and at what speed is invaluable, especially in hazy conditions or, worse yet, in fog.

There are two types of AIS receivers for recreational boats:
- Receive only (known as Class A AIS)
- Receive and transmit your own position so other boats can see you (known as Class B AIS)

I prefer the second type so I know large ships can see me as well as I can see them, but either type is better than not having AIS

Class A: Receive Only

The AMEC CYPHO-150S priced at $239 is an excellent receive only AIS unit. It has an integrated antenna splitter so you can connect it directly to your present VHF antenna.

Class B: Receive and Transmit

We installed a Class B transponder so we transmit our position as well as see other AIS targets. The AMEC CAMINO-108S Class B AIS Transponder with Integrated Splitter priced at $509 is pictured at left. It comes with a portable GPS antenna that may be good enough inside fiberglass boats. If you need an external GPS antenna, then use the AMEC GPS antenna priced at $49. For connection to the chartplotter, it has both NMEA2000 and NMEA0183 output. It will connect via USB too if desired for your laptop. With this unit, you do not need a separate antenna splitter, as it's integrated into the transponder.

Class B Transponder with WiFi and NMEA 2000, 0183, and USB

The Vesper Marine XB-8000 transponder for $740 has it all. It will transmit AIS content to a compatible iPad app such as Aqua Map Master to show AIS signals right on the navigation app screen via WiFi and will also include the boat's AIS details of name, size, speed, direction of travel, etc. If connected to NMEA, it will also transfer the NMEA instrument data to the iPad app like wind speed, boat speed, wind direction, etc. You will need a separate antenna splitter with this unit to use your present VHF antenna. The modern splitters are not like the old ones where you lost 3db of signal. The modern ones actual amplify the signal so there's no loss.

A Couple of 17" Ball Fenders

Of course, you have the standard fenders suitable for your boat on normal docks but a couple of 17" ball fenders really come in handy on face docks. I carry two Polyform A-3 fenders but Taylor makes them too. The 17" ball fenders come in particularly handy when against a bulkhead at Elizabeth City or in going through locks. The 17" size gives a good standoff and absorbs a lot of punishment.

One EasyStow Fender

Wind gusts to 50 kts were predicted from a direction that would push us directly into the facedock. I got out my EasyStow fender, inflated it with my dinghy pump and felt very secure with the extra-long 5 ft x 12 in diameter size between me and the dock. Nothing beats an inflatable heavy-duty EasyStow fender. The 5 ft length allows for boat motion without popping out or missing the piling. It rolls up nicely when not in use but when a major storm comes, it protects your boat like no other fender! You shouldn't even think about this, just buy one. You won't regret it.

Download All Equipment Manuals

If you installed Documents by Readdle per the advice in Chapter 3, then you have a place to put all equipment manuals. I have close to a hundred manuals stored on Google Drive and synced to my iPad. I haven't found an equipment supplier yet who does not offer a PDF download of their manuals. What a space saver! Paper manuals on the boat took up a lot of space and were often out of date, and as my eyes aged, the manuals somehow became harder to read. On the iPad I just do the two-finger expand and the image is magnified. So easy. For those times needing repairs, I often have a manual more up to date than the shop. As an added plus, the text is fully searchable, a great time saver.

Towing Service Contract

You hope you'll never need it but waiting until you do need it is not an option. The only time I used one was the first year we cruised and anchored in Edisto River with 3 kts of current and an opposing wind. I had put out too much rode and the nearly horizontal rode wrapped itself around my keel as the boat turned during a tide change. At 3:00 am I was in the dinghy trying to push the bow around to unwrap the rode but no dice. At the time I didn't know how to unwrap the rode from the keel without help. Later I found out that all that was necessary was to turn the boat towards the anchor while under power to take tension off the rode, which would then drop off the keel. At the time it was counter-intuitive since turning the boat in that direction would wind the rode even more around the keel but it was the right thing to do, and I have since used that technique one other time when the rode wrapped around the keel.

The bill for the above was $1800 since he had to travel about 30 miles, but it was all paid for as part of my $179/year contract with SeaTow. It's $149/year for Boat/US towing, but you have to join BOAT/US first for $30.

Washdown Pump

Many ICW anchorages have mud bottoms and not just any mud but rather thick, gooey, "hard to come off" mud. This assumes you are using some length of chain, which is an excellent mud collector. This stuff doesn't just wash off with a bucket and if you don't want to wind up with an anchor locker full of mud and a foredeck suitable for growing clams, you'll need lots of water at high pressure. Get the most powerful one you can fit in such as the ShurFlo ProBlaster

Holding Tank Monitor

You really do want to know the level of black water in your holding tank to prevent an embarrassing overflow down the side of the boat. That goes double for when you're in a marina with guests on board! There are dozens of systems out there and I've tried several. I didn't want to drill any holes in the tank to accommodate an internal sensor (smell leak?) so I chose a liquid level sensor that is adhered to the outside of the tank. I've been using SeeLevel II with good success for the past eight years. On the downside, you do have to clean the inside of the tank where the sensor is located since adhered "stuff" on the inside can give a false reading. I have to clean the inside by the sensor about every two to three months depending on how good a job I did the first time. I didn't do the first cleaning until after five years but now it's more often. I really should clean the inside of the tank to "like new" condition, but that's for another day.

12v Outlets, You Need More

Most boats come with woefully inadequate 12v outlets. Mine came with a grand total of one 12v outlet at the nav station! I installed two on the binnacle for the iPad and iPhone, two in the forward cabin on either side for our Kindles and GPS for the anchor watch and one in the aft cabin for guests. I should have installed one more in the main cabin on the side opposite the nav station. The one at the nav station powers the 150w inverter to a power strip for charging devices.

Vinyl Tubing, ½ Inch for Shower Drain Pump

Most boats have a shower sump pump with a ½ inch hole to suck water. If you buy some ½ inch vinyl tubing, it can be shoved into the hole and you have an instant overboard pump with a long extension (as long as you want with the tubing). It's very handy for getting rid of water in the bilge that the bilge pump can't reach or any other source of water. While you're at it, buy a three-inch diameter mesh stainless steel shower strainer; the part that dips should be much smaller, see photo at left. Walmart carries them. It saves having to clean the filter under the sink; just clean the strainer, a time saver.

Get a Dinghy with a High Bow and Hard Bottom

I've been through several dinghies and found advantages to dinghies with a high bow. I have to get to shore in all kinds of weather for Hoolie relief and sometimes the weather is rather windy. I prefer a dry ride to a wet ride. A dinghy with a high bow will deflect the waves better and keep you drier. With frequent landings for Hoolie relief, I found that a hard-bottom dinghy lasts longer. You cannot always find a sandy beach and an inflatable dinghy bottom is prone to puncturing. I can't afford the downtime to fix the dinghy so it's a hard-bottom dinghy for me. I had the AB Ventus 10VL with a 6 hp Mercury motor that lasted 15 years but it eventually gave out due to Hoolie wear and tear from leaning on the port side as he rode to shore. I have since bought a new dinghy, a Defender model 300 with a hard bottom (photo at left). It seems of high quality and it saved us a

few bucks. Note the high bow in the picture. It's wise to be prepared so keep a dinghy repair kit on board made for the fabric used in the dinghy. I landed one time on a bed of mussels and proceeded to step off the dinghy by first stepping on the inflated tube, not wise. The dinghy had a hard bottom but stepping on one of the tubes tilted the dinghy and the mussels found soft rubber to pierce. I'm careful to no longer do that. If I need to get out of the dinghy, I go over the bow which is fully protected by the fiberglass bottom. The repair was complicated by the bottom paint I had used, but patience in removing it and careful cleaning won out.

Davits or Trail the Dinghy?

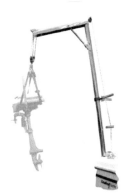

Ann and I have this discussion every season. We currently just trail the dinghy behind Fleetwing. It's instantly ready for Hoolie when we pull into an anchorage and we still can cruise at 7.3 kts under power. We have an unobstructed view aft to see boats overtaking us so it has worked for us. However, we have to hoist the outboard motor off the railing and onto the dinghy every time we stop. You can see the motor and hoist on the starboard side of the boat in the previous discussion of a sugar scoop stern.

On the other hand, davits have a lot to recommend. In going offshore, the dinghy is secure in large seas. Some people will keep the motor mounted on the dinghy when in davits so that's a savings in launch time over trailing a dinghy. I'm sure Ann and I will continue our discussions but we'll probably stay with just trailing the dinghy. If you do trail the dinghy then you have to consider bottom paint for it, another plus for davits. If you store the outboard on the aft rail as we do, then you will need a motor hoist. The one from Garhauer is hard to beat; it has served us well for 14 years

Anchor Alarm set in the Forward Cabin

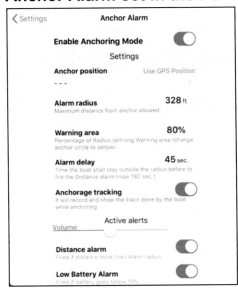

Aqua Map, now has a very sophisticated anchor alarm built-in with many configurable options. It has the same functions as the popular "Drag Queen" iPad app which is no longer offered.

If used on your smartphone, you can set it from the forward cabin. I never had much luck setting the position of the anchor from the helm; I found that the aft end swings too much to be an accurate indicator of distance to the anchor. You're already starting out 40 ft or more farther away from the anchor which requires too much slop before triggering the anchor alarm, not good in a tight anchorage. Note, a GPS will find satellites through fiberglass but an aluminum boat is another story.

Remote Thermometers

I bought two indoor/outdoor wireless thermometers. For one unit, I put the remote in the freezer compartment to keep tabs on our frozen meats without having to open the freezer door and letting in warm air. For the other unit, the remote went in the cockpit to see the outside temperature at a glance when getting ready to take Hoolie ashore in the morning.

Water Filter

I used to lug around water jugs but that changed when I bought the latest Fleetwing. I didn't want to drink water directly out of the tanks even though the boat was new so I installed a house-sized filter at the end of the water hose when taking on water. It serves the double duty of filtering the water and keeps the spout located over the inlet pipe. Once in place, I can walk away and take on fuel. I also installed a drinking water filter right at the sink that's rated to take everything out down to microbes and some viruses as well as all chemicals. I bought the Seagull filter but there are others that are cheaper. The water that comes out is as good as or better than anything you can buy in a bottle and a lot handier. Besides, do you really know where your bottled water comes from?

Mattress Warmer, 12 Volts

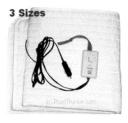

You will not believe how great it feels to climb into a warm bunk on a chilly night going south in the fall. There are 12v mattress warmers used by truckers that will not drain the batteries but will provide a nice cozy bunk. It's great for getting rid of dampness on humid nights too. We don't use it all night; just to warm up the bunk at night and first thing in the morning. Ann loves it!

TV Antenna

We have an LG 32-inch LED LCD TV. The LED version only consumes about 80 watts, something our battery bank and inverter can handle easily. However, what do you do for a TV signal? You could install a tracking antenna for pay TV that might set you back $2500 and a monthly fee for the service. As an alternative, we just put up a 19 inch Shakespeare 3019 $119 disc type antenna and typically get 20 to 30 channels all up and down the ICW (50 to 100 near cities) in full HD. The land surrounding the ICW is fairly flat so even if you don't mount the antenna on the top of the mast, you will still get most of the channels. Ours is about 10 ft high, just above the aft radar. In fact, the picture you will get over the air is superior to cable since the signal is not compressed like cable signals. Once you enter the Keys, the TV signals drop out dramatically. In Miami, you'll get over 100 stations but in Marathon, it's down to 10 or less. In Key West, it's one and it's not one of the major networks.

In 2017, Verizon and many other providers came out with unlimited data plans and they have been a boon to cruising sailors. Even though they are not really unlimited since the LTE speeds are usually limited to the first 22 GB before throttling but they do allow for streaming of HD video from Amazon Prime or Netflix and many other providers. Now there are no more worries about exceeding your data plan, just stream. Verizon only throttles after 22 GB if the cellphone tower traffic is heavy. We've never experienced a problem yet with Verizon throttling. However, the plans keep changing as the providers jockey for customers so you'll have to do your homework to find the best plan for you. We streamed HD TV through Netflix and Amazon Prime all spring, no problems, all along the ICW. We have a TV-out adapter for our iPad or iPhone and output HD video directly to one of the HDMI inputs on our 32-inch LED TV.

Dehumidifier Rod in Closed Compartments

While at a dock you may not get the airflow as you do underway and moisture can accumulate. One aid is to install a dehumidifier rod which is used in keeping closed cabinets dry such as for firearms. I only have one but it's an important one, the Admiral's hanging closet. It works.

Galley Lights

The galley in boats is typically poorly lit, especially in sailboats. A couple of LED light bars do wonders for the cook; now the work area is nice and bright. SuperBrightLED is a good source. They also have LED replacements for all the lights on a boat and they are priced right.

Engine Temperature Gauge

It's surprising how many new boats have no temperature gauge. What's the value of the temp alarm going off AFTER the engine has overheated! You want to know whether the engine is approaching the overheating point BEFORE it overheats!

Mount Your iPad at the Helm

You have a new iPad for navigation, now it's time to give it a mount at the helm, which one is best? I've tried several and settled on the RAM X-Grip series. The advantage of this type is the wide range of iPad sizes and thicknesses that a given mount size will accept. I have the RAM X-Grip Universal Holder for 12" Tablets. It holds my iPad Pro 12.9 in place with or without its case but also will hold my iPad Air 2 when it's in its case. I only use the two top and two bottom arms.

Get a Rolling Cart for Lugging Things to the Boat

They come in all sizes. You want one narrow enough to roll down the aisle of a bus, but big enough to be useful. The Drive Medical Rolling Cart works well. Notice the large wheels, which are good for rolling over gravel, since they don't dig in. Aside from hauling food to the boat, it's handy for lugging LP tanks to and from a refilling station and for lugging laundry by taking the canvas off and using bungees to secure the laundry bag to the frame. The tall, relatively narrow size fits well on a shuttle. Along with the cart, get a small, ice cream size insulated bag for frozen food since it will take a few minutes to reach your freezer.

Solar Light for Your Dinghy

When we leave Poughkeepsie YC in September the days are getting shorter and the trips to shore for Hoolie start to get darker. It is wise, not to mention required by law, to have dinghy lights so other boaters can see you. I've been through four iterations of lights and finally, I found the solution on Amazon.com. It's a truly waterproof solar white light that's very bright and lasts the entire night. It's the S4LN White 1/2NM solar non-flashing LED. It fits on a 1-¼ inch post. I bought an adapter at a local hardware store that accepts the 1 ¼ inch post and mates it to a ¾ inch aluminum pipe that slides into the two ¾ inch brackets on the inside of the dinghy. With a thin aluminum pipe three feet tall, it's above my head and doesn't flood my night vision. The two ¾ inch brackets should be stainless steel, the plastic ones don't last. After I did all this, FWC at Marathon now no longer requires your dinghy to be lit all night as long as your painter is less than 10 ft. Nevertheless, it's an excellent light and I just leave it in the dinghy whenever we're anchored. One more light can't be a bad thing in a busy harbor, especially by an inlet. While you're at it, buy a bow light too. The one I use is available from Amazon, Portable LED Bow Light w/suction cup. Hint, tie a small line around the base so it doesn't go overboard if it loses suction. They also come with a base that you can glue to the dinghy for a more secure attachment.

Inverter, 150 Watts

With cell phones, iPad, printer, and laptops and on and on, you need a lot of 120v outlets but not much current for those devices that don't come with a 12v charger. You can run the main inverter but the idle current is more than what you would use to charge your electronics. A small inverter such as the Foval 150W inverter is more efficient. Plug in a power strip so you have lots of 120v outlets available. I run my 32 inch LCD TV off of one. It has much less idle current than my 2000 watt main inverter and it's more efficient too.

Ravpower to Charge Devices

With a supply of 120v from the Foval inverter, now plug in a Ravpower unit for 6 USB charging outlets. All of the outlets support 2.4 amps, which is enough to fully charge an iPad. Don't confuse this charger with one at Walmart or in a Dollar Store. This is state-of-the-art in fast and safe charging for both Apple and Android devices.

Sundry Items on Board

Spray Nine.

It's our general cleaner; we've tried everything out there. It came in first in testing by Practical Sailor and it especially works great on cockpit floors.

MaryKate On/Off.

It cannot be beaten for removing the ICW mustache on the side of the boat. It's also good for removing rust stains. I use it on the foredeck to get rid of any rust that came off the anchor chain.

Magic Eraser.

It's a great product and works on more stains than you might think. It's made of melamine foam and works like very fine sandpaper and is very good at removing stains from fiberglass. Its hardness is about the same as glass so do not use on vinyl windows or anything painted.

Clorox

Clorox bleach is our cleaner of last resort. We only use it when nothing else works. We've found it's the only thing that will remove purple-colored stuff after it went through a bird. It's also the only thing I found that will remove fuzzy bill stains (when they die on your boat by the hundreds, each one leaves a green, gooey stain).

<u>Tide Pods</u>.

We used to measure detergent but then Tide Pods came out and they are much more convenient and work well.

<u>Metal Spring Clamps</u>.

We've used wooden clothespins in the past but the metal clamps have much better-holding power and don't slip. They are great for holding sunshades in place.

<u>Microfiber Cloths</u>

Where would we be without microfiber cloths? There are a ton of brands out there but some are better than others. The largest supplier of microfiber cloths in the U.S. also sells them direct over eBay. These are a breed apart from the usual fare. They are 330 grams per square meter which is much denser than anything you'll find at Walmart or Home Depot. You get 24 cloths for $20.50 with free shipping, a good deal.

Spares to Bring Along

The extent of the spares to bring will depend on where you're going. The list that I've found useful is just for the ICW. If you are going to the Bahamas or farther, your list will be much more extensive. Along the ICW, there are many places to find parts and to get a boat worked on. There are still a few items you ought to have that fall into the category of "If they fail, you're in trouble."

- Impellers. These things wear out and can ruin your day if you don't have a spare on board. Take along at least two. You might even consider a spare raw water pump; I keep one handy.
- House water pump. A boat with no running water is no fun.
- Washdown pump. You could get along without it for a while but with the muddy bottoms of the ICW anchorages, it's no fun, especially in the Chesapeake.
- Fan belt. Well, there's no fan on an engine but you know what I mean.
- <u>Rescue Tape</u>. This stuff is amazing. It can repair a leak in a hot, pressurized hose.
- <u>Flex Seal Tape</u>. For quick repairs of leaks, nothing beats this tape. It comes in black, white, and clear with different size widths. I used the 4-inch-wide black tape to repair a leak between the seams of my teak rail. It was a quick fix until I could repair it properly but it kept the lockers dry in the meantime.
- Oil filter. It could leak, probably not, but just in case.
- Fuel filters (primary and secondary). If you get bad fuel, it's the primary fuel filter that goes, the one closest to the fuel tank. Usually, bad fuel won't stop you completely but just prevent the engine from revving to cruising speed. You can usually limp into a nearby marina.
- Engine oil.
- Spare head pump (the entire assembly for a fast fix). You don't want to be in a boat with the head not working! While you're at it, stock a few joker valves too.
- Spare running lights bulbs and anchor light bulb. You've got to be seen.

The above would be an absolute minimum although some people would expand the list, on the ICW you're never far from help. Cruisers going to the Bahamas or the Caribbean would carry much more.

Chapter 4: The Cook Speaks
Preparing the Galley

After nine trips up and down the ICW, I've learned to keep a well-stocked galley. I purchase meat and freeze it solid before leaving home so I don't overload our boat freezer. Refrigerator room is in short supply so I keep items like Parmalat milk which does not require refrigeration until it is opened. The taste is better than canned or powdered milk although my grandson, Matt, disagrees. You can always get milk at the nearest 7-11 or even CVS so we don't keep multiple bottles in the refrigerator. Frozen veggies fill in when the fresh runs out. Apples, oranges, and grapefruit will keep on the counter.

I'm a basic cook. Hot, simple, nourishing meals are the key. At the end of a day on the water, I want to use a simple recipe and have a glass of wine while dinner cooks! The computer is a wonderful source of cooking ideas and the supermarket checkout lane has a new supply of cooking magazines every month. A propane stove can heat up the main cabin in a hurry and on a cool day this is welcomed, however, most days are warm going south so I aim for short cooking times. I try to limit cooking to twenty minutes so brown rice which takes 45 minutes to cook and whole chickens are not on my shopping list. Forget about baked potatoes unless they go in the microwave. I use fresh veggies and fill in with frozen ones between shopping trips. Boneless chicken breasts, thighs, and pork tenderloins can be frozen flat and stack well in the freezer. Add a few spices to these and the variety is almost endless. Fruit ripens quickly on the counter and is a magnet for fruit flies. I'm told dipping the ends of bananas in vinegar will kill any eggs. To get rid of fruit flies, put an inch of wine in a small glass, cover it with Saran Wrap and use a toothpick to make holes in the top. Fruit flies go in and cannot get out. They can also lay eggs in sink drains. Close the sink seacock, pour in vinegar and put in the stopper. Vinegar kills the eggs.

Before leaving home, make a list and buy three to four each of all the dry goods. Bread with preservatives will last the longest (we've thrown away a lot of "preservative-free" bread). I can hear someone saying, "There must be supermarkets along the ICW." Sure, there are, lots of them but very few are within walking distance so you have to add in the cost of a rental car or taxi unless you find one of the few marinas with a courtesy car. Juggling bags of groceries on a bike is no fun either. I plan on carrying at least two weeks' worth of meals.

Regardless of the type or size of a vessel, it needs a convenient galley. I have a three-burner propane stove with an oven. Pots with vertical sides use less burner space than the potbelly type. A Calphalon 2.5-quart pan, a Calphalon 1.5-quart pan, and a Calphalon 12-inch fry pan can be in use at the same time and centered over each burner and they come with glass lids so you can see what's going on inside. We found that all non-stick cookware has a limited life span. They become scratched and cooking oil will eventually carbonize and the non-stick quality is lost. Calphalon is neither the cheapest nor the most expensive but it is very sturdy. It has worked well for me. In addition, I have a small 8-inch skillet and a Dutch oven.

Lastly, I have an enameled cast iron brazing pan shown at left. It is cast iron with a ceramic coating that comes clean regardless of abuse although it may take a little scrubbing. The pan can be used on the stovetop or in the oven and can't be beaten for one-pot meals. Unfortunately, the model I have is no longer available but one from Klee is very similar. We do have a gas grill that attaches to the stern rail but with our low-fat diet, we seldom eat steak or burgers so it has seen little use.

I have a small Black and Decker food processor. There's no room for a full-size unit so I have a 3-cup size for the galley. It's great for dicing.

Of equal importance is refrigeration. My freezer is 2.9 cubic ft and larger than the refrigerator but it is shaped like a cube and we've learned to repackage all frozen meats into "pages." That is, lay the meat flat, tightly wrap each one in Saran wrap or equivalent so they don't stick together when you want just one, and put the individual pieces into a one-gallon zip bag labeled with the date. The gallon bag should just be one layer of frozen meat thick so they can be stacked in the freezer to save space. We avoid round-shaped meats like a whole chicken; they take up too much room. When you provision and buy unfrozen meat, do the above packaging but then lay the gallon bag vertically against one of the cooling coils of the freezer, it will freeze much faster that way.

Before leaving, I freeze meat at home so everything starts out cold. I buy family packs of boneless chicken breasts and thighs and repackage them into meal size units. Pork tenderloins in the plastic vacuum wrap also pack well. I also take frozen fish and shrimp along with 3 or 4 family size bags of frozen vegetables. Keeping in mind that we can no longer drive to the supermarket, I have at least two weeks' worth of frozen food. Whenever possible we eat fresh fruit and vegetables. Grapefruit travels well without refrigeration.

The refrigerator is cramped. It opens on the front and has two shelves. We have two plastic trays stacked on each other on the top shelf with room on the side for milk and juice. One tray on the bottom holds veggies and fruit. There is room in the back for a carton of orange juice lying on its side. Salad dressing goes beside the tray. It is adequate but not spacious. Large economy jars, while economical, are not practical.

The final component is dry goods: beans, red, black, or baked, diced tomatoes, and rice, lots of rice. Onions are essential. These ingredients can be combined with chicken, garlic, onions, and spices for a variety of meals. I use lots of Spices. Cuban, Cajun, Caribbean, Mexican provide a variety of choices. Want it hot? I can do that too! At the end of the day, my goal is to prepare a healthy dinner quickly. That small stove can heat up the salon. A twenty-minute cook time is ideal; save those casseroles for a cold night. I've overflowed my spice rack pictured at left but the rack is vital for easy access to spices.

List of Provisioning stops

Grocery stores are not conveniently located at every marina so we plan ahead for provisioning at stops that offer easy access to groceries. I've listed the provisioning stops from north to south all the way to Key West that we have used.

Going from PYC in New York to Key West:

1. We start running out of perishables while in Chesapeake Bay and we've found the Solomons Island anchorage by the Holiday Inn handy for picking up necessities with a Weis Supermarket about a mile walk away via a convenient sidewalk.

2. Hampton, VA, is our first major provisioning stop. We take a dock at Downtown Hampton Public Piers and rent a car from Enterprise just around the corner, less than 200 ft from the marina. There's a wide selection of markets but we usually go to the Walmart Supercenter nearby. They have one washer and one dryer for marina use and bikes to use for minor provisioning.

3. RE Mayo Docks is a good stop for local scallops, shrimp, and flounder. They flash freeze fish in blister packs, perfect for provisioning on a boat since they are frozen flat and pack well. Warning, the docks are not so great but the frozen seafood is.

4. Homer Smith Docks and Marina in Beaufort, NC has a free courtesy car for easy access to a Lowes Foods supermarket nearby and a free washer and dryer with new floating docks, first class.

5. Charleston Marinas are close to several Harris Teeters. My favorite is in downtown Charleston. Charleston Maritime Center has a Harris Teeter within walking distance with a great selection of fresh food. The marina has two free washers and dryers. Alternatively, we can provision at Tollers Cove Marina which provides free shuttle service to the nearest supermarket. Another alternative is St Johns Yacht Harbor which has a free courtesy car for shopping with good laundry facilities.

6. Titusville Marina is another place we rent a car for access to the nearest Walmart. I think you can see a pattern here in Walmarts. Most of the ones down south have excellent food markets and we can pick up most non-food needs at the same stop. They have three washers and dryers, $1.50/load.

7. Vero Beach Municipal Marina has a free shuttle to Publix if there's anything we missed at Titusville. They have many washers and dryers.

8. Marathon has a Publix about a mile from the city docks. The taxi ride is only $5 each way for groceries if you have too much to carry. With the mooring field of 220 boats, they have 8 washers and 8 dryers.

At Key West, we'll just rent a car periodically to provision. There are two Publix stores but the Winn-Dixie store has the best prices and bus stops out front. There is no Walmart at Key West. Use public transportation for $0.50 each way for seniors and skip renting a car to shop at Publix or Winn-Dixie. You can even track when the bus is coming with your cellphone using the Key West Transit app. Each bus transmits its location from an onboard GPS and it's displayed in the app so you know when the bus will arrive. Who thought Key West of all places would be so up to date?

Chapter 5: Staying Informed While Cruising

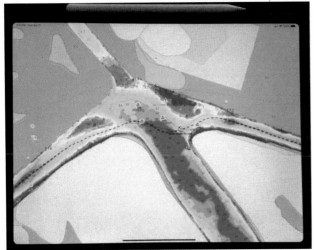

I was brought up as a PC person and Apple products were things to be avoided. As an IBMer at the time, we viewed Apple products as "toys." All that changed when Ann bought me a new iPad for my birthday one year. "Why do I need this…?" However, as I used it, I came to like the simplicity and ease of use.

A tablet is incredibly useful on a boat. I use mine as a replacement for my ancient Raymarine chartplotter in navigation, for email, in weather forecasting, financial status, taking photos – in short – anything you do on a laptop can be done on a tablet.

There are two players in the tablet market: Apple and Android. The Apple products are top of the line and they charge that way. The Android tablets are much less expensive but not as fast so it depends on tradeoffs you want to make. I wanted a tablet to be used as a chartplotter replacement so I chose the 12.9-inch iPad Pro, Apple's fastest and biggest tablet (pictured above with pencil) but there are other choices that may suit you better. Even the Apple entry iPad is only $325 for the 32GB version without a GPS chip. With a GPS chip (needed for navigation) and 128 GB, the price rises to $559. It is possible to buy the non-WiFi version to save money and use your boat's GPS antenna for directional fixes, more on that later. Of course, you can always step up to iPad Pro for better than laptop performance, especially in quick chart redraws but you pay for it.

For Android users, a good entry-level device with a GPS chip is the Galaxy Tab A 10.1 with 32 GB storage (but you can add an SD card for more) for a list price of $230.

Both devices have an app store (tablet software is called an "app" instead of "program") and you will find apps much less expensive than buying programs for your laptop, 10's of dollars vs 100's of dollars, big savings in software! There are still a few things a laptop can do better such as word processing for writing a book or doing a blog but the rest of the areas are shrinking quickly. In fact, I prefer to use my tablet whenever possible which turns out to be about 95% of the time when I'm on Fleetwing.

One advantage the Apple tablets have over the Android versions is the selection of apps. If a new app is released, it will be released for Apple products first. If an upgrade is made to an app available for both product lines, the upgrade will be made to the Apple versions first. This is merely economics since Apple products are so widespread for use in navigation. For a product like Aqua Map which is available in both formats, the Android version will catch up eventually but most likely be one version down-level until the rate of feature enhancements slow down.

The various providers of navigation equipment all get their initial data from charts created and maintained by the National Oceanic and Atmospheric Administration (NOAA). The providers then add their own enhancements to the charts like tides and currents, different color formats, crowdsourced data by Waterway Guide and Active Captain, and other data to personalize the charts for their customers. In the early days, they would physically scan in the paper charts and convert them to digital format for use in their chartplotters. Then NOAA went digital but just converted the paper charts to RNC format (Raster Navigation Charts), which the various manufacturers converted to their own formats that were incompatible between them (of course!) Next, NOAA went fully digital with ENC charts (Electronic Navigation Charts), and over the last two years, most manufacturers have begun using the ENC charts but again only after converting the NOAA ENC format to their own proprietary formats. You can tell when the changeover started; their charts started looking identical to the NOAA ENC charts where depth contours are concerned. There are a few programs that use the NOAA ENC charts directly without modifications such as OpenCPN, which is a free program maintained by users and runs on both Windows and Mac computers. There is no charge for downloading NOAA ENC charts from the NOAA website. I have permission to use the Aqua Map Marine charts in this guide that display the depth surveys by the US Army Corps of Engineers (USACE).

Updating Your iOS on Apple Devices

I have automatic updating for the iOS system selected over WiFi. However, I recently learned that there's a difference between updating your iOS via WiFi vs through iTunes with a USB cable. It turns out that when a WiFi update is done, only the iOS code that is changed is downloaded which saves time. For an update through iTunes, the entire iOS is downloaded and replaces the previous version on your device. If you're having problems with no obvious cause (like losing GPS fixes), there may be corrupted iOS code causing it. If that code happens to reside in an iOS upgrade, then the WiFi update will fix it. If it resides in the code that's not changing, then the WiFi update will not fix it.

With that as background, I recommend iTunes updates if you're having problems with your device you can't find a solution for. In the future, I will only use iTunes updates on my most complicated device, my iPad Pro 12.9, that I depend upon for navigation. I've never had a problem with any other device.

Aqua Map Marine

The program is free and charts for the entire US including Alaska and USVI are only $25. They come with a lifetime supply of updates every three months although you can buy a yearly subscription for less. With the lifetime update feature, there's no more paying for updated charts! The charts are digital and can be downloaded to the iPad or Android tablet so no internet connection is required for viewing once downloaded. They are based on the NOAA ENC digital charts. The charts are not cluttered and, to my eyes, have just the right blend of information, color, and contrast. In Chapter 8, I used the Aqua Map Marine app on my iPad to copy charts to show the hazard areas in this guide. See the link Aqua Map on how to get the most out of the app.

Aqua Map downloads and displays the entire Waterway Guide and Active Captain databases of reviews of marinas, hazards, anchorages, and local knowledge (inlets, harbor entrances, etc.). The database is invaluable for coastal cruising and is stored directly on the tablet, no internet connection is required to view. When you want to sync your database with the Active Captain or Waterway Guide server, then you do need a connection. The program also allows you to input to both databases, but you need an internet connection for that feature. Finally, the program includes a search function for all harbors, marinas, and chart features. The app can be set to automatically sync to both databases once a day or done manually. As of July 2019, the dual capability of displaying both Active Captain and Waterway Guide comments is still unique to Aqua Map. Current and tide icons are also displayed on the chart. The icons show the state of the tide and the direction of current. If you tap on an icon, you can find the tide and current at any time you choose. Importing and exporting of routes, waypoints, and tracks are as simple as can be. Just tap on a route download link using Safari on the iPad, and the route is transferred to your iPad and displayed, ready for navigation. For complete instructions, see GPX File Use.

New for 2019, USACE survey charts can now be downloaded and displayed right on your tablet, ready for navigation. Also added is the display of Automatic Identification System (AIS) with input from an AIS receiver so you know where that large ship bearing down on you is going. Data from your instruments can also be displayed to better keep track of depths as you proceed down the ICW. It's a fantastic program for a super price. If you get just one iPad navigation program, get this one, it has it all.

Navionics

For my second navigation program, I use the Navionics app, which is a yearly subscription of $15 with versions for both Apple and Android devices. It can display three types of charts: the Navionics+ charts, the NOAA ENC charts and what Navionics calls a SonarChart. Navionics puts their own spin on their Navionics charts but the NOAA charts (labeled, "Govt. Chart") are just straight downloads from the NOAA site. The SonarChart is generated by Navionics from the input of the users of their automatic sounding products such as SonarPhone T-Box from Vexilar Marine Electronics. In conjunction with your iPad, it will draw a detailed depth chart of your anchorage as you motor around the harbor. It's an amazing product. It just recently added the ability to import routes, tracks, and waypoints but still only offers Active Captain markers where Aqua Map offers both Active Captain and Waterway Guide markers. Get Aqua Map too with their USACE survey charts and have the best of both worlds. I run both at the helm.

iCab Mobile Web Browser

Why does anyone need yet another browser? The Safari and Google browsers work fine and they now remember passwords and will fill in the blanks for credit cards and address data when ordering by mail. The only reason would be the features iCab has that they do not for the $1.99 price:
- Full-screen display, every pixel goes to the webpage
- Built-in adblocker although there are rumors that Google will add one.

Numbers

Numbers is the free Apple app that's compatible with Microsoft Excel. I use Excel on my Win 10 desktop and copy it over to the iPad and let the iPad convert it to Numbers format and vice versa. I use Numbers on the iPad because it allows full editing of spreadsheets, Excel on the iPad requires a monthly subscription to edit their files. I use the app for keeping track of fuel, engine hours, and cruising budget.

Pages

Pages is the free Apple version of Microsoft Word. It's a one-time buy (I hate yearly fees) and Apple is adding features all the time. I use it for all my word processing on Fleetwing. I do have to admit that I use Microsoft Word for writing my guide. It's the standard of the publishing industry and it's very good for that purpose.

RadarScope

RadarScope at $9.99 provides a radar view of local storms in higher resolution than on the weather channel. I use it all the time to track storms. There's also an in-app purchase to get a real-time display of lightning strikes in approaching storms so you can tell when to duck. RadarScope only displays the output from one radar station at a time. One additional feature I use a lot is the projection of a storm's direction with arrival times at marked intervals. This feature is very useful in timing when to get Hoolie ashore. A distance tool is available to also figure out a storm's arrival time based on the storm's speed, which is displayed for each major storm cell.

NOAA RadarUS

RadarUS for $1.99 is best for an overview of a large area for coming storms. RadarUS displays a composite map of all the radar images in the field of view, which can be just local or even the entire, US.

PredictWind

In the spring of 2019, I conducted a test of weather apps and PredictWind tied for the top three positions and perhaps just a little bit better than the other two. For details on the comparisons, see the Weather App Shootout series of articles I published in Waterway Guide: Round 1, Round 2, Round 3, and Round 4. It was developed for America's Cup races and I've found it to be generally more accurate than the rest although it does require a yearly subscription of $28.99. My longtime favorite, PocketGrib, came dead last in the Weather App Shootout. I no longer depend on its predictions but I do look at it for going up the New Jersey coast, it's not bad for that.

Windy

Windy which is still free did very well in the tests I published on Waterway Guide and it's free. The only slight difference was PredictWind's ability to predict severe weather on occasions.

Windfinder Pro

Windfinder Pro at $5.99 provides easy access to weather buoys and provides a wind display prediction similar to Windy. It's a nice combination of several data sources. It also came out near the top in the Weather App Shootout.

SwellInfo

SwellInfo for $2.99 is a specialized app that's aimed at surfers so it's focused on close to shore weather. Since I seldom go more than 2 to 3 miles off-shore when going down the coast, it's a good indicator to use for near-shore wind and waves. The NOAA forecasts cover a broad area, typically out to 20 NM, much farther than where I go. SwellInfo fills the void, and I've found it to be generally accurate for off-shore passages that stay within 3 miles of shore.

NOAA Marine Text Forecasts

I use a browser (Safari or iCab) to view marine text forecasts for free directly from NOAA. They download fast and NOAA should always be considered although I find them to be rather pessimistic on offshore passages (predicting weather that's worse than what actually happens).

National Hurricane Center

NOAA is the gold standard of hurricane path prediction and should always be considered during the hurricane season. Just use your browser to access the NOAA site at no charge.

Hurricane Tracker

It gives current data and tracks development of potential hurricanes even before they become a tropical storm, complete with potential tracks and winds. I especially like the "spaghetti" predictions for hurricane paths. It's a compilation of all the programs that output the predicted path of a tropical storm or hurricane. You can see how wide the uncertainty is between forecasting programs. The cost is $3.99.

Cyclocane

For the ultimate in spaghetti model tracking (where is that hurricane going?), Cyclocane is the web service of choice for displaying a hurricane's possible paths and even before NOAA predicts a path. You can go crazy looking at all the possible routes but it's entertaining while waiting for a hurricane to choose its path of destruction all at no charge.

Simplenote

I take a lot of notes on a sailboat, recording fuel taken on board, repairs made, spares on hand, various engine and sailboat component part numbers for easy reordering, etc. I need a free-form note-taking application. There are lots of them in the apps list. Simplenote is free for both the PC version and iPad and will automatically update all notes taken on all your computers in real-time. If I update a note on my iPad, I will find it updated automatically on my home computer, my laptop, and iPhone within seconds, very convenient.

Documents by Readdle

I tried a bunch of documentation programs and finally settled on the free app Documents by Readdle. I now have every operating manual for every piece of equipment on board in PDF format stored on my iPad. This feature alone is enough to justify the iPad to me. Not only are all the manuals stored in one place (the iPad), they can be searched (content too!) and type size or illustrations can be easily enlarged with the two-finger expand gesture on the iPad, which is great for aging eyes. It also interfaces with Safari so any PDF file displayed in Safari can be directly stored in Documents. Get rid of all those old, paper manuals with fine print (in dim light), download the PDF versions (they exist, just find them) and you'll never regret it.

An amazing added convenience of this program is the ability to sync any set of folders to your iPad by interfacing with any of the major cloud syncing services for free such as Google Drive (shown at left), Microsoft One Drive, Dropbox, and others. I have my iPad set to sync to a folder called "Files" on my desktop, about 50 or so subfolders with hundreds of files. Whatever I store in those folders will sync to my iPad automatically and vice-versa if I change a file while it's on the iPad. I can't overemphasize the importance of this feature to me. I just can't remember all the files I ought to take along for my 9-month cruises so I just store everything of importance in a folder called "Files" on my desktop and automatically sync all devices to that. No more missing that TurboTax file or scan of a doctor's bill, etc. As long as you don't store photos, you'll have a hard time exceeding 5 GB. I use Google Drive, which gives 15 GB of free storage. It syncs across all of my computers, tablets, and phones. If you need more than 15 GB you can upgrade to 100 GB for only $2/month, the best price out there. You can designate whether a folder stored in Google Drive is private (requiring a password) or public for viewing by anyone.

Apple Calendar

I used Google Calendar in the past but with the latest update to the Apple Calendar that comes with the iPad and iPhone, I just use it instead. It syncs between all my Apple products (iPad4, iPad Air 2, iPhone6, iPad Pro, iPad 2018) automatically. With the latest Apple update, it's easier to use than ever. I keep track of all my stops along the ICW for comparing my progress on the ICW year to year not to mention all those appointments we tend to accumulate, as the doctors we see get younger and younger.

The Weather Channel

The app provides a simple 10-day forecast and hourly forecasts for the first 24 hours with additional Weather Channel content, all for free. It's a good, basic weather app, nothing fancy.

Dark Sky

I supplement The Weather Channel with the free service Dark Sky which provides more detail on future weather that I've found very accurate. It's always good to have a second opinion.

Unit Converter

It can convert any unit to any other unit, handy on a boat and it's free.

Calculator!

I've changed over to a Texas Instrument type calculator; I couldn't get used to RPN types. It only costs $0.99.

uTrendnetCam

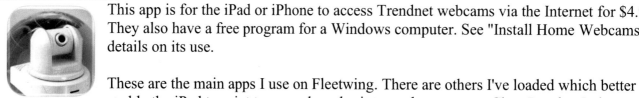

This app is for the iPad or iPhone to access Trendnet webcams via the Internet for $4.99. They also have a free program for a Windows computer. See "Install Home Webcams" for details on its use.

These are the main apps I use on Fleetwing. There are others I've loaded which better enable the iPad to print to my onboard printer and one game, tChessPro that I play occasionally. I'm sure there are many more out there but these are the ones that see the most use on Fleetwing. I also bought the Apple Bluetooth keyboard for those times I do a lot of entry and don't feel like poking around with two fingers on the touch keyboard screen; it works well and has a good feel. Also of use are the various banking apps (e.g., USAA, Chase) that, among other things, allow you to make a deposit just by taking a photo of the check, no trips to a bank required! Now that's a real time saver and it gets that check deposited right away without delay.

Managing Photos on a Boat

I've settled on Amazon Prime Photos which is free for Prime members for storing all my photos I take while on the ICW. I belong anyway to Amazon Prime anyway for the fast, free delivery of boat items as I go up and down the ICW. They are hard to beat in dependability and quick delivery. If you have a Prime account, you already have access to unlimited photo storage and it comes with no reduction in photo resolution like with some of the other services.

You can take all the photos you want and get them off your iPad, laptop and/or iPhone so their storage does not fill up. As a bonus, your photos are now available to your family if you chose to do so on any of their devices too, all at no charge beyond the cost of a Prime membership which I have anyway.

One added benefit is face recognition. If you identify several photos by name, the program goes to work in the background to group your photos by person. If I want to see all the photos of Matthew, then I'll type in his name and photos with him in the picture will be displayed (or Matthew and Nana together, or any other search criteria combination).

US Army Corps of Engineers (USACE) Hydrographic Surveys

The USACE routinely measures depths along the ICW and inlets and makes them available to the public. However, they are displayed in a confusing array of ways. The links in the guide are to the PDF versions of the surveys. Sometimes it leads to the exact chart of interest but sometimes the link will show a PDF file of an entire section of the ICW and you have to hunt for the part that interests you. It depends on how the USACE Districts choose to compile their data; it is not consistent from district to district. There are five districts covering the Atlantic ICW:

1. The Norfolk District covers from Norfolk, VA to North Landing VA.
2. The Wilmington District USACE covers from North Landing, VA, to Little River, SC.
3. The Charleston District covers from Little River, SC, to Port Royal, SC, as far as survey charts are concerned.
4. The Savannah District does not issue PDF survey charts for the ICW. They do issue files that Aqua Map can read and display
5. The Jacksonville District does not issue PDF survey charts but they do issue files that Aqua Map can read and display.

Bridge Heights

All fixed bridges on the ICW are supposed to give 65 ft of clearance at high tide except for the Julia Tuttle Causeway in Miami at 56 ft. Unfortunately, "supposed to" does not conform to reality on the ICW. In the spring of 2018, I took photos of every fixed height bridge from Ft Lauderdale to Hampton, VA. I noted the date and time of the photo and arranged them in a spreadsheet. I then looked up the tide at the time and computed the bridge clearance at the highest tide of the day per the nearest tide station and for a 0.0 tide. Unfortunately, there were 15 bridges that did not have height boards. Obviously, they were not included.

As an example of one with height boards, let's look at the International Speedway Blvd in Daytona at MM 830.1. I came through the bridge on 4/25/2019 at 7:29:21 EDT and took this photo of the height board. I figured the clearance to be 62.8 ft. I then found the nearest tide station, Ormond Beach in the Halifax River which is 4.6 NM north. The nearest tide station to the south is Ponce Inlet on the Halifax River at 9.2 NM away. I chose to use the closest tide station, 4.6 NM north.

Using Aqua Map's excellent tide charts, I changed the date to 4/25/2019 and moved the slider to 7:30 am and found the predicted tide to be 0.6 ft. I also noted the high tide of the day to be 0.7 ft from the text below the graph. Now I had enough data to compute the clearance at low tide and the clearance at high tide:

Clearance at Low Tide = 62.8 ft + 0.6 ft = 63.4 ft

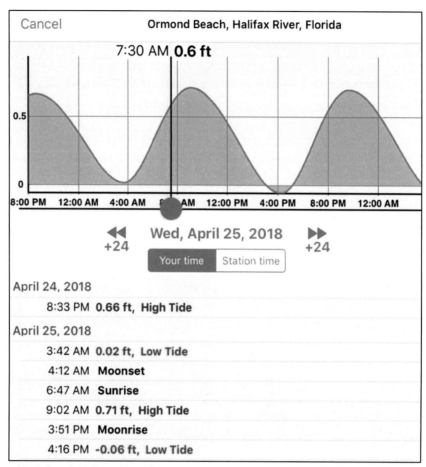

Clearance at High Tide = 63.4 ft - 0.7 ft = 62.7 ft

For the clearance at low tide, I just added the height of the tide per the tide chart at the time of passage to the visual reading of the height board. For the clearance at high tide, I just subtracted the highest tide for that day from the clearance at low tide I had just computed.

I performed the above calculations for each of the 73 fixed height bridges along the ICW based on photos I took in the spring of 2018 as I headed north from Ft Lauderdale. The data I collected was a one-day event. I did not correct for water levels other than predicted tides. So, at most, the charts are an indication, not a promise, but still may be useful in watching out for bridges of concern. The bridges around Coinjock are affected mostly by wind tides which I did not consider in the calculations. I just recorded what I saw on the day I passed under each bridge.

Clearance of ICW Bridges at Low Tide

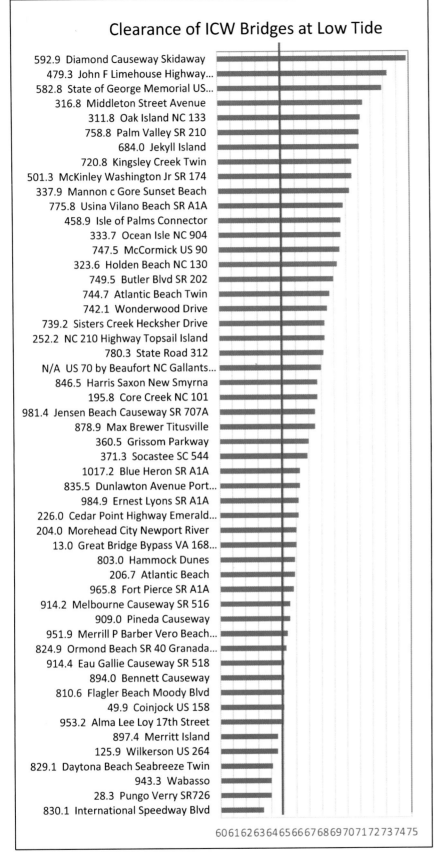

First, the good news, clearance at low tide to 65 ft is good for all the bridges except seven at the bottom in the chart.

830.1 International Speedway Blvd	63.4
28.3 Pungo Ferry SR726	64
943.3 Wabasso	64
829.1 Daytona Beach Seabreeze Twin	64.1
125.9 Wilkerson US 264	64.5
897.4 Merritt Island	64.5
953.2 Alma Lee Loy 17th Street	64.8

Next, we'll look at the high tide clearances.

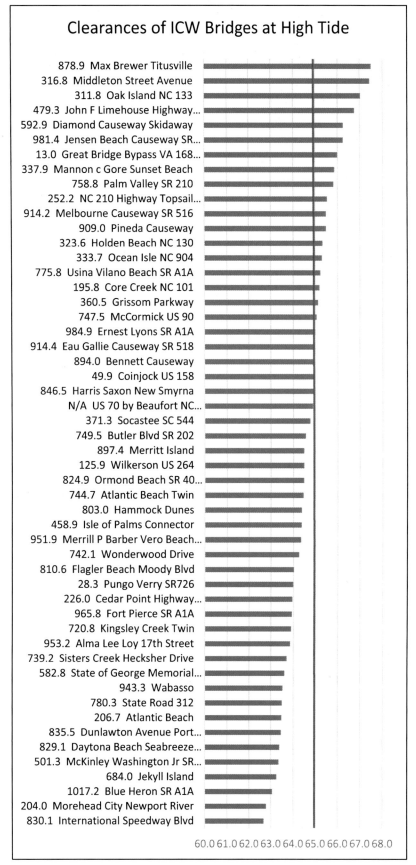

Clearances of ICW Bridges at High Tide

- 878.9 Max Brewer Titusville
- 316.8 Middleton Street Avenue
- 311.8 Oak Island NC 133
- 479.3 John F Limehouse Highway...
- 592.9 Diamond Causeway Skidaway
- 981.4 Jensen Beach Causeway SR...
- 13.0 Great Bridge Bypass VA 168...
- 337.9 Mannon c Gore Sunset Beach
- 758.8 Palm Valley SR 210
- 252.2 NC 210 Highway Topsail...
- 914.2 Melbourne Causeway SR 516
- 909.0 Pineda Causeway
- 323.6 Holden Beach NC 130
- 333.7 Ocean Isle NC 904
- 775.8 Usina Vilano Beach SR A1A
- 195.8 Core Creek NC 101
- 360.5 Grissom Parkway
- 747.5 McCormick US 90
- 984.9 Ernest Lyons SR A1A
- 914.4 Eau Gallie Causeway SR 518
- 894.0 Bennett Causeway
- 49.9 Coinjock US 158
- 846.5 Harris Saxon New Smyrna
- N/A US 70 by Beaufort NC...
- 371.3 Socastee SC 544
- 749.5 Butler Blvd SR 202
- 897.4 Merritt Island
- 125.9 Wilkerson US 264
- 824.9 Ormond Beach SR 40...
- 744.7 Atlantic Beach Twin
- 803.0 Hammock Dunes
- 458.9 Isle of Palms Connector
- 951.9 Merrill P Barber Vero Beach...
- 742.1 Wonderwood Drive
- 810.6 Flagler Beach Moody Blvd
- 28.3 Pungo Verry SR726
- 226.0 Cedar Point Highway...
- 965.8 Fort Pierce SR A1A
- 720.8 Kingsley Creek Twin
- 953.2 Alma Lee Loy 17th Street
- 739.2 Sisters Creek Hecksher Drive
- 582.8 State of George Memorial...
- 943.3 Wabasso
- 780.3 State Road 312
- 206.7 Atlantic Beach
- 835.5 Dunlawton Avenue Port...
- 829.1 Daytona Beach Seabreeze...
- 501.3 McKinley Washington Jr SR...
- 684.0 Jekyll Island
- 1017.2 Blue Heron SR A1A
- 204.0 Morehead City Newport River
- 830.1 International Speedway Blvd

60.0 61.0 62.0 63.0 64.0 65.0 66.0 67.0 68.0

The clearances at high tide aren't nearly so wonderful. I counted 31 bridges that are less than 65 ft at high tide!

830.1	International Speedway Blvd	62.7
204.0	Morehead City Newport River	63.8
1017.2	Blue Heron SR A1A	63.1
684.0	Jekyll Island	63.3
501.3	McKinley Washington Jr SR 174	63.4
829.1	Daytona Beach Seabreeze Twin	63.4
835.5	Dunlawton Avenue Port Orange SR A1A	63.5
206.7	Atlantic Beach	63.5
780.3	State Road 312	63.5
943.3	Wabasso	63.5
582.8	State of George Memorial US 80 Thunderbolt	63.6
739.2	Sisters Creek Hecksher Drive	63.7
953.2	Alma Lee Loy 17th Street	63.9
720.8	Kingsley Creek Twin	63.9
965.8	Fort Pierce SR A1A	63.9
226.0	Cedar Point Highway Emerald Island	64.0
28.3	Pungo Ferry SR726	64.0
810.6	Flagler Beach Moody Blvd	64.0
742.1	Wonderwood Drive	64.3
951.9	Merrill P Barber Vero Beach SR60	64.4
458.9	Isle of Palms Connector	64.4
803.0	Hammock Dunes	64.4
744.7	Atlantic Beach Twin	64.5
824.9	Ormond Beach SR 40 Granada Bridge	64.5
125.9	Wilkerson US 264	64.5
897.4	Merritt Island	64.5
749.5	Butler Blvd SR 202	64.6
371.3	Socastee SC 544	64.8
N/A	US 70 by Beaufort NC Gallants Channel	64.9
846.5	Harris Saxon New Smyrna	64.9

With all that data, how do you use it? It will at least give you a list of bridges to be concerned about if your mast is higher than the high tide clearance. There is room for error in the data since I did not take into account the average water height due to wind or flooding. It's just a snapshot in time around the spring of 2018. If you see something different, drop me a line using the link on my blog site at fleetwing.blogspot.com. Based on input, I'll keep the data up to date. Meanwhile, I have a photo for each bridge. The complete spreadsheet with dates and times for each passage under a bridge is available at 2018 ICW Bridge Heights. I also have all the photos of each bridge height board if anyone is interested. If so, just use the contact form on my blog site and I'll give you a link. Meanwhile, here are some of the more interesting photos:

The Morehead City – Newport River bridge. This is the bridge by the railroad tracks close to the entrance to Morehead City Yacht Basin. I took a piece of paper and marked off the scale and moved it to the bottom of the board to read the height which I arrived at 66 ft. That was on 5/11/18 at 1:34:37 pm with a 1.0 ft tide. The low tide clearance would be 67 ft but the high tide clearance would only be 63.8 ft with a high tide of 3.2 ft.

The Blue Heron (SR A1A) in Palm Beach MM 1017.2. I measured the height at 64 ft when I passed through on 4/17/18 at 11:25:25 with a 2.3 ft tide. At a 0.0 tide, the height would be 66.3 ft but at a high tide of 3.2 ft, it would only be 63.1 ft.

Jekyll Island bridge MM 684 measured to be 64 ft on 4/28/18 at 7:45:31 am with a 7.1 ft tide. The height at a 0.0 tide would be 71.1 ft but at a 7.8 high tide, it would only be 63.3 ft.

The Daytona Beach – Seabreeze Twin bridges at MM 829.1. I measured 63.5 ft on 4/25/18 at 7:37:30 with a tide of 0.6 ft. With a 0.0 tide, the clearance would be 64.1 ft but with a high tide of 0.7 ft, it would only be 63.4 ft. The problem with this bridge is the lack of a large tidal swing. The tide was only 0.7 ft so you have limited help from low tide.

The famous Atlantic Beach bridge at Morehead City, MM 206.7. I took a piece of paper, marked it in line with the height numbers, and held it up against the screen. I got a reading of 65.5 ft from the photo on 5/11/18 at 1:16:22 pm with a 0.4 tide. At a 0.0 tide, the clearance would be 65.9 ft but with a high tide of 2.4 ft, it would only be 63.5 ft.

There are many more examples. The bridges seem to be sinking into their sand foundations. I noticed the newer ones are taller. 65 ft masts are tough on the ICW.

41

When You Need a Doctor but You're Not Ashore

Care On Demand `12+`
Baptist Health South Florida

★★★★★ 43 Ratings
Free

I hadn't slept for the last two nights due to a hacking cough. I was miserable. I had a cold, which is usually no big thing, but this time it developed into bronchitis. I needed a doctor. Unfortunately, I was in the Marathon mooring field with nothing nearby. The local hospital was out of commission due to hurricane Irma and urgent care centers were far away. Calls to local doctors required an appointment and then getting a taxi, I needed help now. What to do?

That's when I discovered "Care on Demand" which is available throughout Florida although there are similar services across the country. When the local hospital was closed due to Irma, they placed a link on their webpage to download an app for your iPad or Android device. With the app, you could see a board-certified doctor 24/7 and get prescriptions sent to the nearest pharmacy of your choice.

I was intrigued. I downloaded the app to my iPad and when I opened it, I was asked to allow the app to access the camera and microphone. I filled in a short questionnaire on medical history any doctor would ask and requested an appointment. You are presented with a list of doctors with their specialties shown to select from (see iPad screenshot at right), I just chose the first one available. After a one-minute wait, I was greeted by a doctor, I could see the doctor, she could see me and we proceeded to discuss my condition. Normally a doctor would feel for swollen glands around my head but she had me press my fingers against my forehead, then sides of my face and my neck, asking each time if I felt any

pain or unpleasantness. Next was the typical, "Say ah" part but in this case, I moved over to directly in front of the camera and "opened wide." She didn't see anything amiss.

After completing the examination, she wrote three prescriptions, which I picked up at a local Walgreens. I also received a detailed report of the diagnosis with the usual medical terms I knew nothing of. I was curious concerning the three prescriptions and I used the patient portal of my medical doctor in New York to get his opinion on the diagnosis (they do not have an on-line service yet) and got an email back after 10 minutes that everything looked fine and the prescriptions were appropriate. With the prescriptions from a board-certified physician and the reinforcement from my own doctor, I took the medicine with confidence and I enjoyed the first good night's sleep in the last three days. I could see where this could revolutionize doctor care for people who can't get to a doctor face to face (although it is face to face over the iPad!) The cost of seeing the doctor was only $59.00 at the time. I believe this to be a great boon that all cruisers should know about!

Chapter 6: Basic Knowledge on the ICW

Aids TO Navigation (ATONs)

ATONs can be buoys, day beacons, lighthouses – anything used for marking a channel or hazard. ATONs marking a channel will be either red (known as a "nun") or green (known as a "can"). When proceeding south from Norfolk to Key West, you will pass red ATONs on your starboard side which will have a yellow triangle and green ATONs on your port side which will have a yellow square. However, there are exceptions when traveling through some rivers where the color rule does not apply but in those cases, you still pass the ATONs with the yellow triangle on your starboard side and the squares on your port side when headed southward – even if the red and green colors are reversed (as they are between the Dismal Swamp and Elizabeth City). The red day beacon shown in the picture has a yellow square so it should be honored as a green marker and passed to port when heading southward on the ICW. When passing across inlets, be sure to look for the yellow squares and triangles to distinguish between ICW ATONs and those marking the inlet channel.

Always Monitor Channel 16

When underway, always monitor channel 16. It's monitored by the Coast Guard and used for distress, safety and for the initial contact of another boat or marina unless the marina posts a different channel on their website. The Coast Guard will issue navigation warnings and other alerts over this channel.

Slow Down When Being Overtaken by a Faster Boat

ICW courtesy is for the overtaking boat to hail the forward boat at low power on channel 16 or 13 (13 is preferred but it's not always monitored) and ask permission to pass on one side or the other, at which time the overtaken boat replies and slows to idle as the overtaking boat passes slowly by.

After 1000 miles of this, the same maneuver is often shortened to the forward boat noticing the aft boat which then slows down to idle, the aft boat then passes slowly on the forward's boat port side, all without use of the VHF. In our experience, about 90% of passes are silent and the overtaking boat passes slowly about 90% of the time. If the overtaken boat doesn't slow down to idle, the overtaking boat will often speed by, in our experience. One more hint, after the overtaking boat passes, the overtaken boat should move across his wake, behind the boat so when he resumes normal speed, the increased wake that results will not wash over the overtaken boat. Don't forget to wave!

Always Ask for a Bridge Opening

There may be four boats ahead of you, and even though each one asked the bridge attendant for the next opening, you still need to call the attendant yourself and identify your boat for the next opening. Use channel 13 for bridge requests in Virginia and North Carolina. Use channel 9 in South Carolina, Georgia, and Florida. Repeat the name of the bridge three times followed by the name of your vessel and a request for an opening and wait for a response. If you get no response, repeat. Call for an opening even if the boats ahead of you already did so. It's important that the bridge tender know that you want to pass through.

Dropping the Anchor

Well, you don't just drop the anchor. Pick a spot where you want to anchor and approach it from downwind or current, depending on relative strength. Then the one at the helm stops the boat and the one at the bow lays out the chain as the boat is backed. The goal is to lay the chain on the bottom in a line from the anchor (no piling up!), snub it at 70 ft or so, and let it out the rest of the way for the depth, usually 80 to 90 ft. I use 5:1 with an oversized anchor and 3/8-inch chain. Then gently back the anchor in, not at high RPMs but enough to be sure the anchor has dug in. In soft mud, an initial hard set may not let the anchor settle into the mud for an eventual good set. In 20 years of anchoring at thousands of anchorages, we've never had an anchor drag using this technique (which of course will guarantee we'll drag all over the place this coming fall. Knock on wood!).

Picking up a Mooring or Weighing Anchor

The key to picking up a mooring or anchor is successful communication between the person on the bow who can see where the boat needs to go and the helmsman. For sailboats, there usually is a good line of sight between the helmsman and the person at the bow. For a powerboat, that may not be the case and wireless communication headsets may be needed. In weighing the anchor (raising the anchor), you want a vertical pull on the chain for least strain on the windlass, and at the end to rotate the anchor out of the bottom. If the helmsman has a clear line of sight to the bow, which is usually the case for a sailboat, then just use hand signals. They are very simple for us; I just point in the direction I want the bow to go. It's up to Ann to figure out how to make the boat go in that direction (ha!). If I want more thrust, I raise my palm; less thrust I lower my palm. Of course, the approach to picking up a mooring or weighing anchor is always into the wind and/or current, whichever is boss.

Dropping a Mooring

You would think this would be simple, just drop the mooring. That part is easy, but now you have to avoid the mooring line, other mooring balls, and moored boats in a crowded mooring field! When I drop the mooring line I then point at the mooring ball since Ann, at the helm, can't see it over the bow but now knows where it's at. I stand at the bow and keep pointing at the ball until I'm sure Ann can see it herself. In a busy mooring field, the helmsman is busy monitoring nearby boats or mooring balls that may be empty behind her or to the side and only has to glance at the bow person to know where the ball they just left is located. We've tried the alternate technique of the bow person pointing in the direction the boat should go, but the helmsman has a better view of mooring balls aft of the boat. If the helmsman knows where the mooring ball just dropped is currently located, then a path out of the field can be found.

Follow the Bends

The current through the ICW will usually cut a deeper path on the outside of curves rather than the inside. It is often tempting to "cut the corners" to take a more direct route between markers, but don't yield to the temptation unless you're in known deep waters. The deeper water is almost always on the outside of a curve in the ICW (never say always).

Swing into a Dock

When we first started out, we would approach a face dock parallel to the pilings. It was tough to estimate the best path and would invariably get a fender caught between a piling and the boat with something giving way and a lot of yelling. So now we come into a dock at a 30-degree angle and at the last-minute Ann will swing the bow over and throw the engine in reverse causing the boat to stop and drift into the dock with no fore or aft motion, all without bow thrusters. This is known as the "Captain Ron Maneuver" for those who have seen the movie, "Captain Ron," which I highly recommend.

Put Strength Where Strength is Needed

This can be a sensitive topic with some boaters. When picking up a mooring, sometimes strength is needed to pull up the rope and tie it off on a cleat. Who's best able to do that? Most of the time for cruising couples, the stronger of the two should be on the bow, not at the helm. The one at the bow can give directions by pointing which way to go for a successful pickup of a mooring and when anchoring or picking up an anchor, the strength should be at the bow for best results. Many boaters don't follow this guide and do okay but some situations do require an added boost of muscle, which one of the crew may have. It's up to you to decide which one. The same comment goes for docking. On Fleetwing, Ann does all the helm work: anchoring, mooring, and docking. I haven't docked a boat in months?

Getting off a Dock when Pinned by Wind and Waves

We were at Fernandina at a face dock when the wind piped up to 20 to 25 kts with wave action pushing us directly against the dock with the wind at a right angle to the boat. There were many boats at the long face dock and we were packed closely so the marina could maximize profit. There was no room for any motion forward or backward along the dock; you had to leave at a right angle to the dock, no other way. We watched with interest as the dockhands helped four large powerboats get off the dock. None used their bow thrusters; wind and wave action were too strong for their high bows. We copied their technique and exited the dock without a problem although we did turn the dinghy upside down. Okay, so what steps did they follow that we copied?

Step 1: Tie a line to the forward cleat on the boat. Check to make sure the end of the line is NOT knotted (does not have a stopper knot).

Step 2: Loop the line to a cleat on the dock about halfway down the length of the boat and lead it back to the same forward cleat on the boat and secure it, don't try to hold it by hand, as you won't succeed.

Step 3: Put a large fender by the forward cleat on the lifeline so it can be moved by sliding it in case you misestimate the point of contact between the dock and your bow.

Step 4: After being sure all other lines are off, power the boat forward and turn the wheel into the dock. This will cause the aft to swing out away from the dock.

Step 5: Wait until the boat has swung out about 45 degrees, turn the wheel in the opposite direction and then power the boat in reverse as the forward line is released. If you have help on the dock, the line can be slipped off the dock cleat, or the crew on the boat can flip it off the cleat. If worse comes to worst, just let the line go, and since you already checked that it has no stopper knot in step 1, the line will slip through the cleat. This latter option is only to be used as a last resort but it does work; we saw one power boater use it when his crew couldn't get the line off the dock cleat in time. Be sure to retrieve the line quickly so it doesn't foul the prop!

Step 6: Go out about twice as far as you think you need before powering forward, turning the boat away from the dock. It's surprising how quickly the wind and waves will blow you back towards the dock you just left so give yourself plenty of room! One large powerboat didn't go out far enough and his transom hit the dock as he looped back to the dock and turned.

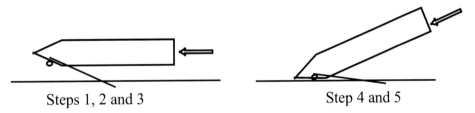

Steps 1, 2 and 3   Step 4 and 5

This technique also works well at Marathon when at the water dock. They even have one piling placed several feet away from the concrete bulkhead for snuggling the bow up against when leaving by backing out.

In calm winds under 15 kts, it's easy to do the reverse by leaving the dock going forward using a line on an aft cleat on the boat to a forward dock cleat and put the engine in reverse. This causes the bow to swing out, but that technique will not work in 20 to 25 kts of wind and 2 ft waves against the dock on a boat with a high bow that catches a lot of wind. You need the power of a prop working in its most efficient direction, forward, to get the aft section to swing away from the dock. Every captain at the dock on that windy day, about a dozen with 40 to 70 ft boats, used this technique. We use it whenever we're in tight quarters and there's no room to go forward. It works every time. You should practice both techniques in calm conditions so you're ready to use either one under more stressful weather. This is an important skill you must know when cruising the ICW.

How to Import Routes Using GPX Data

For several of the shallow spots, it's useful to have waypoints to follow when the route is not well marked. For some areas, I've listed waypoints in the guide that can be entered manually. However, a better way is to use GPX data for the exchange of routes between programs or apps. The format was released in 2002 and is used by all charting programs on all devices including those on the PC, Mac, iPad, iPhone, Android, and so on. The other advantage besides saving tons of time is the elimination of transcription errors. I maintain an updated list of routes that can be downloaded in GPX format on my blog site under Cruising Tips, GPX Routes and in many of the Waterway Guide Alerts.

All chartplotters accept GPX data but the technique varies between manufacturers. You have to consult their manuals to find out how to move GPX data to their chartplotters. What I will cover is how to get GPX routes into the most common apps that allow it. The same technique applies to importing Tracks.

GPX File use:

A GPX file is a universal format used to exchange routes, waypoints, and tracks between navigation apps and programs and is supported by all such programs. Examples for loading a GPX file into sample programs and apps are given below.

Part 1: **Do this first on your tablet**
- Use your browser (Safari on iPad, other browsers may not work) to open GPX Routes.
- Tap on the GPX file of your choice.
- A screen will appear showing the name of the file you just downloaded with an option to "Open in" an app and a second line labeled "More." If the default choice is not the app you want, then tap "More" for more choices and slide the top row of icons until the app you want appears and tap the icon.
- When asked "Import User Data?", click "Import". You will get a success screen.
- See below for further instructions for typical apps.
Alternatively, you can tap on a link in the Waterway Guide Alert for the shallow spot and a choice will pop up on which app to download to.

Part 2: Different for each app as described below
For Aqua Map:
  - The first time you load the route it will automatically appear, ready for navigation. To access it again after the first download, follow the instructions below.
  - Tap on the search icon to the upper, right of the screen.
  - Tap on User Data and Routes.
  - The route you imported will be in the list shown, scroll until you find the route.
  - Tap on the route name and it will be shown on the chart ready for navigation.

For iNavX:
- Tap on Routes at the bottom of the screen if the routes screen is not already shown
- Tap on the route just imported
- Tap on "Scroll To" for the route to be shown on a chart

For Garmin BlueChart: (no longer offered but people still use it)
- Tap on the ship's wheel icon at the bottom, middle of the screen
- A screen showing "My Content" will pop up
- Tap on "Routes"
- A list of routes will be displayed, tap on the one you want to use
- Tap on the "Hamburger" icon at the upper right (three horizontal bars)
 - One choice will be to "View on Chart", tap on that choice to see the route for navigation.

For Garmin Active Captain:
- Tap the Chart tab at the top of the screen
- Tap the "Hamburger" icon at the top left
- Tap User Data
- Find your downloaded route and tap on View on Chart. Garmin Active Captain does not download tracks.

For Navionics – This is a new capability for Navionics as of June 2019
- Tap on "Menu"
- Tap on Routes (or Tracks), your file will be in the list
- Tap on your file, the route will be displayed ready for navigation.

For Downloading the GPX file to your computer
- Click on GPX Routes and click on the GPX route you want to download.
- The downloaded file will appear at the bottom left of the window. It has already been saved in your default download location per your Windows preferences, usually a folder called "Downloads." You have to know this location so you can access it for copying the file to your PC navigation program. A Mac computer has a similar feature.
- Open your PC navigation program and import the GPX file.

To transfer a GPX file from a computer to an iPad:
- Attach the GPX file to an email addressed to yourself.
- Open the email on your iPad and hold your finger on the file icon, a menu will appear.
- Slide the top menu to the left and tap on the app you wish to use.
- If you're asked to okay the import, tap Yes.

Other apps have different ways of accessing routes but once the route is loaded into the app, all you have to do is find the route in the various menus.

Calibrate the Fuel Gauge

If your fuel gauge is like mine, it's woefully inaccurate. The ¼, ½, etc. markings bear little relationship to actual tank volume. However, you can calibrate the gauge to within a couple of gallons easily enough. All you need to do is note where the needle is against some marking on the gauge (I use the letters TANK printed on the gauge) and record how many gallons you take on each time, I use a spreadsheet on my iPad. After about 10 tankfuls at different starting points, you will be able to estimate the fuel remaining to within a gallon just by looking at the gauge. Alternatively, you can use the hour meter with the rate of fuel usage per hour to also compute the remaining fuel. This technique is complicated if you have a genset using diesel fuel out of the same tank. I just look at the fuel gauge while Ann watches the pump and call out how many gallons I expect to take on so she can warn me when getting close to filling up.

Prevent the ICW Mustache

When traveling down the ICW you will run into water with a lot of tannins, especially in swampy areas. The tannin will stain the bow of your boat forming the famous "ICW Mustache." In years past I've battled the affliction using Marykate On/Off which works quickly and does the job. However, it's better to prevent it in the first place. I had always used paste Fleetwax No 885 pictured at left but still had the problem. Last spring, I discovered that if I put on two coats of Fleetwax, I did not develop the ICW Mustache! So last summer when I hauled Fleetwing I put on three heavy coats of Fleetwax at the waterline near the bow it survived the trip to

Key West and about ½ way back before developing the bow stain again. I guess even paste wax eventually wears off. The basic problem is that fiberglass is porous and you need a coating that will close the pores. Wax will work if it's applied heavily enough so it doesn't wear off too soon. I imagine some of the chemical treatments that seal the fiberglass will also work, but I haven't tried them. It's nice to have a clean bow

Put a Waypoint at Every Bridge You Can't Clear

If you use the Aqua Map navigation app, then you have access to the ETA of every waypoint in your route. You've entered a bunch of waypoints to follow the meandering ICW and if you also add a waypoint on top of each bridge location, then Aqua Map will compute the time of arrival to that bridge. This is very handy in judging whether to speed up or slow down to make an opening for a bridge that you can't otherwise clear. If you purchase Aqua Map Master, then it automatically gives you an ETA to each bridge as part of its Route Explorer function but you still have to enter a route, you just don't have to put a waypoint at each bridge.

Pass Dredges on the Side with the Diamond Shapes Displayed

You will likely encounter a dredge or two while traveling the ICW. The first question that comes to mind is which side to pass the dredge on? The first choice is to call the dredge and ask, usually channel 13 but other channels may have to be tried if you get no answer (16, 64, 65, 68, etc.) At last resort, the side of the dredge marked with two diamond shapes are supposed to be the deep-water side as maintained by the dredge operator – circled in yellow in the picture. In the picture, I'm looking out over my bow and approaching the dredge from aft and so I should pass the dredge on my port side.

Traveling with Pets

There are lots of pets on boats. People like their dogs and cats, and there is no reason why they can't happily go with you. Hoolie is a Brittney which is a very active breed and yet on a boat when underway, he just settles down and mostly sleeps. However, he's all alert and active when we come into a marina or drop anchor! He's is also a breed that doesn't bark much. He's a bird dog and I guess they are bred not to bark so they don't scare the birds when out hunting until told to. That's handy on a boat so you can leave him in a marina when you go for groceries and know he's not going to drive all the neighbors crazy.

When we traveling, we get him to shore three times a day. Once in the morning, then when we pull into a marina or anchorage and again before bedtime. We never tried to teach him to "go on the boat." I suppose we should have but just never did. We feed him dog food that we can buy at the local Walmart, nothing fancy. We don't have time to send away for anything special, he seems to thrive on it. He weighs 45 lbs and has for the last 10 years. Negotiating the ladder to the salon is not a problem nor is getting in the dinghy since we have a sugar scoop stern. He occasionally falls into the water and then will swim to the nearest floating object and hangs on for dear life. We now have a harness for him with a loop on top so we can fish him out after such adventures with a boat hook. Hoolie wears a leather collar with a rabies tag, dog license, a tick collar, and a metal tag with his name, our cell phone number, and the boat name. He was "chipped" as a puppy and we carry a list of his shots.

There has never been a problem at any marina. He is leashed when off the boat, and we clean up after him. Hoolie may bark to say hello, but he is not a barker. If you need to leave your dog on board for a short time, make sure he is secure and can't "jump ship." Hoolie is a Brittany so he needs exercise. When possible, we have morning and afternoon walks (we need exercise too). Dog parks are his favorite place where he loves to chase a tennis ball. On a leash, Hoolie is like a thoroughbred before the derby, forty-five pounds of energy. Back on the boat, he stretches out and keeps an eye on the passersby. It's great to have a pet on board; it's part of the cruising lifestyle.

Kids on Board

This could be another whole chapter but I'll keep it short. A rite of passage in the Sherer family for grandkids is to spend time on Fleetwing for one of the legs going south. The tradition started with Matthew and was kept alive by Sarah and Finn. Last year, all five grandkids joined us for a cruise on Long Island Sound. Here's the bare minimum you need to do to promote harmony on board.

You need a charging table with an ample supply of USB outlets for charging. The kids live by their phones and tablets. The Ravpower unit is the best charger available. You will still need some 120v outlets, not all the kids will have 12v USB chargers. The Foval 150W inverter is a good unit. It's efficient and doesn't use much idle current. I plug a six-outlet power strip into the output of the Foval inverter for lots of plugs. Keep in mind that it's only good for low amp uses but 150 watts is plenty for charging kids' devices.

You need a hotspot for kids to log into with their phones and devices. One might declare that all phones and tablets, etc., must be stored and not accessed while onboard so the full enjoyment of being on a boat can be experienced. Okay, after the total mutiny, you might want to reconsider such a strategy. The internet connection is part of their world now. I use the hotspot feature on my iPhone and also the iPad. With the Verizon unlimited plan, I no longer have to track usage.

Naturally, everyone has an assigned duty when docking and anchoring. They all want to be part of the action and the most popular action is driving the dinghy when I take Hoolie ashore. One of their duties is to write their part of the blog every night while Ann and I enjoy wine in the cockpit. They all like to be in the water but along the ICW, we don't allow that due to the threat of alligators except in known safe waters like Marine Stadium in Miami.

They all take part in boat chores and rotate through tasks like washing dishes. As for entertainment, they bring a lot of books and DVDs and I provide some nautical DVDs. The titles I've found the most popular are Captain Ron (with the Captain Ron maneuver), Overboard, and Hot Pursuit. Unlike adults, the kids like to watch these movies over and over and over (ugh) but Captain Ron is by far the favorite.

Chapter 7: ICW University

I've assembled a variety of topics that may interest those traveling in-shore along the ICW. They are aimed at boaters with on the water experience but with additional information, they may have not encountered if they haven't cruised the ICW extensively.

Topic 1: Resources for ICW Navigation

Some say, just follow the Aid to Navigation (ATONs). Others say pay more attention to the chart. Others have favorites like SonarChart from Navionics. The surveys from USACE are also popular to follow. Then there are the crowdsourced data from Waterway Guide and Active Captain. There are also many guide books, including my own ICW Cruising Guides. The choices can be bewildering, there are so many. I've collected a list so you can decide for yourself what to use.

Charts

First, let's address definitions so we're all talking about the same things. A chart can be on a chartplotter, a tablet (e.g., iPad) or on paper, it doesn't matter as far as accuracy if they are all up to date and viewed at the proper zoom level. National Oceanic and Atmospheric Administration (NOAA) develops and maintains for free use the coastal charts for the US, updated every seven days. Not every chart is updated, only the ones with changes, perhaps 10 to 15%. Even then, the changes usually affect only small areas of the updated chart, most areas are the same. How those updated charts find their way into navigation programs and apps vary between the providers.

Some use the raw charts from NOAA: Raster Navigational Charts (RNC) that look like their paper counterparts or Electronic Navigational Charts (RNC). iNavX will display the RNC chart for free once you buy their app. Likewise, SEAiq will display either format for free once the app is bought. Both apps read the raw NOAA chart catalog and after an update (press a button), your charts will be to the same level as on the NOAA site. Charts other than NOAA are available for an additional price from each app.

Other navigation apps take a different approach. Their starting point is still the NOAA database but the charts are formatted into a seamless whole so when you zoom or pan, there's no hesitation in the screen display. Also added to the chart in several cases are Waterway Guide and Active Captain icons as well as tide and current markers and other information. With the formatting and additional icons added, the cost is in the additional processing required by the provider so the frequency of updating cannot be the same day the updated NOAA charts are released as is the case with iNavX and SEAiq which uses the NOAA format directly. Aqua Map rebuilds its charts directly from the NOAA source every three months, no change is missed since the rebuild is directly from the NOAA standard. Navionics depends upon manual updates to their Navionics+ charts based on changes to the NOAA charts and, in some cases, from other inputs. The changes lag NOAA but can be close if all the changes are caught during the manual corrections which is not always the case.

In a league by itself are the SonarCharts from Navionics. They receive inputs from boaters using chartplotters they partner with that upload soundings to Navionics as they navigate along the ICW or anywhere else they go. Navionics takes the uploads and constructs their SonarChart product with 1 ft depth contours. Updates are provided upon clicking (or tapping) on the "Update All" button in their app. Be ready for huge updates, usually in the 300 to 700 MB which can be even higher if you let the updates go longer than a couple of weeks. The algorithms used by Navionics to create their SonarCharts are not shared so I do not know how they do it or the weights they may give to different inputs, I can only see the results in the examples that will follow this discussion.

US Coast Guard (USCG) ATONs

ATON is short for Aids TO Navigation and they are maintained by the US Coast Guard (USCG). Most of the weekly corrections to the NOAA charts are for changing ATON positions, new, or destroyed ATONs. One might think that ATONs would be more accurate than the charts since it's the charts that are being updated, not the ATONs which have already been repositioned by the USCG. However, there are many places where there are no ATONs and the charts can be useful for staying centered in a narrow channel or when crossing an area with strong currents. There are also some cases where the ATONs will lead you into shallow water. I would expect that to eventually be corrected but the USCG has a huge workload and can't always move or add every buoy as needed. I will cover all this in more detail later with examples.

US Army Corps of Engineers (USACE) Depth Surveys

Another source of very valuable charts are the soundings taken by USACE districts along the ICW. They have survey boats that pass through the areas of their responsibility and take soundings to a resolution of 1 ft and map the locations of all the ATONs. The soundings are published and available for everyone to use. The Wilmington USACE will survey the inlets as often as needed, sometimes multiple times a month such as at Shallotte and Lockwoods Folly and even publish recommended routes through the shallows. It is invaluable information and Waterway Guide includes the most recent soundings in the form of a chartlet in the alerts for each area and a GPX file of the USACE recommended route available for downloading off the Waterway Guide site. The Charleston USACE does a survey of the ICW about once a year, not as often as Wilmington but still very useful since they cover the Isle of Palms and south of Charleston down to Port Royal. The Savannah and Jacksonville USACEs do spot surveys of some shallow spots but coverage is missing in many areas. The Wilmington and Charleston USACE districts publish PDF charts of their surveys but the other districts only publish the underlying data. Aqua Map Master imports data from all districts (the five I mentioned but also from other districts across the US) and displays it ready for navigation in their app. One advantage of the PDF charts by the Wilmington district is that they show the updated locations of the ATONs, ahead of when NOAA charts are updated.

Crowdsourced Data

Waterway Guide and Active Captain are the two biggest collectors of crowdsourced data. Both can be useful in avoiding shoaling areas as well as general information about marinas, anchoring, and other items of interest. Active Captain accepts all inputs as is but Waterway Guide editors look over the input first before publishing. An input like, "Came through at high tide, no problems" is not particularly informative and we've all skipped over such reviews when reading Active Captain posts and maybe even looking for a post by Bob423. In Waterway Guide, an editor, often an On The Water Editor (me for the ICW), will contact the poster for more information on the actual depth readings, tide level, depth of keel, etc. to make the post more useful and roll the results up into a unified guidance post at the beginning of the hazard alert. Since I personally maintain the Waterway Guide alerts, I naturally look first at the latest information from that source since I know it will be up to date and as accurate as I can make it. I access both sources in deciding the best way to negotiate a shallow area. The great advantage of crowdsourced data is immediacy. It's the "it's happening right now" that's important and is usually in advance of NOAA or ATONs position updates and even USACE surveys.

Given this background, how do you proceed to find the best path for navigation for a day's run? In the next topic, I'll examine that question with examples.

Topic 2: Considerations in Navigation

Let's examine four examples of navigation where there's conflicting information on how to proceed.

Example 1: Browns Inlet in North Carolina at MM 238

Below is the 6/12/2019 NOAA chart for Browns Inlet downloaded directly from the NOAA server. As you approach Browns Inlet, The ATONs look nothing like you see on the chart.

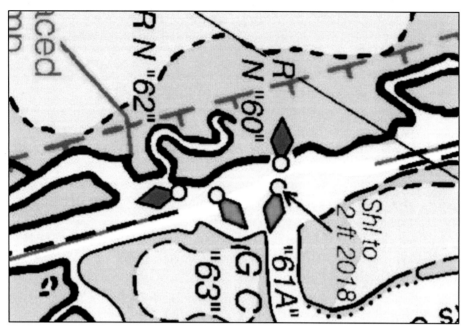

Let's look at what the area really looks like in the USACE survey of 4/16/2019. It shows the current positions of all the ATONs, the depths to 1 ft readings, and a recommended route in blue.

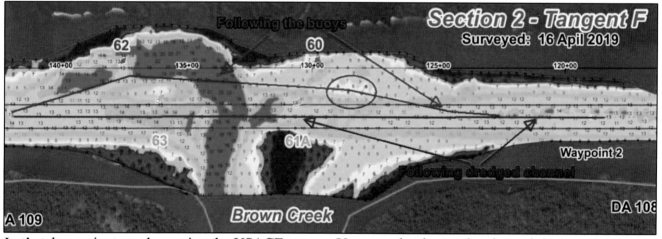

Let's take a minute and examine the USACE survey. You can clearly see the channel that was just dredged. It's right down the middle of the survey in a straight line. You can also see that the buoys have not been moved to show the newly dredged route. The dredging was completed in January 2019 and yet the Coast Guard still had not moved the buoys to guide boaters through the dredged channel as of 6/15/2019! Although the labels for G61A and G63 are on the south side of the channel, if you look closely, you'll see that the buoy symbol is on the other side of the channel. The blue line shows the correct, deep water path. The red line shows the path if you honor the buoys – right into shoal water (circled in red)! The Coast Guard even issued a shoaling alert since boaters were following the buoys they neglected to move and running into the circled shoal in the chart above! Given the above discussion, what would you do at Browns Inlet on 6/10/2019? If your preference is to always honor the buoys, you would run into shoal water at low tide. Let's look at another asset used by many boaters, the Navionics SonarChart.

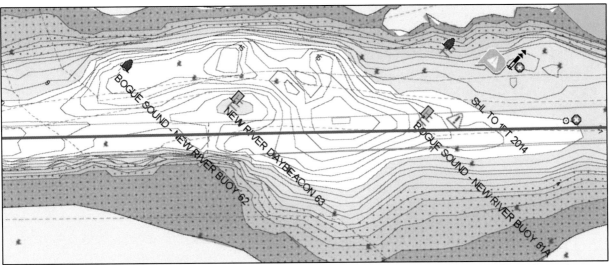

There has been enough time for SonarChart to update their charts based on soundings from boaters with compatible chartplotters that passed through Browns Inlet. The blue line is the straight-through path and SonarChart shows it as being at least 10 MLLW.

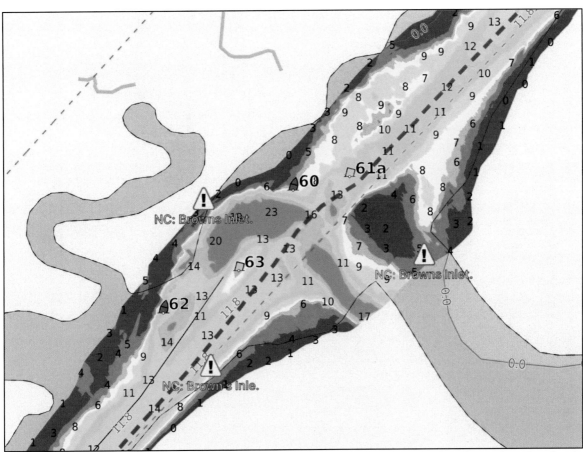

Aqua Map Master is shown above as it displays the USACE survey chart (north up). It also clearly shows the dredged channel and the placement of the buoys. The blue dotted line shows the correct deep-water path. Having looked at USACE, NOAA, and SonarChart, where does crowdsourced data come into play? From Waterway Guide, you would know that the buoys had not been moved as of 6/15/2019 and that the best strategy is just to go straight through the inlet crossing. The bottom line for Browns Inlet on 6/15/2019 is that the USACE survey charts, the SonarChart, and Aqua Map Master would show you the deep-water path through but if you followed the buoys, you would find shoal water at MLLW. Score a miss for following the ATONs.

Example 2: Altamaha Sound by R208 in Georgia at MM 659

Below is the NOAA chart of the area, 11508 cleared through 5/18/2019. You wish to travel from R206, by R208 and finally by G209. If you just exited R206, you would be sorely tempted to just head for R208. If you did and it was low tide, you would go aground at the 2 ft MLLW spot. This is a case where the NOAA chart is correct but the ATONs are not placed correctly to guide the boater safely through.

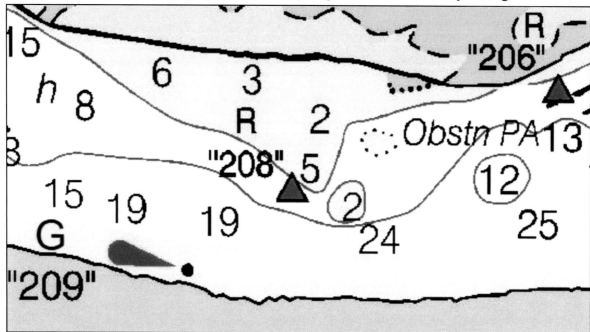

Both the Navionics SonarChart and the Aqua Map Master charts will guide you through to avoid the shoal. The Aqua Map Master chart with the USACE overlay is shown below.

There is no ambiguity here. Don't go over the shallow area shown in red! The blue line is the correct path.

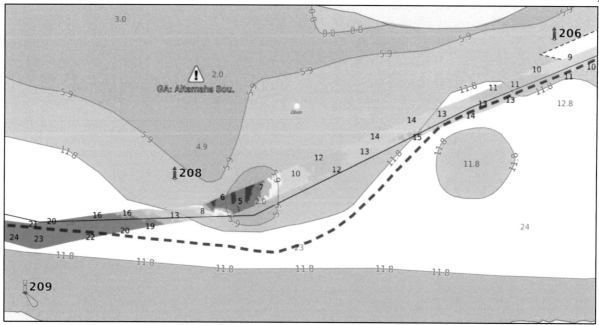

Crowdsourced data like Waterway Guide or Active Captain would both give you guidance to pass R208 far to the green side, by about 300 feet. This example is yet another strike for "just follow the ATONs." This shoal and R208 have been here like this for at least the last five years.

Example 3: New River in North Carolina at MM 244

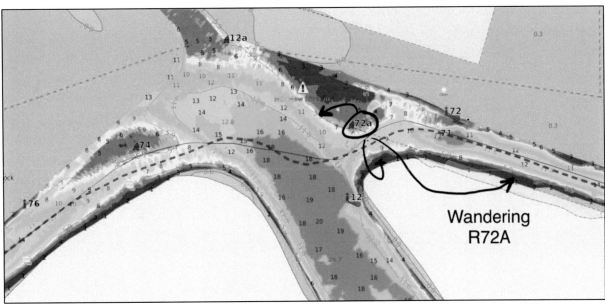

A third example is one area that has given cruisers fits over the last two years, New River. R72A has been a wanderer of the first magnitude. At various times over the last year, R72A been reported at three locations shown in the Aqua Map Master chart above.

Getting through the inlet is just a matter of following the deep water as shown in Aqua Map Master but if you follow the ATONs, then you could have run aground when R72A is off station. How would you know? Well, that's the value of crowdsourced data, reporters in the field (boaters) post what they see as they go through shallow spots on the ICW Cruising Facebook page and hopefully on Waterway Guide and Active Captain. The New River area is confusing enough without having to contend with missing or drifting buoys.

Example 4: Lockwoods Folly in North Carolina at MM 321

The NOAA charts are not useful at inlets where there's rapid shoaling so I won't even show an example. In the chart above, the 6/6/2019 USACE survey is shown. You can see that a spur of shoaling (circled in yellow) has developed at G47A right into the channel. That spur was not present three weeks ago.

In the previous examples, SonarChart also had the right path shown, how about in this case? Let's take a look.

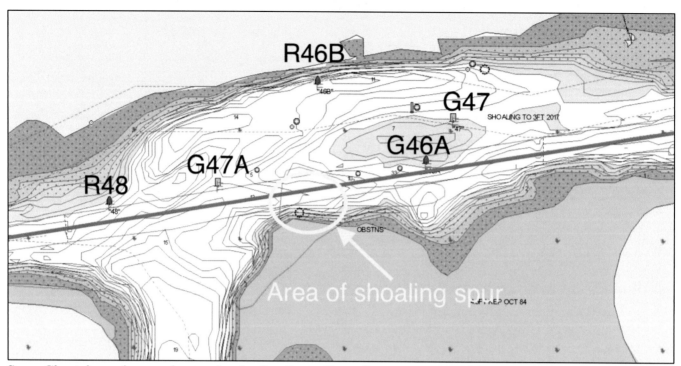

SonarChart depends upon boaters' uploads of soundings. It cannot respond immediately to rapid shoaling; the process needs multiple inputs and time to integrate the depth data into SonarChart. If you followed SonarChart in this case, you would have run into the spur of shoaling at low tide. Confusing the matter further are the ATONs, they are not shown in the correct locations. R48 is too far to the east, G47A on the wrong side of the channel, R46B is not there, and G47 is not there. Do not take this criticism as a knock against SonarChart, it is a valuable resource 95 % of the time and it has a home at the helm on Fleetwing, you just need to be aware of its limitations.

What is the point of all these examples? What I've been trying to illustrate is that it's not a good strategy to just depend upon one source for your navigation data. In brief, I would suggest a priority approach when planning a day's run:

Priority One: Use Aqua Map Master to display USACE surveys if they are current as the number one priority and the GPX routes based on their waypoints. Aqua Map Master will display the surveys for navigation and accepts GPX routes and tracks as aids to navigation. The USACE surveys are updated once/week in Aqua Map Master. The GPX routes will change throughout the year as new surveys are completed.

Priority Two: Use the crowdsourced data, be it either Waterway Guide or with less detail, Active Captain. There is no substitute for on-the-water reporting. I have a bias towards Waterway Guide since I personally maintain the alerts for the ICW but Active Captain can be useful too if you have confidence in the poster.

Priority Three: Use SonarChart, it's good for 95% of the ICW. Check it against priorities one and two to be sure it's telling you the right path to follow. Navionics recently fixed their greatest limitation, their latest release as of June 2019 now supports the importing of routes and tracks. Take note: Immediately after dredging, SonarChart will not be accurate, it takes some time to collect boaters' depth data and fold that into SonarChart. Eventually, it will self-correct. It will not show a rapidly shoaling area like in example 4. A USACE survey, on the other hand, will be accurate on the day it's published.

Keep in mind that iNavX and SEAiq are other options and will always have the latest raw NOAA charts upon hitting the update button. Aqua Map follows with a complete update every three months (weekly for surveys). Whether you prefer the user interface and ease of operation of iNavX, SEAiq or Aqua Map depends upon your personal preferences. All three will accept loading of GPX routes.

Topic 3: Units of Measurements on the ICW

Distance: The worldwide unit of measurement of distance on water is the nautical mile (abbreviated NM). The original reason for the unit can be traced back to the early days of celestial navigation where it simplified distance measurements on a chart with lines of latitude (enough said, this could consume a book). Unfortunately, the unit of measurement on NOAA charts along the ICW is the statute mile and is displayed every 5 miles along the ICW. You will find all references to anchorages, marinas, and hazards made in statute miles from the starting point by Hospital Point in Norfolk, Virginia. One nautical mile equals 6076 feet. To convert statute miles to nautical miles, multiply by 0.87. I use both measurements in this guide.

Speed: Speed on the water is measured in knots. A boat going one knot will cover one nautical mile in one hour. Wind on the water is also measured in knots.

Direction: The directional readout on an electronic compass is in degrees, either true or magnetic. True is referenced to the Earth's north pole. Magnetic is referenced to the Earth's magnetic pole. There can be a difference of a few to 10 to 20 degrees between the two. The mechanical compass at the helm points to Earth's magnetic pole. The electronic compass in the boat or as part of your phone or tablet can be selected to show either one in Aqua Map and most other apps (the app applies an internal correction if magnetic direction is desired).

Topic 4: What is MLLW and how do I use it?

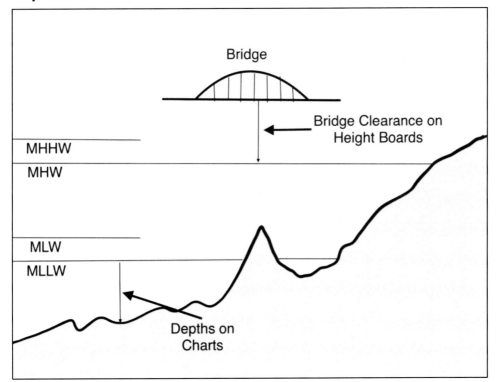

We have all used tide tables and have seen references to MLLW or MLW. What do they mean and how can I use them?

The tide tables or graphs you see in popular navigation apps like Navionics or Aqua Map predict the height of the tide above Mean Lower Low Water (MLLW).

Where does that come from? If you look at a series of tides at a location along the east coast, you will generally see two low tides for any given day. One tide will be lower than the other one. If you take the lowest tide of the day and average that reading across 19 years, then the resulting value is MLLW for that tide station, it's called the MLLW datum. The various datums are illustrated in the graphic above.

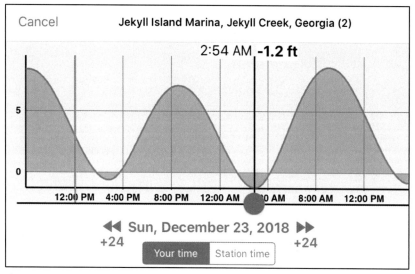

The value given by the tide chart or graph at any given time is the height of the water above the MLLW value calculated over the last 19 years. So, with the tide table readout in hand, what use is the height above MLLW? It turns out that it's very useful since the depths shown on the charts are also referenced to MLLW. A depth of 3.0 ft on the chart means that spot is 3.0 ft above MLLW. If you are going through Jekyll Creek and the tide is at 2.0 ft above MLLW and the charted depth is 3 ft, then you'll have 5 ft of water depth total. Knowing your draft, you can figure whether or not that's enough.

You will see from the tide charts that the MLLW number can be positive or negative. What does that mean? If it's negative, then the height of the tide is even less than the 19-year average of MLLW. In the above example, if the tide was -1.2 MLLW (a drain tide), then the 3.0 reading on the chart will mean there's only 1.8 ft of water for your boat! In short, just take the tide reading from the nearest station and add it to the depth reading shown on the chart (from high school math, adding a negative number looks like this: 3.0 ft + (-1.2 ft) = 1.8 ft.

There are other datums such as MLW (average of both low water readings per day over the last 19 years), MHW (average of both high-water readings over the last 19 years) and others. MHW is of value since that's

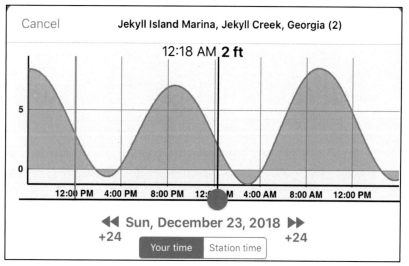

the reference for the height of bridges! Unfortunately, the easily accessible tide tables in nav apps only show water height referenced to MLLW. The MHW level is nowhere to be found. NOAA does publish MHW data which could be used to calculate bridge clearances but they only do that for the main tide station (Harmonic) in a given area.

We are getting more complicated here. NOAA has a main station and then there are subordinate stations based on a delta off the main station. Most likely, the tide station of interest to you by a bridge will be one of the subordinate stations which only has a reference to MLLW. Only the main Harmonic station has a selectable reference, one of which is MHW. It's not practical to track that down but they are available from NOAA. In my 2019 ICW Cruising Guide, I have a photo of every height board I found on the ICW in the fall of 2018 and calculated the clearance at MLLW based on the nearest tide station. It could be of use to those with masts taller than 63 feet.

Knowing the tide is well and good but there also other components to consider: wind and rain tides. How do you figure those effects? That's the subject of another article. Until then, just use a rule of thumb that an on-shore wind around 15 kts will raise water up to a foot and an off-shore wind will do the opposite.

Topic 4: Wind Tides – What are They and How Do They Affect Me?

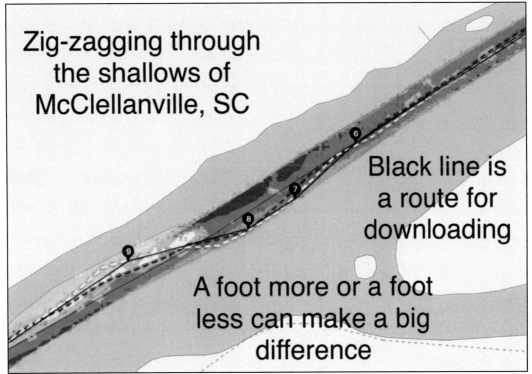

Everyone knows how to account for tides when traversing shallow areas of the ICW by looking at the nearest tide station but how does one account for wind tides? We all are aware of a "rule of thumb" that an east wind will push water into ICW inlets making shallow passages easy and that a west wind will do the opposite. The trick is in gauging how much the water level varies due to the wind. One could take the "rule of thumb" approach and take note of winds greater than 15 kts and expect 0.5 to 1.0 foot of water difference (east wind = more, west wind = less). The higher and longer-lasting the winds, the greater the difference.

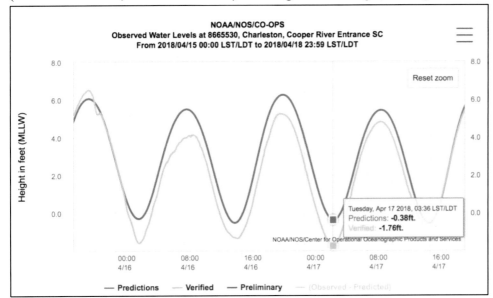

However, I think we all want something more definitive, a number to go by, and it turns out that there is a resource that's readily available over the internet. Let me share some examples with you. Here's the Charleston, SC tide station showing predicted (blue line) vs actual (green line) water levels for 4/16 – 4/17/2018.

Lurking nearby is the Isle of Palms and McClellanville. You can expect that the lower than normal water

level at Charleston will be reproduced along the coast, at least in my experience over the years. A boater traversing the area could see **1.38 feet less water** than what the nearest tide station predicted based on the previous graph! That's an enormous difference for the shallow areas along the coast approaching Charleston. I would imagine there would be some surprises in store for those cutting it close on bottom clearance through there. What could cause such a difference in water level? Let's look at the wind for that time period.

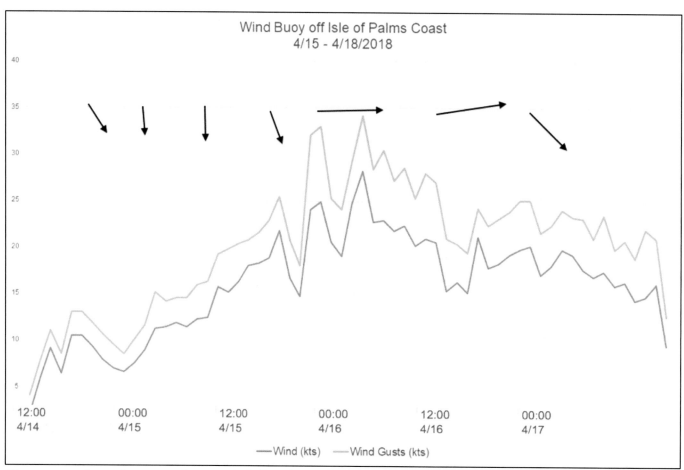

The arrows show the approximate wind direction (I had to enter them manually off NOAA logs). The previous chart of actual vs predicted tide level shows an expanded scale around the time of interest but you can compare the two charts by referring to the times across the bottom. Note the rapid drop in water level in the top chart in the early morning hours of 4/16/2018. That corresponds to the change in wind direction to out of the west and the increase in wind above 20 kts with gusts to 33 kts. Once the water drained out, it stayed out for a couple of days given the west winds around 20 kts keep the water from coming back in.

Next up, we'll look at a tide vs actual chart on the next page where the tides are a lot higher than predicted and see if we can determine the reason why.

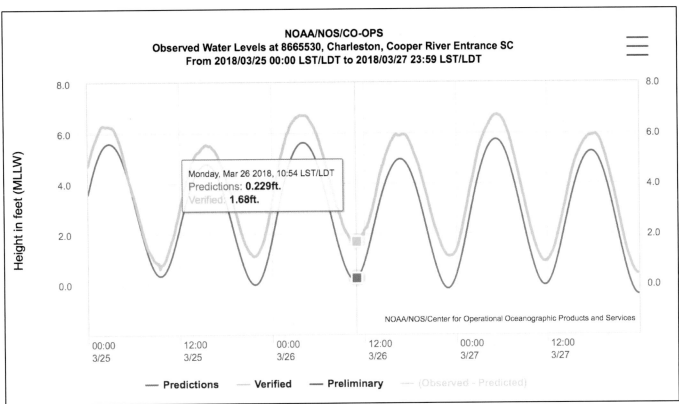

NOAA/NOS/CO-OPS
Observed Water Levels at 8665530, Charleston, Cooper River Entrance SC
From 2018/03/25 00:00 LST/LDT to 2018/03/27 23:59 LST/LDT

On March 26, 2018, right at the start of the spring migration last year, those cruisers going through the Isle of Palms and McClellanville area enjoyed a real boost in water depth above and beyond anything they got from the tides. At 10:45 am, they had an **extra 1.45 feet of water** above what was predicted by the tide charts.

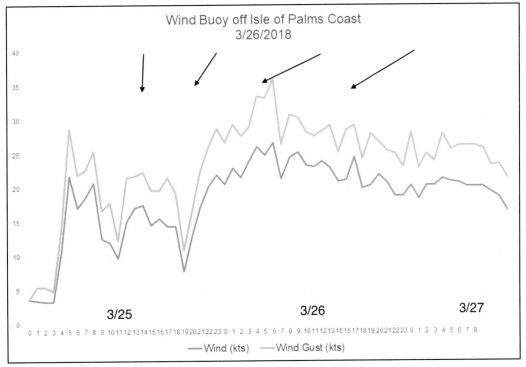

As you can see from the chart above, a strong east wind pushed water against the coast and into our ICW, especially around areas close to the coast like Isle of Palms and McClellanville. The two examples should give you a feel for how winds affect water level. The effect varies somewhat for areas farther away from the coast but there's still a delta, although perhaps a little smaller elsewhere.

This is all interesting but how can it help me? Well, for one thing, be aware of the wind direction. A strong (15 kts and greater) wind will move water around, especially if it's blown for several days. Remember, an east wind blows water in, a west wind blows water out. With winds 20 kts and greater, you can expect up to a foot change in water level vs the predicted tide which can make a huge difference at McClellanville! There are also more tide stations like the one I used at Charleston, SC that will show the predicted tide vs the actual water level that you can access over the internet. For example, click on Charleston Tide Station to see a graph like the ones I showed above. You can check it anytime but it's especially useful just before you transit the Isle of Palms or McClellanville, SC. It will give you a sense of whether the water level is higher or lower than predicted by the tide charts.

NOAA maintains a whole list of such stations across the US and they can be accessed at NOAA Tides and Currents for Water Levels.
The ones I use the most are:
Cape May (figuring whether or not I can get under the 55 ft bridge at low tide with my 55 ft mast)
Hampton, VA
Beaufort, NC (for sections of the ICW close by and the Atlantic Beach Bridge which can less than 65 ft)
Charleston, SC (for Isle of Palms and McClellanville, SC)
Savannah, GA (for Hell Gate)
Fernandina Beach, FL (for going through Fernandina shallows)
Vaca Key, FL (for general water levels in the Keys)
In closing, if you have a near low water passage ahead, just take a moment and access one of the sites above to see if it's a day of especially low water beyond the tide table prediction. As the old saying goes, an ounce of prevention is worth avoiding a pound of mud...

Topic 5: How to Recover from a Computer Crash

This may be a bit much for most people but then what do you do if you're in a remote anchorage and everything is fine – except – your laptop just crashed! It may be the hard disk or just a corrupted file but, in any case, your computer is dead. Your first response might be to load a restore point (after a few choice words...) After all, doesn't the computer automatically create restore points whenever a major update is installed? If you have a Windows computer and have Win10 installed, the answer is no. The automatic creation of restore points is turned off by default in Win10 to save a few seconds in booting up since the computer has to wait to see if F8 is being depressed. So now you have no restore point to fall back on, and if it is a hard disk problem, you don't have a spare hard disk either. To make matters even worse, you can't access the "Advanced Startup Options" in Win10 since it's accessed by pressing F8 during the boot process which is turned off by default.

With no CD of Win10 (it's back at home) and no programs CDs (also back at home), no restore point and no way to access the Advanced Startup Options, what do you do? I spent a lot of time stepping through how to bring my laptop back to life and documented the procedure under Recovering from a Disk Crash on my blog. The instructions are best read before disaster strikes but that probably won't happen because you're too busy getting ready to cruise just like I was. Nevertheless, they can still be used to breathe life back into your laptop even without all of the above; it just takes a little longer.

Topic 6: Socastee SC 544 Bridge Clearance in South Carolina at MM 371

Wouldn't it be nice if there were bridge height boards that automatically adjusted for water level? Better yet, why not put the readout on the internet so you could confirm that your mast would clear the bridge before you left the marina or anchorage? A solution to this problem actually exists for some bridges, and one of those is the Socastee SC 544 high bridge. As we know, the height boards don't transmit their readings of bridge clearance via the internet but there is a water depth gauge next to the bridge that does. Therefore, if

you took a photo of the height board as you passed under on a low-water day and noted the date and time, then you could look up on the internet the water level reported by the water gauge at the bridge the day or our next passage. There will be a correlation between reading on the bridge height board and the reading on the water level gauge.

For example, if the height board reads 65 ft. and the water gauge shows 12 ft. of water depth, then when the water level goes up to 13 ft. the bridge clearance should decrease by the same amount to 64 ft. Sounds simple. The solution is getting enough data points to establish a correlation and a graph.

We are interested in the Socastee SC 544 high bridge so let's find a water gauge nearby. Let's link to USGS 02110725 AIW at Highway 544 at Socastee, SC.

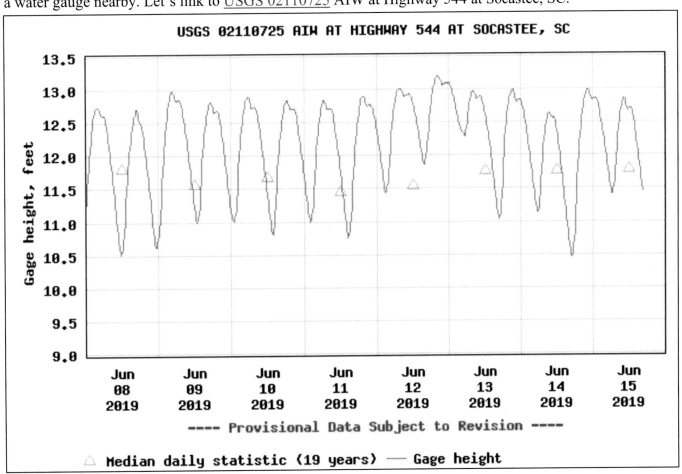

I enlisted the help of members of my ICW Cruising Guide Facebook page in taking photos of the bridge height board as they passed under the Socastee SC 544 bridge on a normal water day. Knowing the date and time of their passage, I then accessed the chart above to find the water gauge depth.

Having in hand the photo of the bridge height board and also the water gauge level reported, I then constructed the graph below.

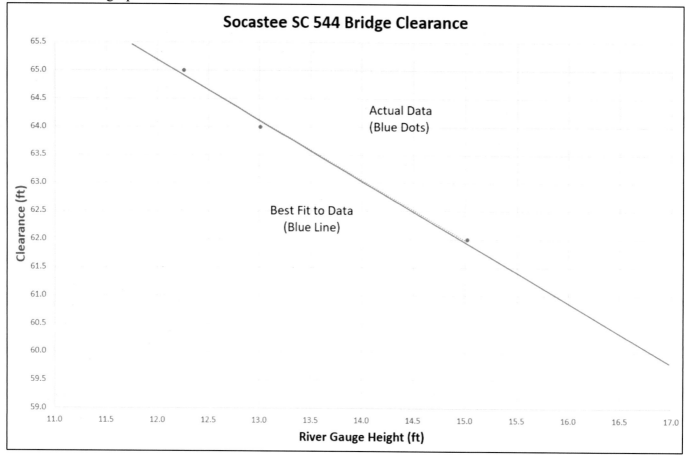

To find the bridge height, you first find the River Gauge Height for Socastee SC 544 Bridge (this is a direct link). For better accuracy, you can request a table instead of the graph so the exact water depth at a given time can be found. On the horizontal axis above, go up to the blue line and then over to the left to read the predicted bridge clearance.

For example, if the river gauge height was 15 ft., then the bridge clearance would be predicted to be 62 ft. The chart and links in this article have also been posted as a Nav Alert in Waterway Guide so all cruisers can take advantage of the information for convenience and safety.

With all this information available over the internet, you can find whether you'll clear the Socastee bridge from the comfort of your cabin in a marina or at anchor before you cast off. Don't you wish every bridge had this data available? In fact, there are several more that might and we at the ICW Cruising Guide Facebook page and Waterway Guide are working to produce more graphs for other bridges that sometimes don't meet the 65 ft. minimum at high water. Feel free to help out and stay tuned.

Topic 7: Tracks vs Routes – What's the difference?

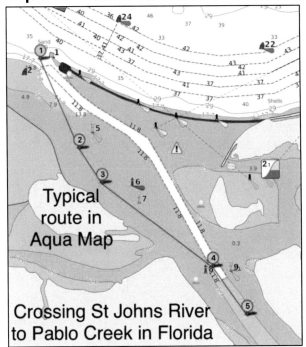

Typical route in Aqua Map

Crossing St Johns River to Pablo Creek in Florida

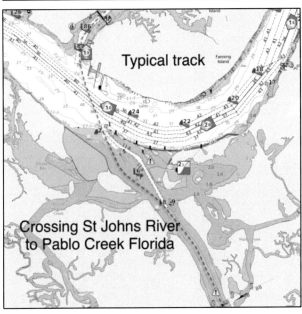

Typical track

Crossing St Johns River to Pablo Creek Florida

Both types of files are available through this site but which type is best for you? First of all, what's the difference? A track is like a crumb trail of where your boat went and is usually just a recording of your boat's progress for any given time period. In Aqua Map, it shows as a dotted line on the chart. A route is similar but it's planned in advance so the captain can follow a path from point A to point B without having to do real-time adjustments for shallow water or other charted obstructions.

If you had a successful day and recorded your track, you can send it to others, likewise for a route and now importing also works with Navionics with their recent update. I use routes to plan a day's path. I don't necessarily fine-tune the route to include every single small turn. I don't publish these routes since I usually make real-time adjustments as I proceed. Another type of route available is for passages through specific shallow spots along the ICW. Examples include routes through the shallows south of Fernandina Beach in Florida, Hell Gate in Georgia, Dawho River in South Carolina and many others. They are short routes only through the hazard and they make a lot of turns to follow the deepest water based on my past experience through the area and USACE surveys.

To summarize, I have long routes I use for general point A to point B navigation and short routes specifically aimed at shallow spots. The short routes are listed on my blog page at the left under GPX Routes with a short description for each. Each route has a timestamp in the title such as BLock120718 which stands for Lockwoods Folly route as of 12/11/2018. The routes can be accessed at GPX Routes. If you use these routes, be sure you have the latest one by looking at the time stamp in the name since I update the routes as new information and surveys come in. At the bottom of the page on the link, there are additional instructions on how to download GPX routes into various apps and programs.

This spring I recorded my tracks as I headed north and made them available at Bob423 ICW Tracks. They are divided into daily segments with a description for each track and mile marker coverage at 2019 Track Descriptions. Aqua Map wrote a lead-in for my webpage to display the tracks and provided a download button for easy downloading into various programs and apps, especially Aqua Map. Instructions on how to download tracks are at Download Instructions. The link is also located under the header for the main webpage. You can see in the graphic that a track is longer than the GPX routes I publish since a track is an entire day's run, not just through a shallow area. The tracks can be followed or just used for reference and can be thought of as a "New Magenta Line" that actually worked for good depth (outlined for each track in the description) as of the date of the track. It incorporates all the GPX routes through the shallow area automatically since I went through everyone on the way north in the spring of 2019 There will be new tracks from my run south this fall of 2019 and will be posted on the same page.

Finally, to help in planning your day, a compilation of Waterway Guide Alerts is given on the download page under, Waterway Guide Shoaling Alerts. I personally keep these alerts up to date with the latest information from USACE surveys, personal data, and high-quality reviews by those transiting the areas.

Topic 8: Using Tracks in Aqua Map

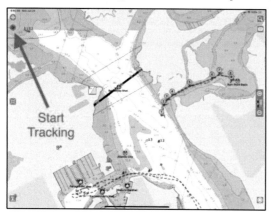

Aqua Map has a red button in the upper left corner of the screen that when tapped, starts creating a track of your boat. The button will start to blink to indicate active tracking is taking place and a track is being recorded. You can change to another app (e.g., Navionics, email, browser, etc.) and the track continues to record without interruption.

Aqua Map Master added the ability to use NMEA data with an appropriate interface such as the Vesper XB-8000 AIS transponder. It not only transmits AIS data over WiFi but also all NMEA data connected to it like depths from your depth sounder, wind speed, and wind direction.

If you already have AIS or just want NMEA data fed to Aqua Map, then there are other less expensive options like the Digital Yacht Smart WLN10.

That's all very nice but why do you need NMEA fed to Aqua Map? You already have instruments that display the data, why another display on your iPad or iPhone? The answer lies in some unique enhancements to Aqua Map in track recording. When connected to NMEA instruments, Aqua Map records the depth at points along the boat's track.

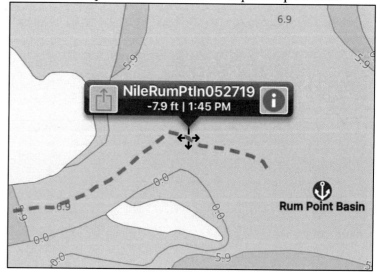

With the track displayed, you can tap on any part of the track and a pop up will show the depth and time at that point as shown at right. You can use the time to figure the tide and the depth to figure MLLW. That's neat!

But wait, there's more! Aqua Map produces a summary graph with the date, time and least depth seen shown at left below. Tapping on the "i" icon by the depth summary will display another graph shown at right.

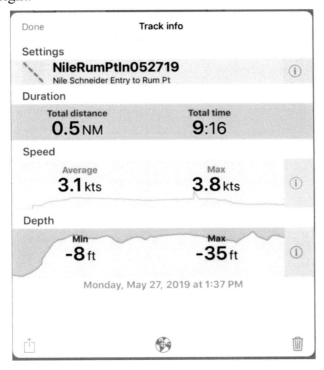
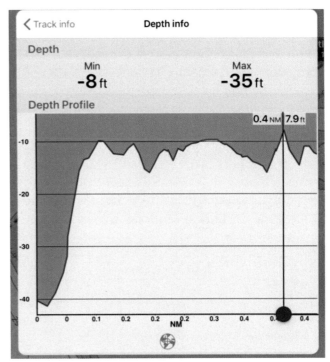

The graph at right has a blue dot you can move with your finger to find the least depth manually and to inspect the depths seen all along your track. When you find a depth of interest (7.9 ft in the example), you can tap on the globe icon and the chart will appear showing the location of that depth point (see the chart displayed earlier in this article, I found the 7.9 ft point by this procedure.

The example I chose is from Nile Schneider who has NMEA connected to Aqua Map and recorded a track that may be of interest to those wanting a protected anchorage in Atlantic City, namely the Brigantine anchorage by Rum Point. Nile corrected his depth sounder to read the depth to the surface of the water. The least seen on his track was 7.9 feet at 1:45 pm on 5/27/2019, Memorial Day. The tide at that time was 2.7 ft. That would make the least seen depth to be 5.2 ft but it occurred after entering through the channel.
I've created two downloads:
NileRumPtTrack.gpx
NileRumPtRoute.gpx

You can download the track into Aqua Map and see for yourself the depths that Nile Schneider saw on 5/27/2019. Or you can also download the route that duplicates the track and follow that instead.
Wouldn't it be nice if everyone connected their copy of Aqua Map to NMEA and shared their tracks over this Facebook forum? We would all benefit from the real-time information. Think about adding NMEA, it would cost about $200 or less and be of good use to all of us navigating the ICW.

Topic 9: Planning a Typical Cruising Day

Now that you know all the basics, let' go over one way of planning a day's cruise.

1) Plan the route per the weather and where you want to wind up for the night and perhaps a couple of bailout points along the way if the weather is not as expected (when has that ever happened? Ha!)

2) Note the mile markers you plan to cover in your cruise for the day

3) With a range of mile markers in hand, check the Waterway Guide Shoaling Alerts for the latest information. Most will also include a GPX route for downloading if desired.

4) Check the tide level through the shallow areas you plan to transit against the MLLW listed in the Alerts above to be sure you have enough depth for your draft. You can fine-tune these estimates from the tide tables by noting if there are high winds predicted. An east wind will push water in and raise the water level, perhaps up to a foot or more. A west wind will do the opposite and push water out, decreasing depths by up to a foot. It usually takes winds of 15 kts or more to make a difference in depths. The more wind, the more the effect.

5) Finally, look at the available tracks for the mile markers you plan to cover for the day and consider downloading the tracks. The track can be followed or just used as an additional reference while underway.

With 1 through 5 done, you are current with all the information on the ICW available. Now go out and enjoy the scenery and the thrill of traveling one of America's greatest waterways and enjoy an ICW sunset!

Chapter 8 - ICW Hazards with Charts

All of the comments in Chapter 8 are from our October 2019 and January 2020 trip on the ICW to Key West. They are our observations as we transited the shallow spots with depth recordings from the NMEA interface to Aqua Map Master. They have been reduced to mean lower low water (MLLW) per the nearest tide station.

You will also find anchorages scattered in amongst the shallow spots. I've included our favorite places to drop the hook marked with an "X" where you'll likely find us if you are in the area when we're anchored. The hazards and anchorages are ordered from north to south for the fall cruising migration.

GEC Products was gracious enough to allow me the use of their charts as displayed in their iPad app, Aqua Map Marine. The charts are reproductions of NOAA ENC charts, but improvements have been made for better color contrast and display. Active Captain and Waterway Guide comments have been added and I've been working with Aqua Map programmers over the past year to enhance the product for cruising sailors. I believe their charts are the best on the market. An amazing feature of Aqua Map Master is the ability to display USACE survey charts showing recent depths which are a great help in safely navigating the shallows of the ICW.

Before continuing with the details of each hazard I need to include the standard disclaimer, this one from Aqua Map Marine but you will see similar disclaimers from all charting programs. I don't know why they feel the need to print the disclaimer in all caps but I see the same trend in all programs. The disclaimer covers both the use of Aqua Map Marine and myself, Robert Sherer.

THE AQUA MAP PRODUCT IS TO BE CONSIDERED AN AID FOR LEISURE NAVIGATION. IT CAN CONTAIN ERRORS AND CANNOT SUBSTITUTE FOR THE OFFICIAL GOVERNMENT CHARTS. ONLY OFFICIAL GOVERNMENT CHARTS AND NOTICES TO MARINERS CONTAIN ALL THE INFORMATION NEEDED FOR SAFE NAVIGATION. THIS DATA ARE DERIVED FROM OFFICIAL CHARTS BUT CAN CONTAIN INACCURACIES AND MAY NOT CONTAIN THE LATEST UPDATES. IT IS THE USER'S RESPONSIBILITY TO USE THIS PRODUCT PRUDENTLY.

IN NO EVENT SHALL GEC CORPORATION OR ROBERT SHERER BE LIABLE FOR ANY DIRECT, INDIRECT, INCIDENTAL, SPECIAL, EXEMPLARY, OR CONSEQUENTIAL DAMAGES (INCLUDING, BUT NOT LIMITED TO, PROCUREMENT OF SUBSTITUTE GOODS OR SERVICES; LOSS OF USE, DATA, OR PROFITS; OR BUSINESS INTERRUPTION) HOWEVER CAUSED AND ON ANY THEORY OF LIABILITY, WHETHER IN CONTRACT, STRICT LIABILITY, OR TORT (INCLUDING NEGLIGENCE OR OTHERWISE) ARISING IN ANY WAY OUT OF THE USE OF THIS PRODUCT, EVEN IF ADVISED OF THE POSSIBILITY OF SUCH DAMAGE. THIS LIMITATION SHALL APPLY TO CLAIMS OF PERSONAL INJURY TO THE EXTENT PERMITTED BY LAW

The main reason for the above disclaimer is the changing nature of the ICW. What worked yesterday may not work the next day due to tides, currents, wind, wave action, and who knows what else. Of course, I'll also be updating Waterway Guide Alerts as I go along so you can look for new information there. By the way, if you find yourself behind me and want to follow, be aware that I may wander a bit to explore the channel and not necessarily take the deepest path. Some have found that puzzling in the past.
If you agree to the disclaimer, please continue.

Background on Charts and Guidance

I use have used screenshots of Aqua Map charts throughout this guide. It is available as an app for both Apple and Android products. Their source charts are from the National Oceanic and Atmospheric Administration (NOAA) in digital format. Aqua Map assembles the NOAA charts into one seamless chart for use in their app. They also provide several options in the display of their charts as to colors and warning depths. I've kept a consistent look to the charts in this guide. If you want the same look, then set Map Style to "Standard," Land Data to "Hidden" and Safety Depth to "11.0 ft." Of course, you can vary the settings to suit your tastes but I thought the settings I used may help you in following along a route I've illustrated in the guide.

I've used the feature in Aqua Map that allows a satellite overlay on the nautical chart. The crucial feature difference between Aqua Map and others is that the overlay can be varied in transparency. This allows a chart to show satellite detail on the water and adjacent land without wiping out all chart detail on the water. Where this comes in handy is in the use of US Army Corps of Engineers (USACE) survey charts that are shown with satellite detail outside the channel. When a shallow spot is nearby a land feature, Aqua Map can display the feature (e.g., a dock) and the chart details (e.g., buoys) on the same screen to better place the location of a trouble spot.

I have selectively used USACE survey charts that show great detail of shallow areas. The areas that shoal rapidly are often surveyed every few months, while others have a longer timeline. Where available, I've entered the USACE recommended route based on their survey in a GPX route which is available for downloading at GPX Routes from my blog site at fleetwing.blogspot.com. They are also available through the Waterway Guide Alert icon for a shallow area. Just tap on the icon and then tap on the highlighted GPX route for instant route download into Aqua Map. You do need an internet connection for the download so plan ahead.

The guidance in this guide can be supplemented by accessing Waterway Guide Alerts. Aqua Map is the only app that offers both Waterway Guide and Active Captain reviews within their app with all data downloaded and stored on your Apple or Android device for instant access.

Conventions used in this guide include:
- My route south in October 2019 and January 2020 is plotted as a dotted blue line.
- NOAA charting formats are used such as R18 for red buoy 18 and G17 for green buoy 17.
- The "Recommended track" is shown as a thin, black, solid line in Aqua Map. It is drawn by NOAA on their charts, but in Garmin charts, they show up as the famous magenta line.
- When USACE survey charts are used, the depiction of their recommended route is a yellow dotted line with a yellow dot for each waypoint. Most USACE charts are shown as displayed in Aqua Map Master without the yellow line. In that case, a red line with waypoint numbers is used to show the GPX route.
- USACE uses the coordinate format of DD MM SS.SSS. Aqua Map has a preference switch to choose between DD MM SS.SSS or DD MM.MMM for coordinate entry and display. When given, I've copied the USACE Lat/Long and pasted in the guidance page for a given area.
- Soundings are always to mean low lower water which I abbreviate to MLLW.
- An "R" at the end of a title of a hazard indicates there's a GPX Route available for that hazard.

Always check the Waterway Guide Alert icon in Aqua Map for the latest GPX route for the area. If you have questions about any of the content, please send me a note (in the left column on my blog site).

Leg 1 PYC to Cape May 209 NM

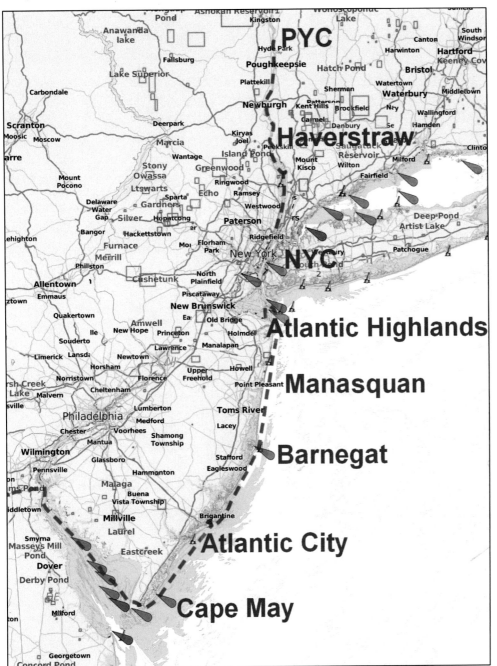

In September we start looking at coastal weather for our trip down the coast of New Jersey. We want calm seas and wind out of the north or we'll move our September 15 departure date plus/minus five days to find good weather or even delay it for two weeks as we did in 2018 when the hurricanes were vying for dominance on the Jersey coast at migration time.

We use all of the weather apps and services I've listed earlier in this guide. We have found them all to be valuable. Ideally, you would like them all to agree on a good day for going south. For us, that means winds of less than 10 kts and out of the north for the 11.5-hour passage. We'll settle for winds out of the northwest or northeast but we do not want a wind with a southerly component. We've done that and it's not what we prefer for an 11.5-hour ride.

With all the apps and services, we monitor, how could we go wrong...?? Now that you've stopped laughing, there are lots of ways. We left in the fall of 2014 with all our ducks in a row but the weather refused to believe the ducks! Winds were predicted out of the west, not the best but should have been okay. Instead, we found winds on the nose and instead of clocking to the west it backed to the east and increased in a non-predicted squall. The first six hours of our run down the coast was miserable with the waves washing over the bow and heavy rain. Eventually, the wind did change to the west and the rest of the trip was okay. Out of twelve trips up and down the New Jersey shore, I would say the weather behaved as predicted about 70% of the time. Still, you do the best you can.

From Atlantic Highlands, we will make the 81 NM to Atlantic City in 11.5 hours and then the 37 NM to Cape May in 5.5 hours. We cruise at 7.3 kts but there is a shore current against us most of the way. I don't use Manasquan or Barnegat inlets since if it's calm, I'd rather push on farther south and if it's rough, I don't trust them to be safe.

Poughkeepsie Yacht Club – Our Home Port

We have great sunsets at the <u>Poughkeepsie Yacht Club,</u> my home port. It is a working club; we do everything ourselves. We haul and launch our boats with a 25-ton travel lift, we make our docks, moor them in March, and take them out in October. There's a face dock parallel to the current flow for guests and there are several guest moorings. There is also an anchorage just north of the club that's protected by an island from wakes produced by river traffic. The showers have just been renovated and we have a new washer and dryer for guests to use at no charge. Best of all, we have a great deck for watching sunsets with a drink in hand!

If you can spend a few days, there are some great attractions in the area. Consider a visit and a dinner out at the world-class <u>Culinary Institute of America</u>, known locally as the CIA. It is a college where chefs are trained from all over the world in 2-year or 4-year programs. The campus is located 5 miles south of PYC on 170 acres by the Hudson River and has graduated over 50,000 chefs. They have 5 restaurants on-site staffed by students earning their degrees, be sure to dine at one while you're here. It's an experience you'll get nowhere else.

If world-class food is not your scene, consider visiting the mansions along the Hudson River that include the home of <u>Franklin D. Roosevelt</u>, the <u>Vanderbilt Mansion</u>, or the <u>Mills Mansion</u>. The first two are national historic sites and they all offer stunning views of the Hudson River and the Catskills in the distance. You can also get a great view of the Hudson River from <u>Walkway Over the Hudson</u>.

Haverstraw Bay on the Hudson River

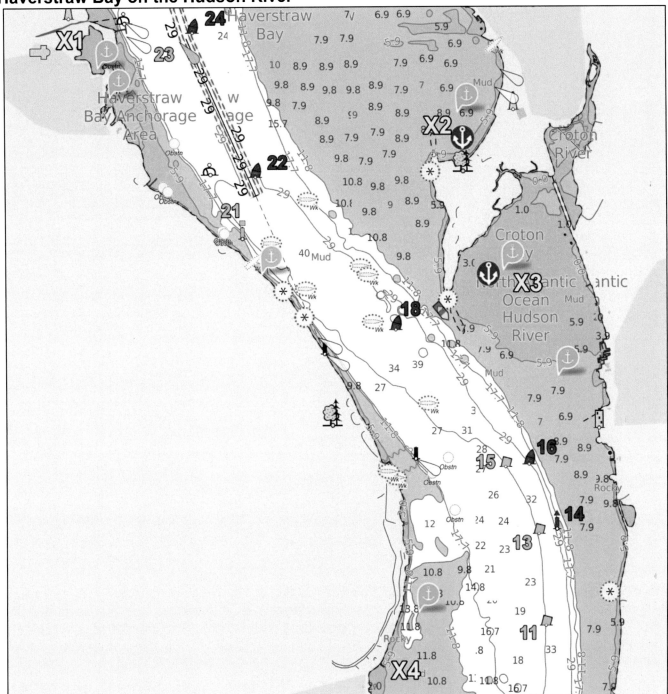

41 NM south on the Hudson River there are four anchorages available depending upon wind direction. The four major anchorages are shown in more detail on the following pages.

X1 - Haverstraw Cove

At the upper left in the chart is Haverstraw Cove. If there is bad weather in the bay, this where you want to be! It has 360° protection.

X2 - Croton Point North

This is the most popular anchorage with good protection from the south and east but open otherwise.

X3 - Croton Point South

Good protection from the north but very shallow. We've never used it.

X4 - Hook Mountain

Good protection from the west but beware of wind changes in the night. I suffered through a few here.

Haverstraw Cove – X1

This chart shows the approach details to Haverstraw Cove mentioned on the previous page. You will find the approach takes you over a bar of soft mud if you happen to find it, as I have at times. The depth over the bar is usually 5.3 MLW but can drop to 4.5 MLW with a strong, north wind. The path will take you close to the south shore to avoid a brick wall extending from the north entrance. Also, note "Obs" on the chart (a pile of bricks) that's sometimes marked with a buoy. I usually turn south between marks 5 and 6 and then proceed 100 ft and anchor in 15 ft of water. The holding is excellent and you are shielded from the wakes of passing boats that plagues the Croton Point anchorage. I anchor at the yellow X. Note the red roof in the photo.

I have personally sounded the entire anchorage area and found 15 to 30 ft everywhere. Just avoid the "Obs" mark; there are no other obstacles. Unfortunately, you cannot land at the park. There's even a dock but it's posted with signs to stay off by 200 ft! There is a small beach by the south entrance that can be used for pet relief. The GPX route shown above is available at BHavCove.gpx.

Atlantic Highlands

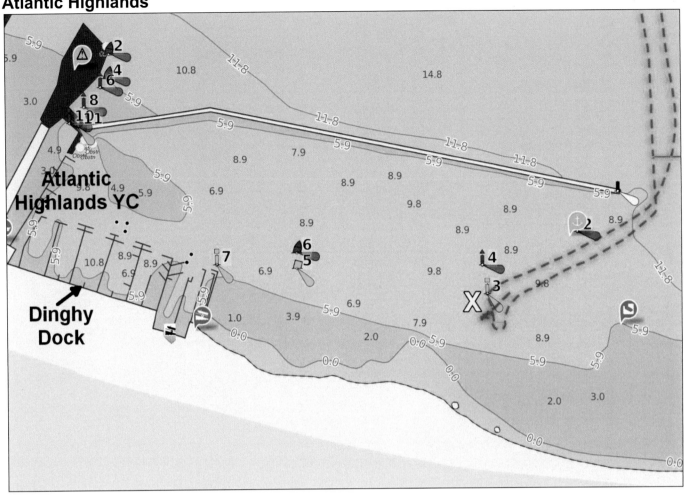

From Haverstraw Bay to Atlantic Highlands is 50 NM. I prefer this anchorage with protection from the north and west. There is some exposure to the east and you have to deal with the high-speed ferry that sends small rollers into the anchorage every hour or so until evening around 10:00 pm. However, I can always count on a good night's sleep before the 81 NM trek to Atlantic City, my next stop. There is a sandy beach just south for pet relief or use the dinghy dock shown on the chart. There are moorings available from the Atlantic Highlands YC, but who wants to pay $50 for one night? We always prefer to anchor whenever possible. I've sounded the area and the 6ft MLW line shown on the charts is accurate. We prefer to anchor west of the green buoy by the yellow X. The track we took in May 2018 is shown in the red dotted line. There is a public dinghy dock further in (2nd fairway past the fuel dock and turn to port) if you need ice or just want to go ashore. The holding is good.

The trip down the New Jersey coast is a study in weather planning. I've recently tended towards PredictWind as my main weather reference. You can read the evaluations I've done on my study published on Waterway Guide. We like winds behind us or at least off land for the trip south and waves less than 2 ft. We also look at the iPad app SwellInfo that covers in-shore wave action. One of the problems with the NOAA coastal forecasts is the area covered, out to 20 NM. We don't care what's happening 20 NM off the coast, we keep within 3 NM of New Jersey on the way down and SwellInfo covers that area well and accurately. We allow 11.5 hours for the passage at our cruising speed of 7.3 kts. There are inlets along the way but we've never felt comfortable using them. Besides, in calm weather, it's just as easy to make it a long day and reach a good harbor at Atlantic City. If the weather is not so good, then the inlets are not so good for entering. There is always a current running and you never want wind against current when transiting a small inlet.

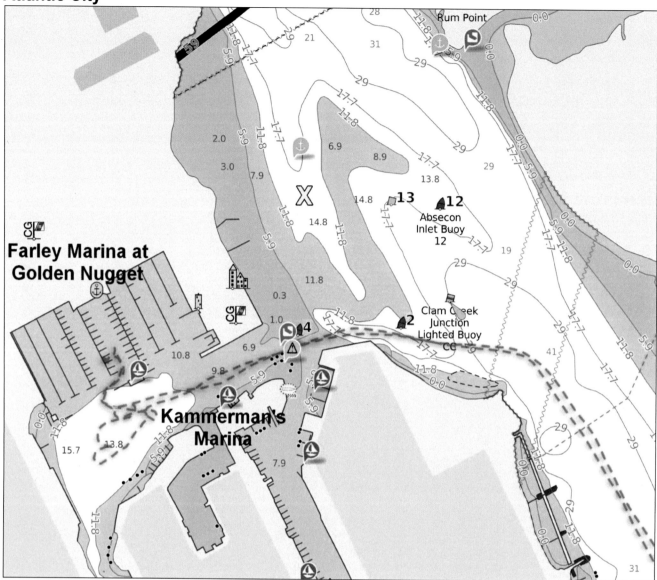

From Atlantic Highlands to Atlantic City is 81 NM, so prepare for a long day.

Coast Guard Station anchorage

A yellow X on the chart marks it. In most conditions, it is a calm anchorage even though you will swing with the current but the holding is excellent, though sometimes it's not so calm as in Atlantic Coast Guard station rocking. There is a sandy beach nearby for pet relief. You can also tie up at the Golden Nugget but call ahead. They like people who spend money but there's no charge to use the dinghy dock.

Brigantine anchorage

It's accessed by passing Rum Point to port and now there's a GPX Route at BBrig062419 for a minimum of 5.2 MLLW. The navaids are private and the last time I checked they used green Sprite bottles and red Coke bottles on poles for ATONs.

Senator Farley State Marina, aka Golden Nugget Marina

We've stayed here in the last few years. If you belong to Marina Life you get a 25% discount on dockage but only from Sunday through Thursday. Friday and Saturday are full price. You have access to the swimming pool on the 6th floor as part of your dockage fee and the WiFi even works. The Charthouse restaurant is excellent! We always dine there on our way south or north. There's a circle of casinos by the Golden Nugget that seems to do okay but many on the boardwalk are closed. Going to the boardwalk should only be done by jitney, don't walk, not advised any time of the day.

Cape May

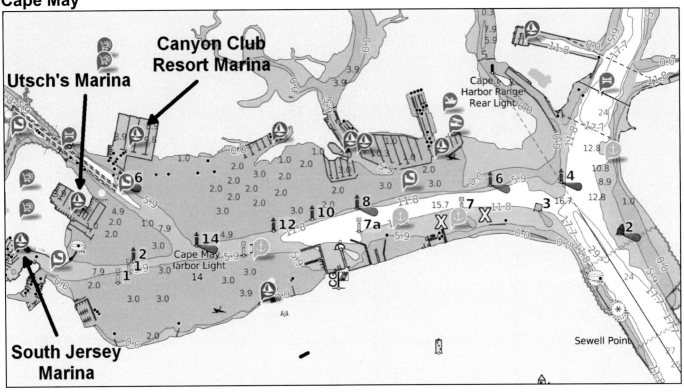

From Atlantic City to Cape May is 37 NM. We either anchor by the yellow X's or take a slip at Utsch's Marina and refuel. Just be careful when entering Utsch's due to shoaling. Ask in advance on the depths for entering. In the spring of 2018, I only found 5.0 MLLW along the entrance (deeper inside) so you might want to play the tides. When anchoring by the yellow X's, we used to just dinghy over to the beach off the Coast Guard station but then two uniformed guards chased us off last time. Now I take Hoolie over to the far side by R4, but then that's not good at low tide. There's a sandy beach across the channel to the east by R2 that I've used at low tide but it's a hike. Be sure to pass R14 on the south side, as it's shoal on the northern side.

Utsch's Marina is a family-owned business and they are very accommodating. The $2/ft dockage fee is very reasonable for the area; the other marinas are much higher. The approach has to be followed very strictly. Make the turn at R16 and keep 20 ft off the wall. The turn into the marina is very sharp by the miniature lighthouse and hard to see if you haven't been there before. There is an excellent laundry on-site with commercial-grade spin washers and dryers although the washers are $2.75 to $3.75 per load depending upon size. The dryers are huge, the size you will find in a commercial laundromat and they work well

At Utsch's Marina, you can rent a car from Enterprise and explore the area. They will pick you up for the rental. There's a Westmarine within a mile over the bridge and there's a good marine store right at Utsch's. If that's not enough, there's a marine store, Sea Gear Outfitters, that specializes in serving the professional fishermen and crabbers about ½ mile away on the road Utsch's faces. Just walk towards the bridge and around under it. You can't miss it. It has everything.

Of course, there's always the Lobster House for good seafood. It's right across the backyard from Utsch's, about 1000 ft. They also sell seafood if you want to have dinner on your boat.

Leg 2 Cape May to Chesapeake City 64Nm

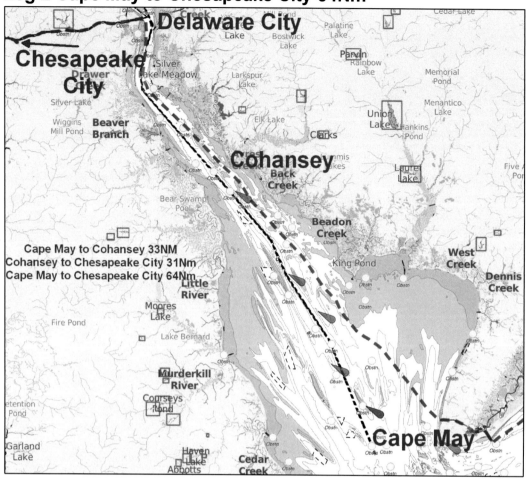

Delaware Bay has currents up to 3.5 kts! You do not want to be bucking such a current; it would take forever to get anywhere. Time your departure from Cape May to use the current in your favor. However, even worse than that is wind opposing the current direction. You may have a 3 kt current in your favor but if you have a 15 kt wind or greater against you then you will understand how rough the bay can get, and it can be downright dangerous. Ideally, you want a following current and either no wind or wind behind you. A headwind of less than 10 kts can be tolerated but not advised since it could increase once you're out in the bay. You have two main choices for stops:

1. Make it to Chesapeake City, 69 NM away
2. Split the trip up and stop at Cohansey after 36 NM and anchor.

We've done either option about half the time depending on how we hit the currents and weather. Cohansey is the only midway anchorage of note. There is also a marina down the Cohansey river we've used in the past which is adequate but nothing special. We just anchor out by the island. We haven't anchored at a very popular stopover at Reedy Island since when we come up the bay with the wind and current behind us and don't see the point in stopping; we just go on to Chesapeake City. On the return trip in the spring of 2015, we left Annapolis and kept going until the Cohansey anchorage since we had current with us and no wind all the way.

We almost always take the Cape May canal instead of going around the cape to enter Delaware Bay. Our mast is 55.3 ft above the water and the height boards on the bridges show 58 ft at low tide so we clear with a couple of feet to spare. We've been through twelve times without a problem but always within 1 foot of low tide. If you've never done this before, it will look like you're going to hit as you approach the bridge due to your perspective, but rest assured you are not if your height is less than what's shown on the boards by the bridge. One time I even had the boat behind me call on VHF and in a rather urgent voice told me I was going to hit the bridge and wanted me to stop! Having been through many times, I proceeded without a problem and never heard from the boat again. Be sure to read through the guide on how to figure the bridge heights in the Cape May Canal.

Cape May Canal Bridges

The easternmost bridge on the Cape May Canal

If your height is less than 58 ft then you may be able to take the Cape May canal between Cape May and Delaware Bay. There are three factors to consider:

1 - **The tide**. It's simply the predicted tide out of a tide table; it's easy to find for any time with a charting program that allows the time to be varied with a display of the tide height. For the bridges, I use the Cape May Harbor tide station since it's much closer to the two bridges than the ferry terminal station.

2 - **The actual vs predicted water level.** NOAA maintains a family of tide stations that show the actual water level vs the predicted water level. They are not generally known but there is such a station at the ferry terminal at Cape May. It will display either a graph or a spreadsheet showing the actual vs predicted tide height. Most helpfully, the data can be accessed in real-time over the Internet at NOAA Cape May water level site. The water level varies due to weather conditions such as a strong on-shore wind blowing water into the bay or a heavy rain upriver when the flow reaches Cape May. An easterly 15 kt wind will easily raise the water level a foot, as will heavy rains up the river. During tropical storms and winds greater than 20 kts the water level can be dramatically higher, 2 to 3 ft or more.

3 - **The real bridge height**. Unfortunately, the data does not support a 55 ft bridge height at high tide provided the height boards are accurate.

The picture above was taken at a high tide of 4.0 on 5/23/2016 of the easternmost bridge. There's not 55 ft clearance here! Note also that 4.0 ft is not a particularly high tide, it was predicted to be 5.2 ft later that night.

The picture above was taken at a low tide of 0.4 ft on 5/23/2016 of the same bridge. It looks like 57.2 ft.

The water level as reported by NOAA at the ferry terminal station was running 0.7 ft above the predicted tide level. There had been heavy rains up the river the day before. So, what is the real bridge height? Over the years I've used 58 ft at low tide as the starting point for figuring passages. Take a look at the low tide picture. The total water level above MLLW was 0.4 + 0.7 = 1.1 ft. If you add that 1.1 ft to the displayed number on the height board (57.2 ft) then you get pretty close to 58 ft at 0.0 MLLW with no water level delta (actually in this example 58.3 ft). With the three numbers I've developed an equation for computing bridge clearance:

Clearance under bridge = 58 ft - (Tide Height) - (Water Level Delta of predicted vs actual)

Note that the "water level delta" is positive when the water is higher than normal. The positive number then gets subtracted from "tide height" per the equation. In the example above:

$$\text{Clearance} = 58 \text{ ft} - (0.4 \text{ ft}) - (0.7) = 56.9 \text{ ft}$$

As long as your mast height is less than the clearance from the formula above, you'll clear the bridge. Note that the tide height and water level delta can be positive or negative. The equation works either way. The crucial bit of information is the real bridge height of 58 ft at MLLW. The number came from my experience with a dozen transits and it looks to be a little conservative by 0.3 ft. I haven't yet confirmed this but you probably have a few more inches if you avoid the red light hanging down from the middle of the bridge. Although height boards have been added, they have not been cleaned and the bottom 2 ft is even missing on several. Just follow the formula and you will be fine but you will still have a little tension as you approach. From your angle of view, you would swear you're going to hit but you won't if you follow the formula – just double check your figures! Caution: the height boards have been removed due to bridgework as of 5/2018. Hopefully, they will be back in place soon.

Standard Disclaimer: The captain always takes full responsibility for his actions. I believe the above advice to be accurate and I've followed it myself many times in my sailboat with a 55 ft 3-inch mast, once with the height board reading 56 ft.

Utsch's Marina as shown at left has reserved slips for cruisers with two fuel docks. They also have a dredge!

It's a short walk over to take a look at the 55 ft bridge and where the tide stands against the 55 ft height.

Cape May Canal

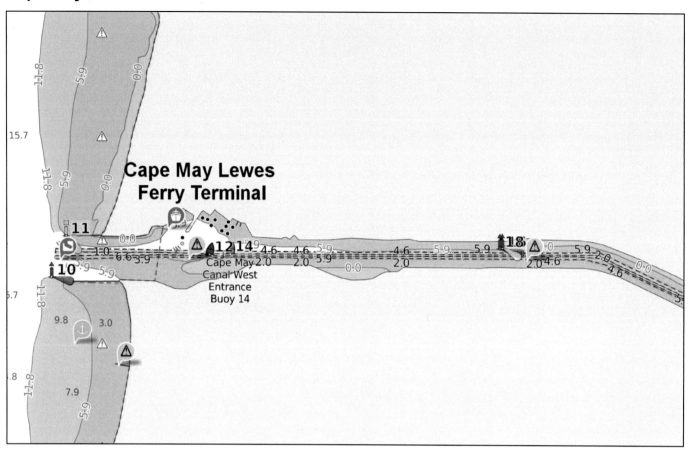

The canal is fine until you start the straight stretch between the two shoal marks shown above. The canal shallows to 7.0 MLLW for several hundred feet. Follow the channel per your chartplotter or use SonarChart (which works well through here) between the two shoal marks. If you get over to the red side you will find shoal. You also have to be careful to stay close to the ferries on the way out and at the exit channel, move to the center of the channel for 6.9 MLLW. This is an area that is often dredged so check with Active Captain or Waterway Guide for the latest information.

With a storm, the clearance can really get low. There had been strong east wind and a lot of rain, a double whammy along with a high tide. It was a no go for me at this time under the bridges in the canal.

Cape May Outside Passages

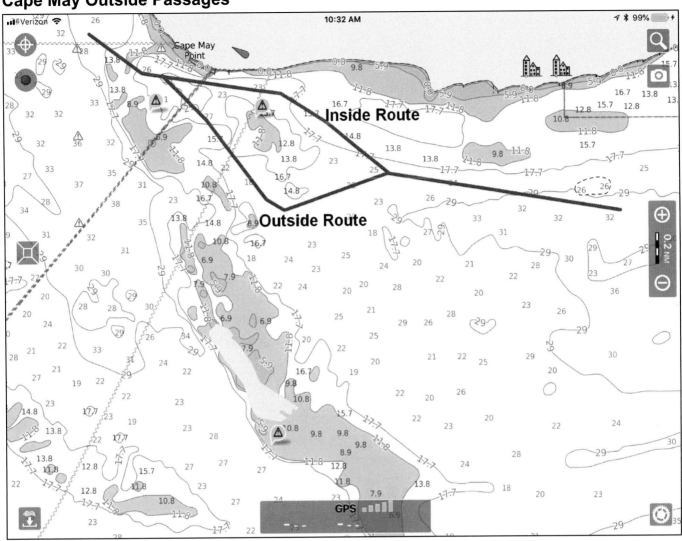

There are three routes around Cape May if you can't fit under the two canal bridges.

Inside Route: this is the route taken by the whaleboats and has been stable through several hurricanes but it's a test of nerves since you get so close to land. You will find 15 MLLW here. However, I have always taken the Outside Route to get farther away from shore.

Outside Route: I just wanted to be a little farther away from land and I've taken this route several times but only on calm days. Wind against tide can get very exciting, even dangerous! With 2 to 3 kts of current and a strong wind against the current, you will get standing waves that can be dangerous to your boat, not to mention, yourself; Cape May standing waves. On calm wind days or at slack tide, it's fine.

The Big Boat Route: This route is not shown but it's on the charts. It's the longest path, around all the shoals, but you'll still have to contend with strong wave action if you happen to take the route when wind is against the current.

Cohansey Island

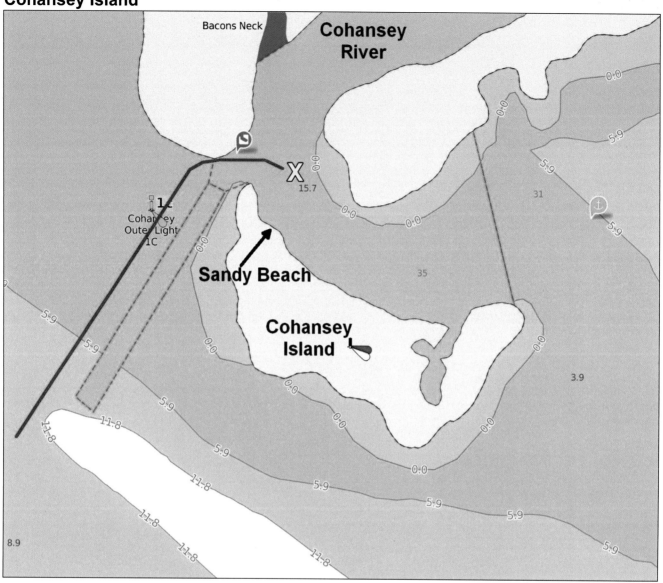

Cohansey is 33.4 NM from Cape May and provides an anchorage halfway up the Delaware Bay if needed. Approaching the island, pass by the lighted green tower within 30 ft for 20 MLW following the red line. The chart will show you outside the channel; the chart is wrong. Then aim for the left side of the visual opening between the island and the neck of land to the left for 18 MLW. If you wander too far to the right, near the island, you will see the depth decrease to 7 to 8 MLW. Once past the opening, the bottom drops out with depths from 25 to 50 MLW. We wanted to anchor just off the island but the depths were too great (35 to 50 ft!) so we backed off to the yellow X. You can safely anchor anywhere behind the island, lots of room. We've never anchored where the green anchor marker is on the chart. We were there in May 2019 at the yellow X and put out 100 ft in 30 ft of water and held fine with 60 ft 3/8" BBB chain and a 66 lb Spade anchor. The anchor came up clean.

You are protected from south and east winds to some degree but it is rather open. We usually don't have a problem since we wait for calm weather anyway before going up the bay. There is also a marina on the river we've used once; Hancock's Harbor Marina is adequate but I wouldn't recommend it although it's only $1/ft. If you're caught in a storm on the bay, it's a good refuge, totally protected. Just be prepared for a rustic atmosphere and not much help coming in. A better option if you don't need pet relief is just to run up the river and find a place in a bend. There are several anchor icons that will help find a spot. It is much better protected than behind the island although there's lots of current.

Chesapeake City

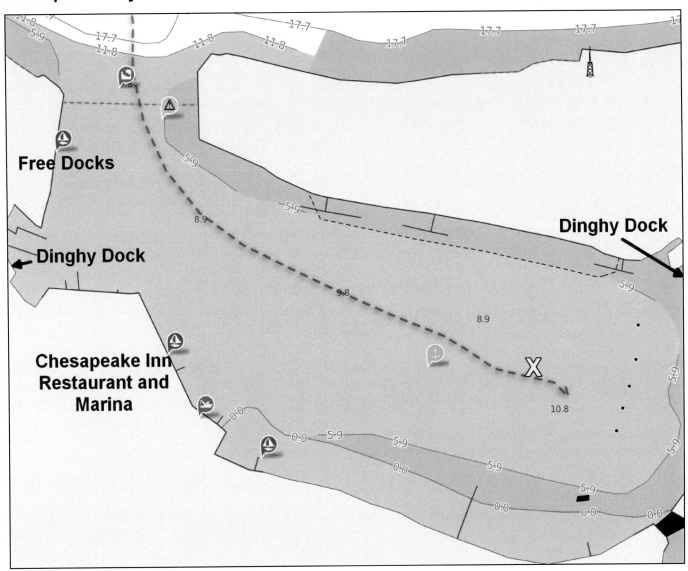

Chesapeake City is 31 NM from Cohansey and 62 NM from Cape May. The anchorage has been dredged and in May 2018 the entrance was 10 MLLW all across the width. There was 9 MLLW by the free docks. At the anchor marker (yellow X), I found 13 MLLW. The bottom is thick, gluey mud and you'll have fun cleaning your anchor and chain in the morning. However, the holding is fine with a good, heavy anchor.

There are two dinghy docks, one by the town and another at the east end by the boat ramp. With the dredging, the free docks for boats are now available. You can stay there overnight at no charge, but if you want electricity, it's extra at $15 and the use of water will cost $5.

There are two USACE boats on the north shore and when the anchorage starts to silt in, as it eventually does every few years, the best path is to hug the boats since they keep a path clear just by plowing through the mud. For now, don't worry; it's still deep but do check the hazard marker at the entrance just in case mud has piled in again.

Leg 3 Chesapeake City to Hampton VA 195Nm

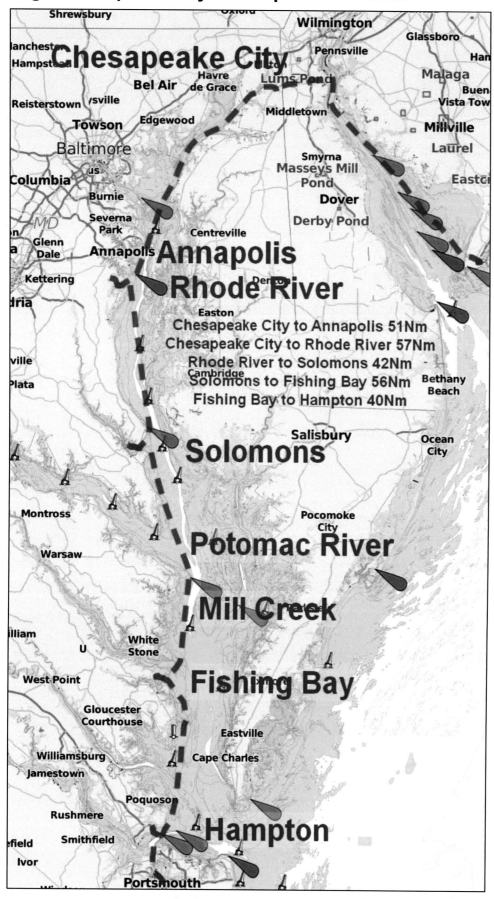

Chesapeake City to Annapolis 51Nm
Chesapeake City to Rhode River 57Nm
Rhode River to Solomons 42Nm
Solomons to Fishing Bay 56Nm
Fishing Bay to Hampton 40Nm

When I first started our ICW trips, I had daydreams of wonderful sails on Chesapeake Bay. In my visions, I would crisscross the bay in 12 to 15 kts winds with little wave action and have an idyllic experience.

Reality disagreed with our expectations, at least at the times of the year that we go through the Chesapeake. Maybe it's selective memory but we always seemed to have strong headwinds for days at a time, the 20 to 30 kt variety with accompanying waves. We waited for a weather window and when it finally came, we were in a hurry to get down the bay before the adverse winds picked up again. There are some great places to visit on the Chesapeake but we were usually in too big a hurry to see them.

From Chesapeake City, we'll aim for Annapolis 51 NM away or Rhode River just a little further. Then it's 44 NM to Solomons Island followed by 57 NM to Deltaville and lastly 40 NM to Hampton where we take a dock, rent a car and provision. A good intermediate stop is at Mill Creek just south of the Potomac River.

Predicting the weather seems to be somewhat of a challenge for the local weathermen here. I found PredictWind to be the most accurate for this area.

Annapolis

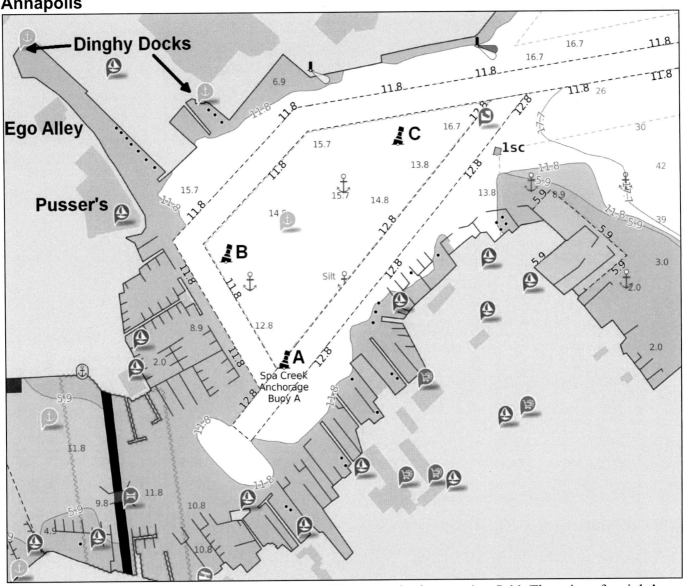

As you can see, you're right in the middle of things if you stay in the <u>mooring field</u>. The price of a night's stay on a mooring has gone up in recent years and now stands at $35/night. There's a weekly rate of $210 but you have to sign up for it when you first arrive.

There are two dinghy docks: one at the end of Ego Alley and another one east of the harbormaster's office as shown above. I always use the second dinghy dock since the Ego Alley dock is always crowded and ducks like to sit on your dinghy and decorate it. They are attracted by people feeding them. You can also take a dock in Ego Alley at $2.75/ft but it's right in the middle of town and people wander by all hours of the night and day. It's not well patrolled at night.

You will often see very expensive, racing sailboats go by the mooring field, just beautiful.

Rhode River

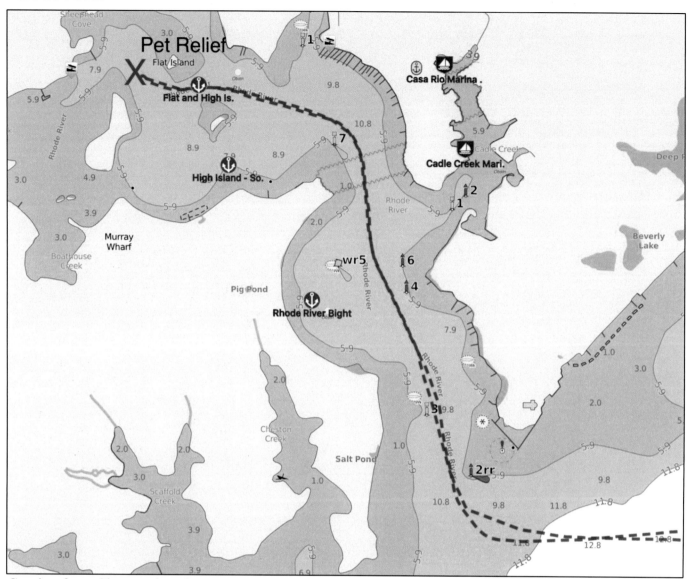

Coming from Chesapeake City, we either take a mooring at Annapolis (51 NM) or drop the hook at Rhode River (56.8 NM). With the recent price increase for the Annapolis moorings to $35/night, we've been coming here instead. We anchor by Flat Island so we can be close to the sandy beach for pet relief pictured below. However, the entire area is fine for anchoring, nice and calm.

We were here three years ago with a dozen other boats waiting out 35 kts winds on the Chesapeake, and yet in the anchorage, the winds were 5 to 10 kts. More than a few boats, we included, thought the NOAA forecast was far too conservative and hauled anchor and motored out expecting light conditions on the bay. It was not to be. We met boats coming back to the anchorage on our way out and as we neared the bay, the winds started to pick up ("Where is that wind coming from?") and sure enough, it was howling 25 to 30 kts at the entrance on the nose with 3 to 4 ft waves. We turned around and came back along with every other boat that tried to leave. A calm anchorage on the Chesapeake can be very deceptive relative to what's happening on the bay.

Solomons Island

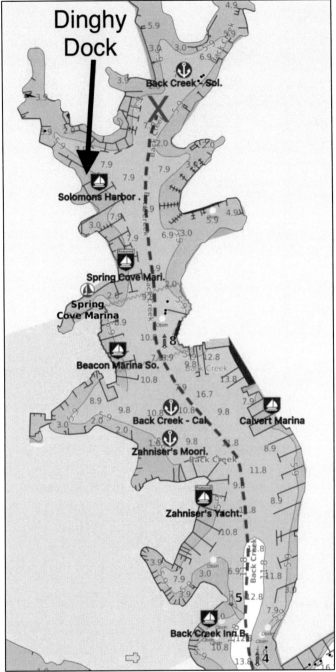

We always refuel at Solomons. There are several fuel docks but we use the one is at Harbor Island Marina located to port upon entering Solomons.

From Annapolis it's 44 NM; from Rhode River, it's 42 NM. There are lots of places to anchor or take a dock. We favor the Back Creek anchorage at the blue X with 10 MLLW since it's close to the Holiday Inn dinghy dock which only costs $2/day. The anchorage is protected from all directions and has good holding.

There is a West Marine to the south down the road about 1/4 mile after walking through the Holiday Inn parking lot and a Weis supermarket off to the north about a mile along with a bunch of fast food outlets. This is a great place to wait out weather.

When heading south, you would like to time your passage across the mouth of the Potomac so there is no wind against current effect. Otherwise, you will have a bumpy ride for about 10 NM.

In the spring of 2016, I needed repair work on my main, as the top strap on the sail let go, and the main halyard was no longer attached to the sail. I found a sail shop at Zahniser's Yachting Center, Quantum Sails, and they did a fantastic job. They were at my boat within 30 minutes and took the sail down, repaired it, and put it back up later that afternoon. The entire job took less than five hours and the cost was less than I expected.

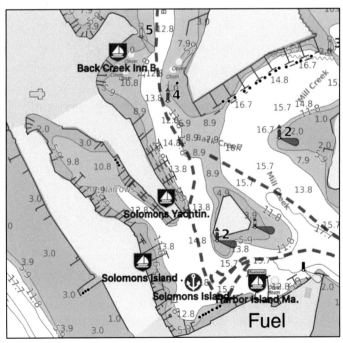

Mill Creek

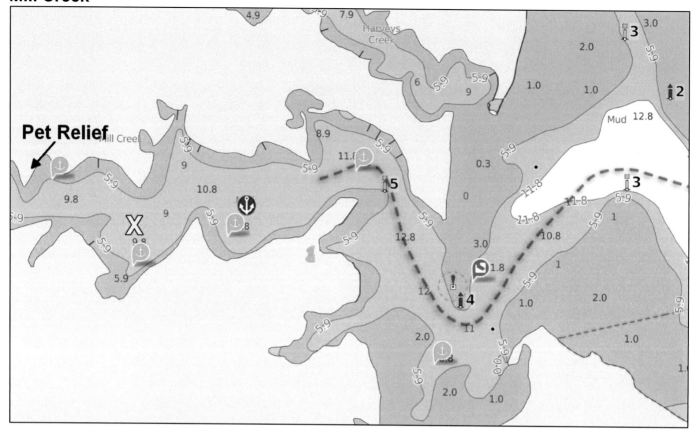

We either stop at Mill Creek at 42 NM or go on to the Fishing Bay Yacht Club at 57 NM. Mill Creek is full of anchoring spots and very well protected. There is a place to take pets at a deserted beach marked on the chart, but be sure to be neighborly and pick up. We anchor by the yellow X, tucked in a little closer to shore for 10 MLLW with excellent holding. High banks with towering trees surround the anchorage so the wind protection is outstanding. We like to anchor by the "X" because it's closer to pet relief, but the other anchorages are fine too.

Here is one place you really, really need a washdown pump. Your anchor and chain will bring up the thickest mud you've ever seen. In fact, you can't see the chain links at all and I could only see the anchor because I have an oversized, 66 lb Spade anchor; anything smaller it would just be a blob of mud. A high-power washdown pump will clear up the mess but it takes a little bit. We enjoyed the calm sunset above.

Jackson Creek

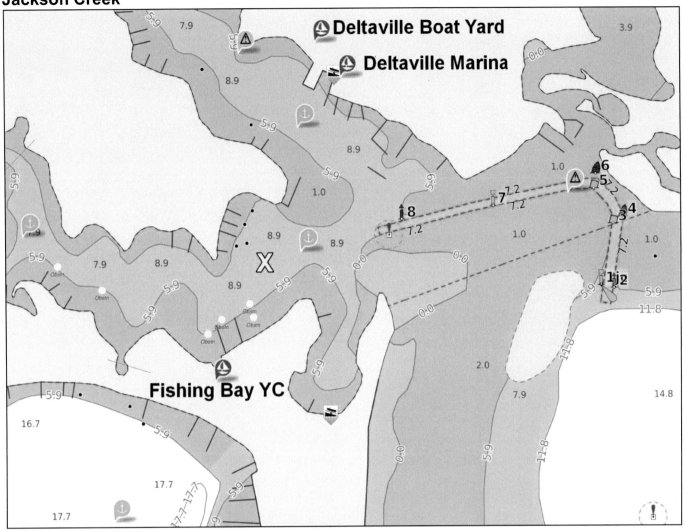

From Mill Creek, it's 32 NM to the Fishing Bay Yacht Club in Jackson Creek or the anchoring spot marked above. From Solomons, it's 57 NM. We usually take a dock at the yacht club. There is no charge for the first

night if you're a member of a recognized yacht club. If you stay longer, the fee is $1.50/ft. Otherwise, you can anchor out with many spots to choose from. The most popular one is highlighted with the yellow X but the Active Captain anchor marker at Fishing Bay is also popular but is more open to adverse winds and waves.

Jackson Creek Entrance

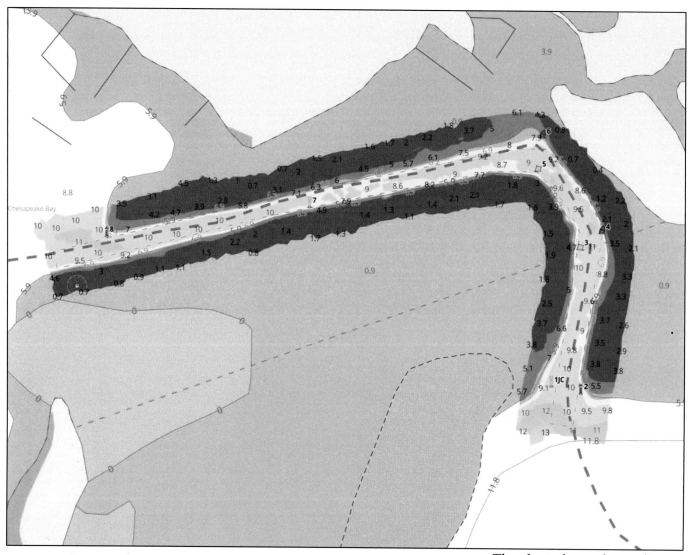

The chart above shows the shallow, twisting channel into Jackson Creek. The USACE survey of 9/17/2019 is shown as depicted in Aqua Map Master. All you have to do is stay in the green. My track of 10/4/18 pretty much did that when I didn't have the benefit of the USACE survey to follow. It gets shallow in a hurry outside the green path!

As a reward for our efforts, we had a great sunset that night.

Onancock

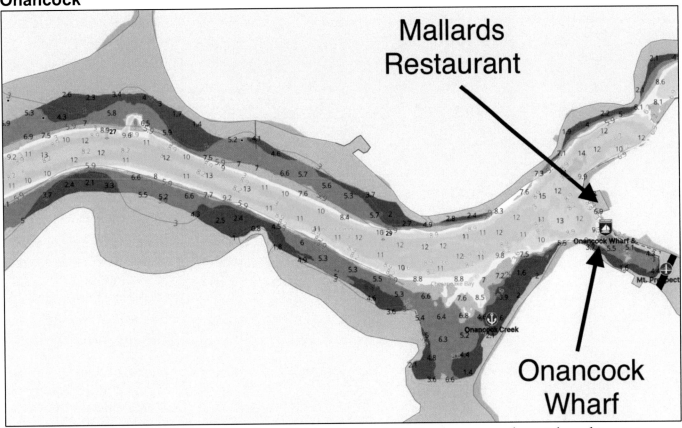

Instead of heading directly to Hampton from Fishing Bay or Mill Creek we sometimes take a detour to Onancock for the sole purpose of eating at <u>Mallards</u>, the home of the musical chef Johnny Mo pictured below. It's a long way into the anchorage or the town docks but the meal at Mallards is worth every penny in my book. Besides, it's a good way to avoid the wind against tide effects of crossing the mouth of the Potomac although it's a long and winding way to the town dock. The USACE survey of 4/3/2019 is shown.

The town of <u>Onancock</u> is a pleasant walk and the town docks have recently been rebuilt but you can always anchor out if you want and still dink into Mallards for dinner.

There are many other anchorages and towns on the eastern shore of Chesapeake Bay which I am not doing justice to, but we've been intent on heading south or north most of the time and seldom stop elsewhere. We usually have to wait for weather anyway and when the weather clears, we're off to the races north or south.

Downtown Hampton Public Piers

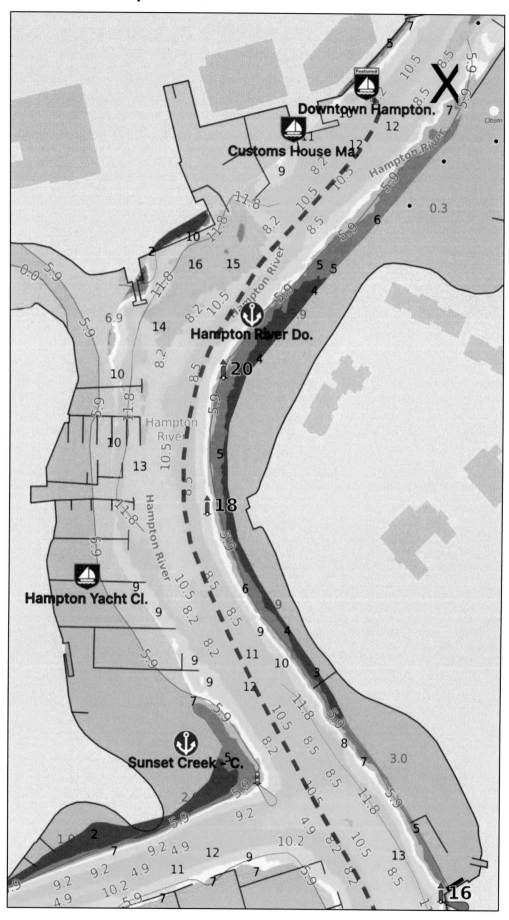

Hampton is 56 NM from Mill Creek and 40 NM from Fishing Bay YC. There is the choice of anchoring in Hampton off the Downtown Hampton Public Piers or taking a dock. At our visit on 5/2019, we saw 8 boats anchored across from the docks.

Hampton is one of our provisioning stops so we take a dock and rent a car from Enterprise which is just around the corner. If you stay over a weekend, you can get a car from Friday to Monday for just $12.50/day, depending upon the time of the year, on some weekends it's more.

There's a Walmart, Home Depot, etc. nearby but too far to walk but the marina has free bicycles for use by boaters. Hampton Public Piers maintains a dinghy dock for use by those that anchor out at no charge although you can buy access to showers for a nominal fee.

The marina has an "Annual Preferred Guest Program" where for a $75 fee (varies by boat length) covering the next 365 days you can dock for $1/ft with the 5th night free vs $1.75/ft per night. ($1.50 with BoatUS) for non-members.

One word of warning, the docks are not as easy to enter as they appear. The river has current at right angles to the docks and the fingers are only 1/2 length, so put your fenders far forward and be ready to loop a piling. The current is not a lot, perhaps 1/2 kt, but it's enough to set you off your mark. The marina will have someone to help you in, and you'll need it.

Downtown Hampton Public Piers is famous for its herb garden free to boaters.

Don't forget to visit the downtown area about three blocks away for a fine selection of restaurants. We enjoy the Taphouse, not fancy but good fun and lots of beers on tap!

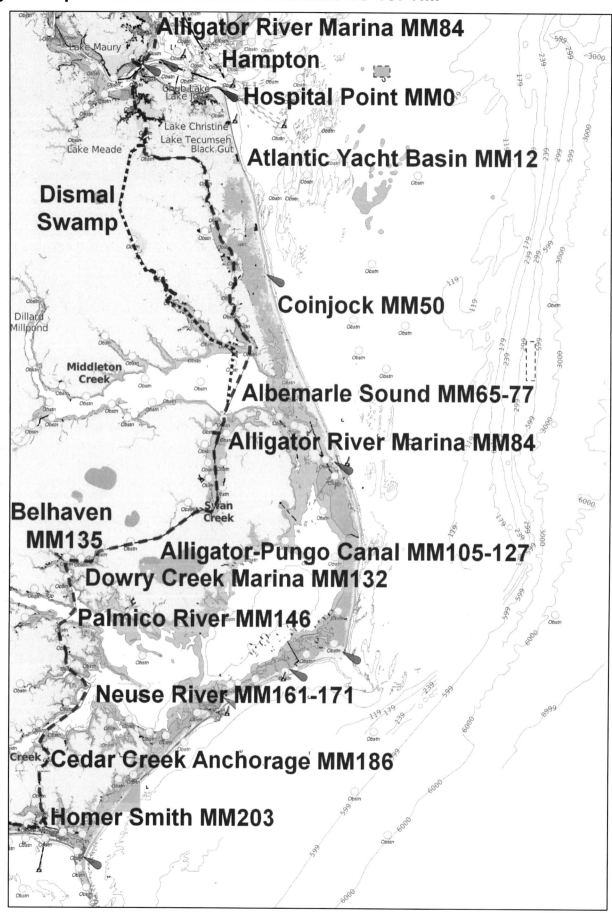

There are two choices in going south from Hampton
1) The Great Bridge to Albemarle Canal which goes through Coinjock, also called the Virginia Cut.
2) The Dismal Swamp Canal.

Despite the name, we've enjoyed the Dismal Swamp Canal but it's not for everybody. It's shallow at 6 ft for controlling depth supposedly but I've never gone through the canal without hitting something on the bottom and I only draw 4' 9"! However, the hits are mostly just bottom logs and you'll get a few thunks if you take this route. There is no commercial traffic for obvious reasons. It's just us boaters overnight at the North Carolina welcome center free face dock. If there are a lot of boats, it's common to raft up, so everyone puts out fenders on the outside when they dock. At times, the boats can be three to four deep but usually no more than three boats on the dock and one or two rafted.

Our next stop on the Dismal Swamp route is Elizabeth City 36 NM away, which has free docks all over town. It's their tradition. Our next stop after that is usually Alligator River Marina, which is 30 NM away, but you have to be careful in crossing the Albemarle. It's 15 NM wide but only 15 feet deep. If there's a wind greater than 15 kts, it can kick up some nasty waves in the shallow water. A good rule of thumb is not to cross the Albemarle with a headwind 15 kts or greater, it can be very uncomfortable. Any winds of 10 to 15 kts will cause a bumpy ride.

If you take the Virginia Cut, then you'll pass through Coinjock and have an opportunity to eat at their famous restaurant serving prime rib—very good. The route is deeper with no worries about shallow water like the Dismal Swamp route but you still have to be on the lookout for floating stumps.

From Alligator River we anchor at the Pungo River 39 NM away, then we cross the Pamlico River to the RE Mayo Docks 27 NM away. We like to stop there to take advantage of the local seafood frozen in blister packs, ideal for a boat's freezer. They have local shrimp, scallops, and flounder, just great. The $0.40/ft dockage price is not bad either, especially since it comes with free electricity. This is not a regular marina. The restrooms are outhouses! The docking is do-it-yourself when you come in; however, they have the best fuel prices in the area but they are not open on Sundays.

From RE Mayo we check for good weather for the 20 NM run on the Neuse River, another stretch of water that can get nasty with winds above 15 kts if it's on the nose. I heard a report from an experienced cruising couple that went to the Bahamas and back that the worst ride they had the entire trip was on the Neuse River when they motored against winds over 15 kts. We drop anchor at Cedar Creek, 27 NM from RE Mayo. If we're making good time, we will continue to Homer Smith's Marina in Beaufort.
We're always relieved to get through North Carolina with the large, shallow bays that can kick up good-sized waves with just a little wind.

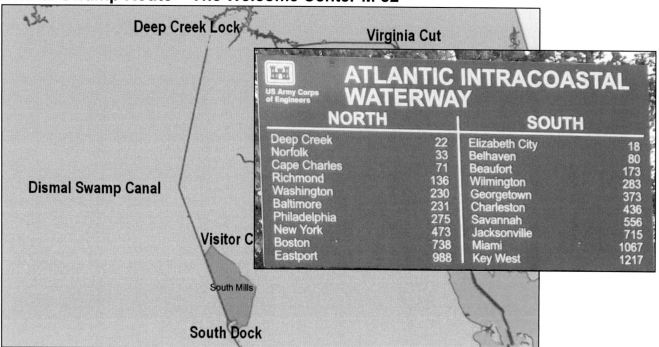

At last, you now enter the ICW; Mile Marker 0 is off Hospital Point in Norfolk. It seems they are always working on one of the numerous bridges through here. Be sure to check for the latest status in on Waterway Guide. From here you have a choice to proceed through the Dismal Swamp or the Albemarle and Chesapeake canal also known as the Virginia Cut. If you draw more than 6 ft you have no choice, it's the A&C. You really want 5 ft or less for the Dismal Swamp even though they claim a 6 ft controlling depth. You need a keel for the passage, something to protect the prop. I've been through the Dismal Swamp canal a dozen times and have never made a passage without hitting something, and I only draw 4 ' 9". Usually, it's just a "clunk" and you go on. Being the lead boat in a line of boats is best since logs lying on the bottom tend to be stirred up by boats passing over them.

I like the passage. It's beautiful and the Visitor Center (36 NM from Hampton) is an experience.

There's room for 3 or 4 boats and if there are more, you raft-up, sometimes three abreast. If you are lucky enough to get a face dock it's considered polite to put fenders out so the next boat after you can raft up. They have a wonderful nature center that's free to explore and lots of trails. There is no electric at the face dock but then there's no charge for staying there either. It's also a rest area for cars, and you'll see many people strolling along and curious about the boats, asking questions, etc. You also get the entertainment of passing through two locks. You have a bow and stern line that you hold up for the lock tender to snag with a hook, and he puts it over the cleat with the end back to you. As the boat rises or falls with the lock, you take up the slack, one line at the bow and one at the stern. Tip: stop your engine. There's crud stirred up with the water gushing in or out that you don't want in your engine intake.

Elizabeth City Docks MM 51

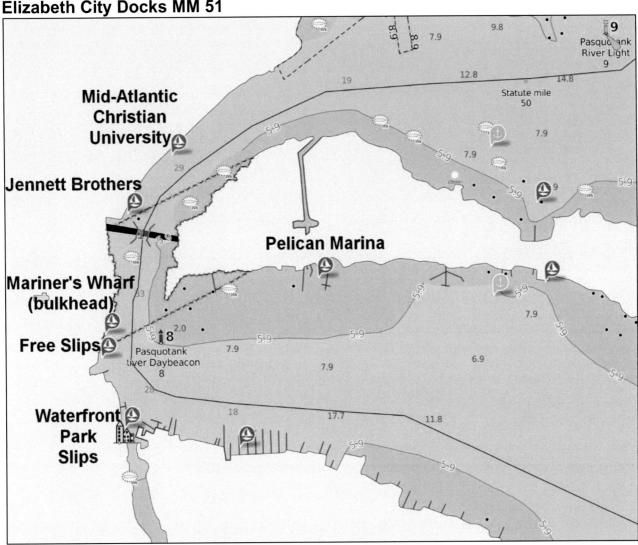

Elizabeth City, 20 NM from the Visitor Center, is full of free dockage. All the red icons you see are all free except the Pelican Marina. You may or may not get help docking but then it's free. There's no electric and mostly no water. You will go bow in for the Mariner's Wharf slips with signs giving the width for each slip.

Some of the docks are bulkheads like Jennett Brothers where you need good fenders. They are not refined and the pilings are covered in creosote.

The docks south of the bridge are exposed to southeast winds and can get rocky if the wind pipes up. For that reason, we usually take the Jennett Brothers bulkhead. We have a dog and they've been okay with us walking him through the property quickly on the sidewalk to get outside. It's a food supply house so they are sensitive to waste. On weekends the Jennett area is closed. You can still dock there but there's no access to town unless you launch your dinghy. The boats in the picture are by the free slips in town.

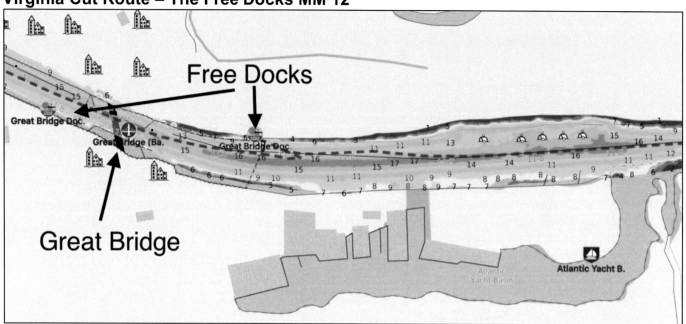

An alternate route to the Dismal Swamp is the Virginia Cut. It's east of the Dismal Swamp route and has deeper water but is also taken by all the commercial traffic. It's only 23 NM from Hampton to the free face docks across the channel from the Atlantic Yacht Basin but it's a convenient stop. The free docks are part of a park where there are hiking trails and a place to walk Hoolie. You can cross over the bridge if you want to shop for 7/11 type items. There's room for about four or five boats depending on how closely they are docked.

You could skip this stop and move on to Coinjock Marina but it's 32 NM farther, which is what we did on the way back north this spring. On the way to Coinjock, there are a few hazards that I'll cover before I get to Coinjock itself. There are several obstruction markers before you get to MM32, but they can be avoided by just staying in the channel per your chartplotter.

During the cruising season, there are usually three to four boats at the free docks.

There's another set of docks north of Great Bridge but they are just pilings, no dock to walk on.

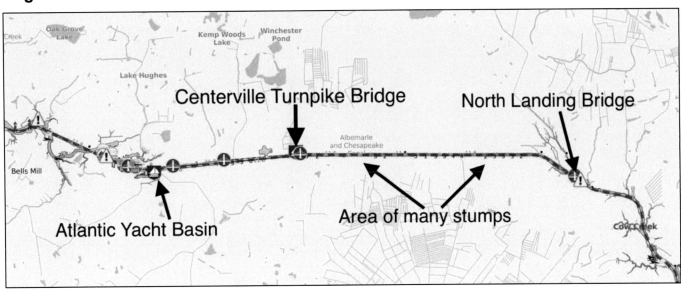

This section of the ICW between the Centerville Turnpike Swing Bridge and the North Landing Swing Bridge is a dangerous area for floating stumps that are barely above water. The hazard warnings will come and go but the danger is there all the time. You have to pay careful attention and go slow so you have time to react. Many boats bend props through this section if they wander off the centerline of the channel. What adds to the problem is that many boats are usually waiting between the two bridges and may wander outside the channel. In my passage in May 2019, I counted at least a half-dozen stumps floating in or near the channel. I just went around them, carefully!

Be sure to call ahead for the operating schedule for both swing bridges. They are old and are constantly being repaired. When headed north and approaching the North Landing Bridge, you will often see a large barge that looks as if it's coming around the bend in the channel. It's not. It's a mooring dock for barges in the area. The sight gave us quite a start the first time we came north!

Here we are going through the locks and the lockmaster stands ready to catch our fore and aft lines with his hook. He'll place the line around the yellow cleat and then hand the bitter end back to you to hang onto. As you rise or fall with the lock, you keep constant tension on the line. It takes two people to do this comfortably.

Virginia Cut Shoaling MM 40.8

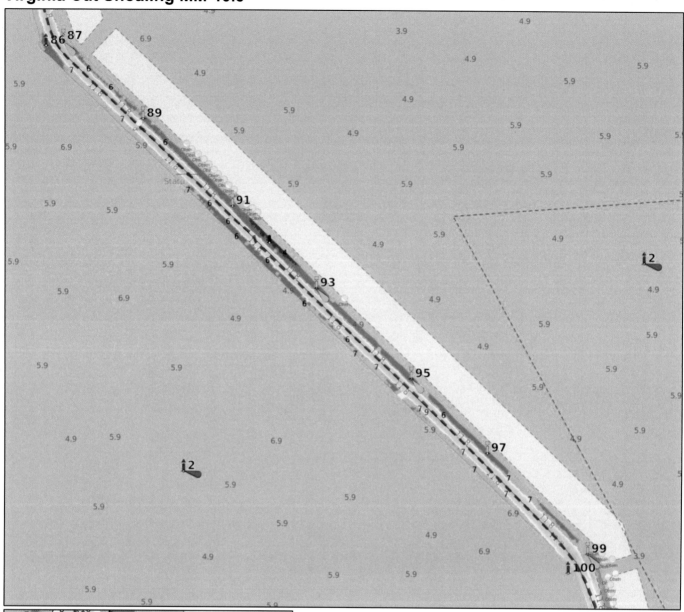

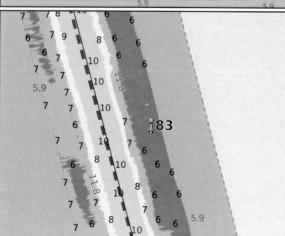

Notice how narrow the green, deep part of the ICW is through here. You will see many hazard markers, especially from Active Captain from boaters who have come to grief. The problem is that the channel is narrow (but deep to 10 MLLW!) and the green markers seem to be too far away. Many boats tend to wander over to get closer to the greens and find shoal water.

For this section of the ICW down to the southern exit to the Albemarle, your chartplotter is your friend. Just stay in the middle of the channel as shown on your chartplotter and you'll see no less than 10 MLW which is what I saw in October 2019. There's no need to be concerned about the hazard markers if you just stay in the middle of the channel per your chartplotter! Note the closeup of G83, it's sitting in shoal water, that's common along here.

Virginia Cut Shoaling MM 44.4

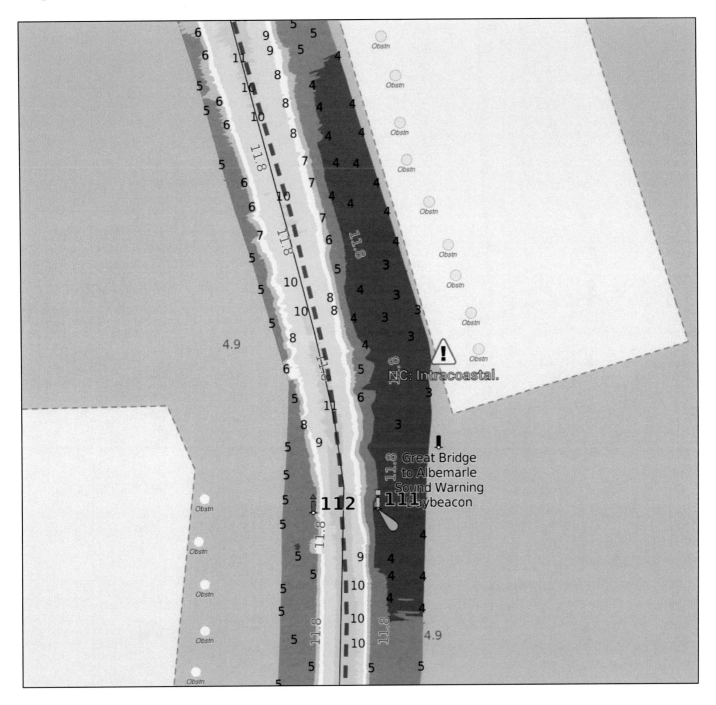

However, by G111/R112, do favor the red side of the turn close to R112 as highlighted by the Waterway Guide Alert icon. There is shoaling to 3 MLW on the outside of the turn by G111. This is one of those rare cases where it's deeper on the inside of a turn.

Here you can see the great advantage of having Aqua Map Master that downloads the USACE surveys right to your tablet (Apple iPad or Android). All you have to do is stay in the green! You can see my track of 10/6/2019 is pretty well centered.

Coinjock MM 49.3

[Coinjock Marina](#) is one very long face dock and they will tie you up very tight to get the maximum number of boats possible docked.

I would have put my dinghy on the outside but they wanted me to raft up with another boat later on. They were so crowded that about ½ the boats were rafted. Be sure to have the prime rib!

Virginia Cut MM 65

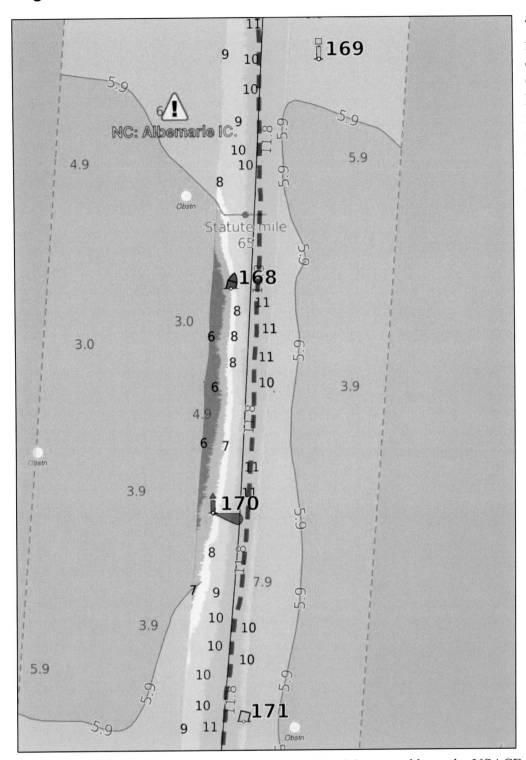

The one exception to just following your chartplotter is along G169 to G171. The hazard by R168 shows an interesting case of where the chart is shifted westward (the chart is shifted; the buoys are not). Looking at the chart, you can see the red buoys 168 and 170 are in the channel and the green buoys are out of the channel, especially 169. To compensate for the offset, travel down the green edge of the channel as shown on your chartplotter. You will find 11 ft. If the channel was plotted correctly, you would be in the middle of the channel. This is a NOAA problem and most chart suppliers just duplicate the offset.

You will often see this chart shift along the ICW. Take a cue from the buoy placement on the chart and mentally correct for the best line (centered between the buoys).

On the other hand, why not just invest in Aqua Map Master and have the USACE chart in front of you as you travel through here. Just stay in the green!

Alligator River Marina MM 84

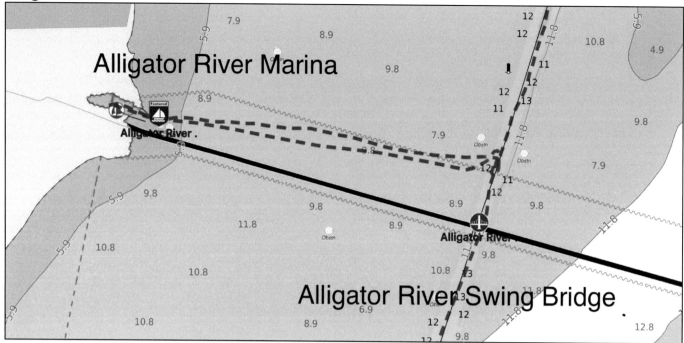

Pick a calm day to cross the Albemarle. You do not want 15 kt winds on the nose; it can get very rough in the shallow waters. The entrance to the Alligator River used to be a problem since the charts were wrong, but the Coast Guard has since moved the markers so all you have to do is follow the markers. Just draw a line between G7 and G9 and follow it to avoid all shallows.

We usually stop at the Alligator River Marina, 30NM from Elizabeth City at MM84.2. They have fuel and a face dock. It's nothing fancy, just a gas station with docks, but it's in a good location for us and it's a good refueling stop. Miss Wanda sold the marina two years ago but it's still in operation.

Alligator River Hazard MM 96.7

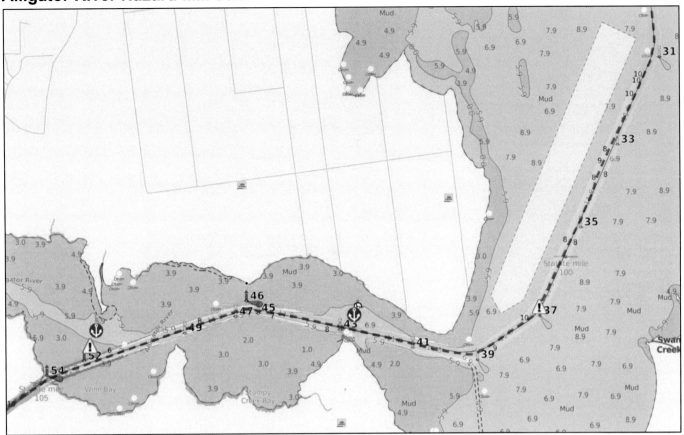

You will always see many Active Captain hazard markers along the channel in the Alligator River. Be sure to read the Waterway Guide Alert (by G37). It will summarize the guidance for the entire area. The area is prone to floating logs and stumps. The best you can do is stay in the channel per Aqua Map and keep a keen watch out for floating debris. It's not advisable to cut corners. Old markers may be present right along the channel but not visible after they've been cut off. Just stay in the channel for the best water.

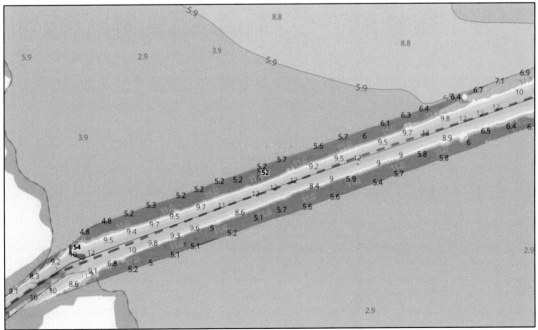

There were at least a dozen boats that reported shoal water through here last fall, the northern entrance to the Alligator-Pungo Canal. There is deep water in the middle of the channel but it's narrow. Just stay in the middle of the green. The 7/2/2019 USACE survey is shown with my 10/11/2019 track.

Pungo River Anchorage MM 127

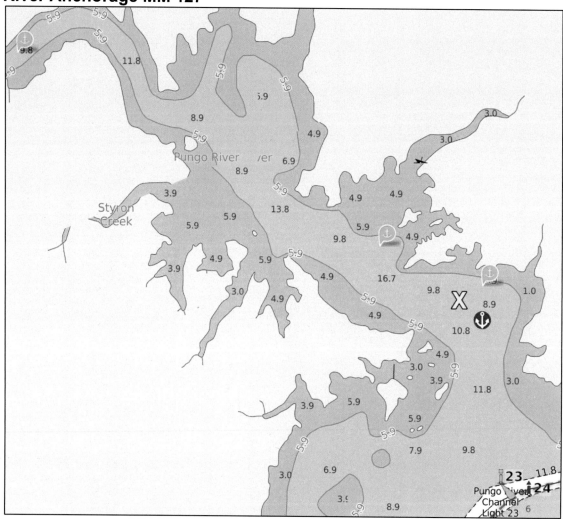

The Pungo River anchorage is 39 NM from the Alligator River Marina. We anchor near the yellow X above in 10 MLW. There's a small, sandy beach for pet relief nearby. You can anchor farther in if there's a south wind blowing. Another option is to take a dock at Dowry Creek Marina or Belhaven with many fine marinas, but the Pungo anchorage suits us fine.

Notice the color of the water from the tannin here at Hoolie's sandy beach.

RE Mayo Docks MM 157.4

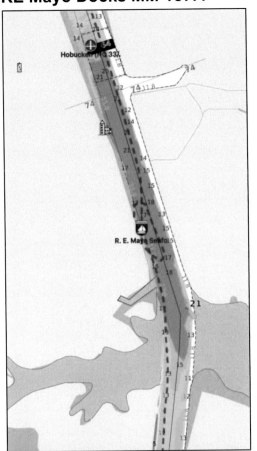

From the Pungo River Anchorage, it's 26 NM to RE Mayo Docks, a good staging area for crossing the Neuse River, which is another river you want to cross in calm weather. We had friends that sailed to the Bahamas and back and said their trip up the Neuse River was the roughest stretch of water they encountered. Don't sell it short; wind against current is not fun. The Campbell Creek or Gale Creek anchorages are a good alternative if RE Mayo doesn't suit you. Both have pet relief.

RE Mayo is a working dock for very large shrimp boats, the Bering Sea type of boat; several from this marina have fished there! Other than the $0.40/ft dockage fee with free electricity, the main attraction is the frozen seafood in blister packs that are ideal for storing in your boat's freezer. The fish is locally caught and flash frozen. We always stock up on scallops, shrimp, and flounder, the best ever. Don't be put off by the docks; they are sturdier than they look—just consider the very large shrimp boats they support—but they are in various stages of disrepair. While we were there one summer, we saw one of the 90 ft shrimp boats barrel into the docks after losing reverse gear. The dock took damage. As for the boat, the gear cable had separated and no longer was connected to the gearbox. By the way, how's your transmission cable? Have you checked it recently?

Although the electricity is included in the $0.40/ft rate, there's only one outlet and it's 30 amps. If other boats try to connect to the two regular 120-volt outlets with an adapter, then no one will have electricity.

There are no showers and the bathroom facilities are meant as a practical joke, brightly colored outhouses complete with painted flowers, etc. Still, the people are nice and the frozen seafood can't be beat.

Gale Creek Anchorage by G23 MM 159.6

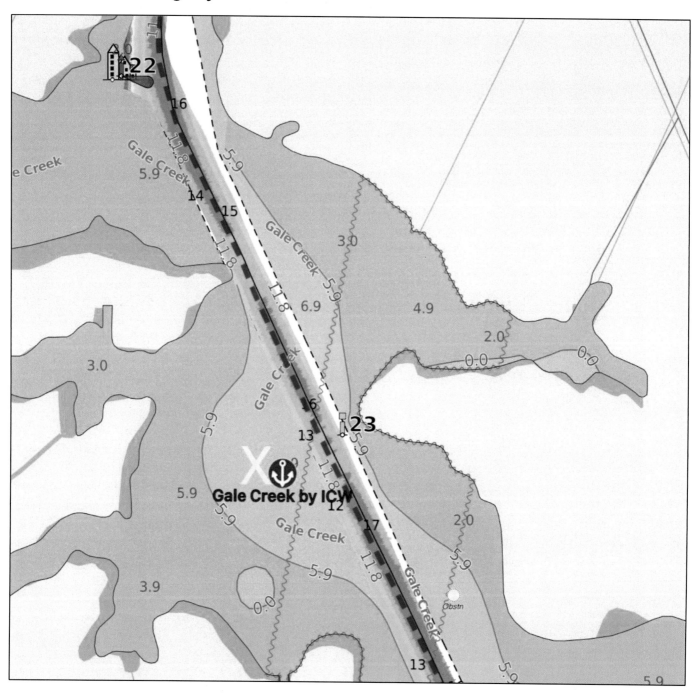

If you don't stop at RE Mayo, then Gale Creek anchorage is a good choice about a mile farther south. It's completely protected and is also a good staging area for crossing the Neuse River. I found pet relief by pushing the dinghy into one of the mosquito canals where I found dry land for Hoolie.

Be careful crossing the Neuse, because it can be rougher than you think. Look for a following wind or no wind. There are several other choices along the way to Cedar Creek. River Dunes Marina is a very popular choice as is Oriental. I've always been in too much of a hurry to stop at either place, but maybe someday.

Cedar Creek Anchorage MM 187

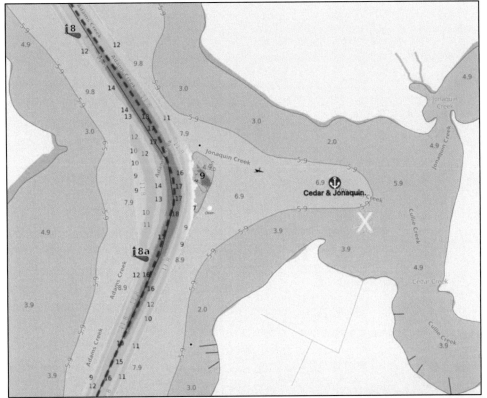

From RE Mayo Docks to the Cedar Creek anchorage it's 26 NM. After crossing the Neuse, we may anchor in Cedar Creek by the yellow X for 7 to 8 MLW. It's deeper by the yellow X than shown on the charts although it's shallower getting there, with more than 6 ft along the way. There's a sandy beach southwest of the X where you can land your pet.

We were hauling anchor one morning when we saw this shrimp boat come in through the still waters. There's a shrimp fishery in Cedar Creek Cove. You can anchor there in 6 MLW if you hug the northern shore.

The entrance to Jonaquin has a 4 MLW bar you have to get over. Both offer better protection than Cedar Creek but we've never tried them.

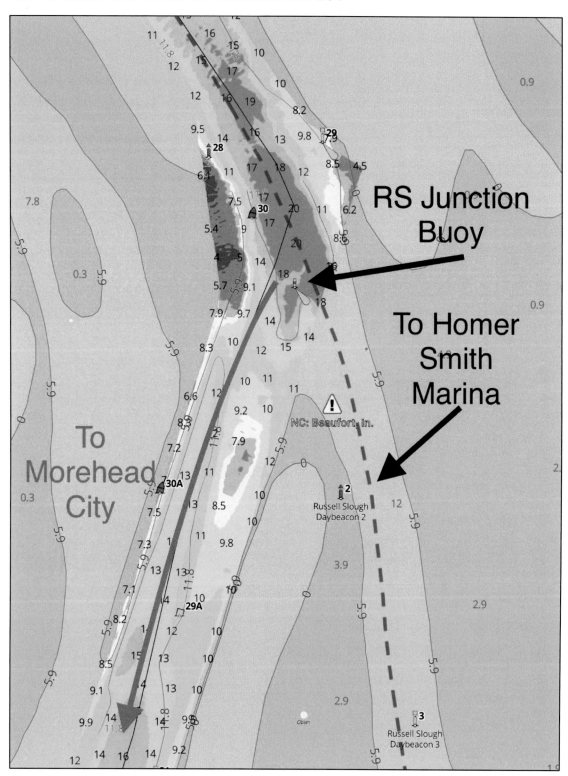

This is a confusing area for first-time ICW cruisers. The channel splits here with one continuing on the ICW and one going to Beaufort.

When going south, you will see a profusion of buoys and it's not clear visually how to proceed. Use your chart plotter with updated charts that show R30 and R30A in the correct positions. If you see R30B on your chartplotter, the charts are outdated. If your chart shows 2.0 MLLW between R30 and R30A on the red solid line, then you still have outdated charts. Buy a new set. Aqua Map shows the correct buoys and depths and is updated four times a year at no additional

charge. The 10/29/2019 USACE survey is shown.

Going south, the channel curves to starboard. I've highlighted the route in red to continue on the ICW to Morehead City and also the route taking you to Beaufort shown by a blue dotted line which was my route on 10/12/2019. Note the green/red/green marker RS. It's known as a junction buoy and can be passed on either side. For the route labeled ICW, I measured a minimum of 11.5 MLLW. On the route labeled Beaufort, I measured 10 MLLW in the spring of 2019. If you just follow your chartplotter, this is easy.

Homer Smith Docks and Marina MM 205

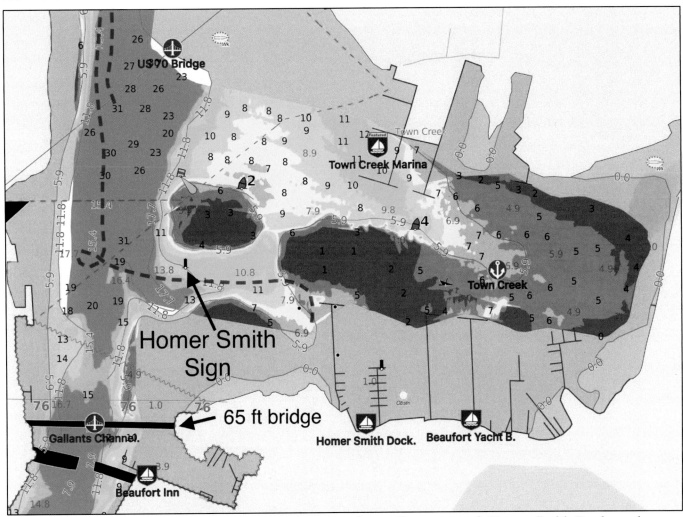

There are many marinas in Beaufort, NC, but there is only one I recommend, Homer Smith Docks and Marina. I heard about the marina from another boater and have stayed there several times. Just follow the Homer Smith route shown on the previous page, pass Homer's sign to port, and follow the local buoys. Mention Bob423 for the best service.

Features:
- Completely protected.
  - $2/ft
  - Within three blocks of downtown Beaufort
  - Brand new floating docks with ipe wood, top of the line.
  - Free spin washer and dryer with A/C and TV.
  - Free courtesy car.
  - New, clean showers but only one. A new clubhouse is being built, scheduled to open the fall of 2019.
  - Pump out and fuel available.
  - Great WiFi by OnSpotWiFi.

The marina is a shrimp boat dock and that Tony is upgrading to service transients. He has an on-site dredge to maintain depths. He added another row of floating docks with ipe wood this spring with full-length fingers. We always make a special effort to stop here and relax with a walk into downtown Beaufort. Be sure not to miss the NC Maritime Museum! Tony and Matt run the marina and will personally see that you are happy.

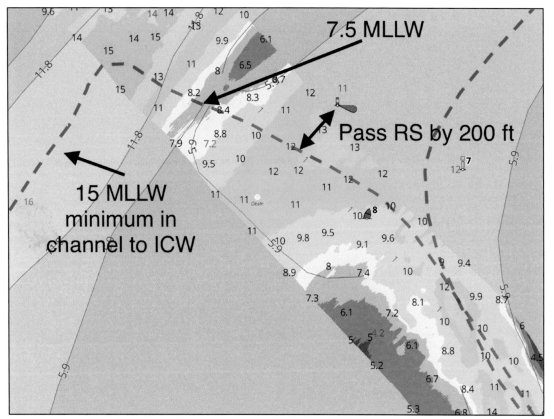

7.5 MLLW

Pass RS by 200 ft

15 MLLW minimum in channel to ICW

When it comes time to leave and head south, it's very convenient to use the same exit the locals use. You passed it on the way down if you came from the north. Head up the channel to R10 and then favor R8, heading to pass RS (red/green/red) buoy by 200 feet off. Then head for the end of the channel as shown on your chart plotter for 7.5 MLLW as the minimum seen as of 10/14/2019.

This passage saves time from having to detour farther south to Beaufort or north to the Crossovers to return to the ICW. The 11/7/2019 USACE survey chart is shown as displayed in Aqua Map Master. It's easiest to just load my fall 2019 track from BobICW (2019 Fall folder).

The new ipe wood floating docks are very nice and come with full fingers and no current for easy docking.

The WiFi is supplied by OnSpotWiFi and is the best in the industry.

I always fill up my dinghy tank with his non-ethanol gasoline.

Leg 5 Cedar Creek or Beaufort NC to Carolina Beach 92 NM

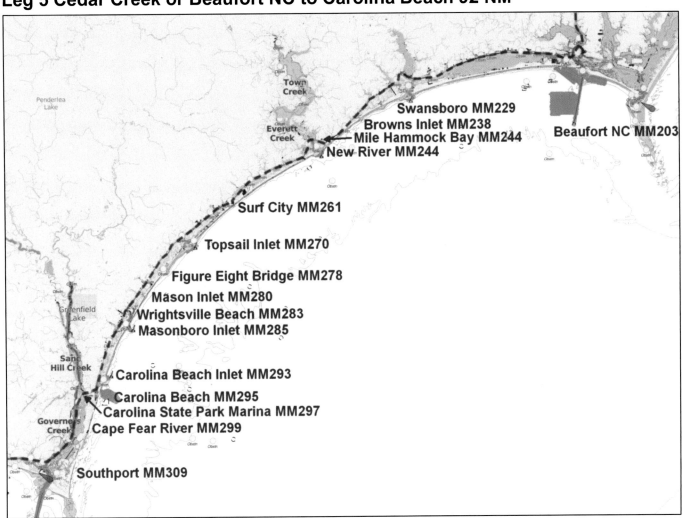

Now we're in the ICW proper with no more open waters until Cape Fear River, just beyond the Carolina State Park Marina which we'll use as a staging area for choosing a favorable tide for going down Cape Fear River. Most recently we've been skipping the Cedar Creek anchorage and continuing on to Homer's Smith Docks and Marina in Beaufort. His docks are new and well protected with the benefit of being only three blocks from downtown Beaufort. The great news for 2019 is the removal of the swing bridge at Surf City that only opened on top of the hour. That leaves only two bridges to get through: the Wrightsville Bridge that opens on top of the hour and the Figure Eight Bridge that opens on the hour and ½ hour. Again, there are many choices, so I'll cover where we usually stay on the trip south.

1. From Cedar Creek to Swansboro for a run of 37 NM and anchor out and run to Carolina Beach the next day for 50 NM. If you want to go further than Swansboro and don't need shore access, then you can anchor at Mile Hammock Bay, a US Marine area which is the reason for no shore access. It's 16 NM farther for a total run of 53 NM.

2. From Homer Smith Marina to Topsail Island Marina in Surf City for 60.5 NM. and then on to Carolina Beach the next day for 35.2 NM. at Carolina State Park Marina. Another option is to pick up a mooring at Carolina Beach for $20. Again, you can break up the trip by stopping at Swansboro if you want or anchoring out at Mile Hammock Bay.

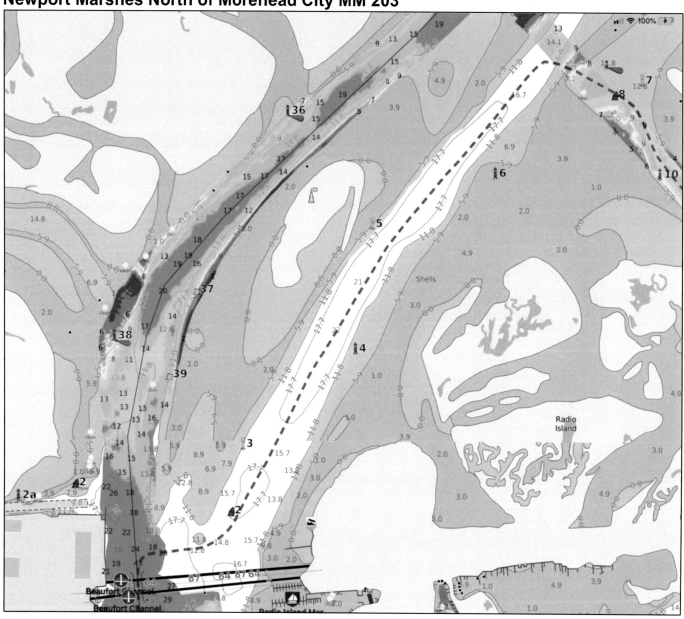

This used to be a problem area when boaters got too close to R38 but with the Coast Guard repositioning G37 and G39, you just favor the greens somewhat and you're fine.

Another marina I recommend is <u>Morehead City Yacht Basin</u>, pictured at left. They have a courtesy car ($10 for 2 hours), floating docks, and two washers and dryers. They charge $1.95/ft if you have a BoatUS, SeaTow or Waterway Guide membership.

Peletier Creek Shoaling by G7 MM 209

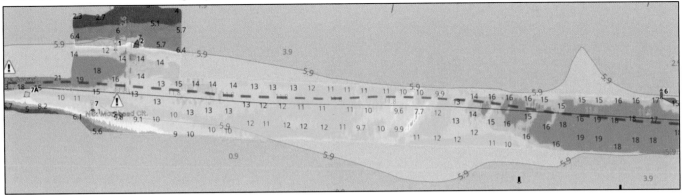

Just run on the red side through here. The least seen was 10.1 MLLW in the green area between R6 and G7. The shoaling is coming from the green side. The dotted line is my track of 10/14/2019 for the deepest water. The Waterway Guide icon by G7 will be updated as new surveys are made by the USACE throughout the year.

Fish markets in the area typically have a layout like in the picture; fresh fish on ice. You seldom see coolers like in a supermarket. The ice is plentiful since it's used so much by the shrimp fleets. This display is from the Independent Seafood Inc market in Georgetown, SC.

Spooner Creek Shoaling by R12/R10A MM 211 R

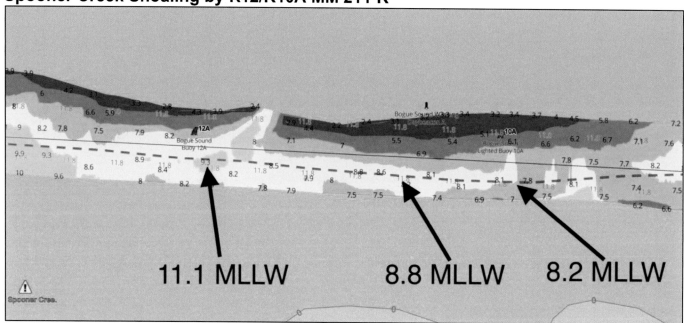

11.1 MLLW   8.8 MLLW   8.2 MLLW

The 1/31/2020 USACE survey is shown in the picture as it appears in Aqua Map Master. There is shoaling from both the red and green side by R10A. Do not hug R10A, pass by 100 ft off. This is a difficult passage to eyeball. Go slow and side to side a little to find the 8.2 MLLW channel by R10A. The easiest thing to do is just to load my track of 10/14/2019 or the BSpooner101618 GPX route, either one will guide you through. Check the Waterway Guide alert icon for the latest information, I will be updating the info as conditions change.

Swansboro Shoaling by R40A to R40 MM 224.4

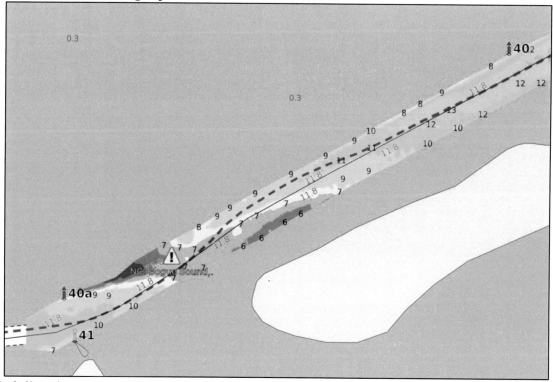

Verbal directions are tough here due to a lack of ATONs. Let's try. Going south from R40, stay centered until ½ way to R40A, then watch your depth and feel your way between two shoals as shown above in the chart. The blue line is my track of 10/14/2019. The least seen was 7.7 MLLW in the orange part of the track. The Waterway Guide alert may have an update.

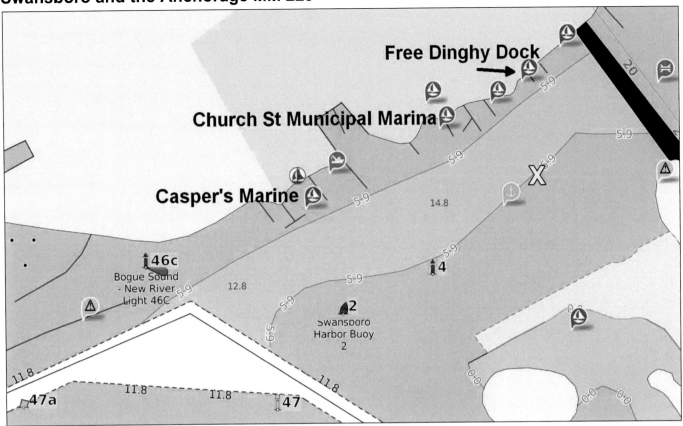

It's 38 NM to Swansboro from the Cedar Creek anchorage and 24 NM from Beaufort. There is a choice of several marinas and a good anchorage marked with a yellow X if you have faith in your ground tackle.

We've anchored here many times with no problem, as the bottom has good holding. It may be a little unnerving to some to have a bridge behind you with a 1 to 2 kt current running, but with a good anchor and chain, there's no problem. But then look at that bridge!

We like the free dinghy dock where you can tie up, explore Swansboro, and walk your pet. Casper's Marina is a good alternative that we've used in the past if a storm pipes up. For the last few years, we've skipped Swansboro and continued, most recently to Topsail Marina in Surf City which I'll cover later.

Goose Creek Shoaling by G55 MM 233.5

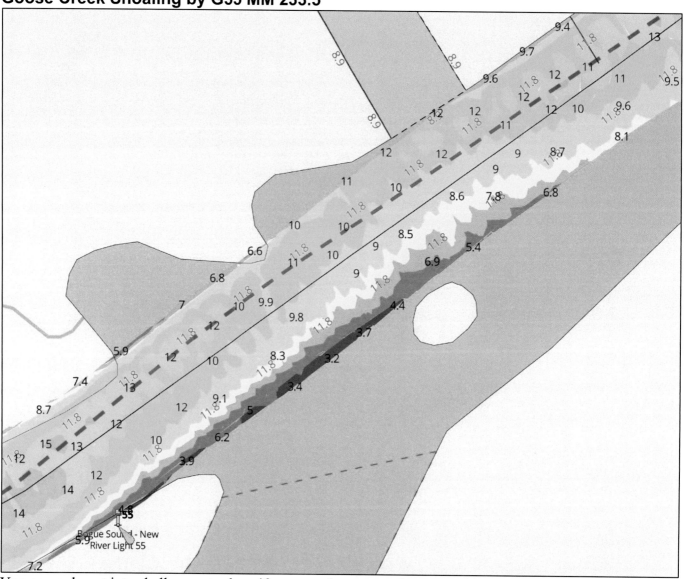

You can only get into shallow water here if you wander over to the green side too far. I saw nothing less than 13 MLLW along the blue dotted line, my track of 10/14/2019 with the 12/16/2019 USACE survey.

Camp Lejeune live firing may close the ICW at times. You may have to wait an hour or so, but in nine years of passages, we've never been delayed. You can call the range office at 910-451-3064 after 3:00 pm the day before to see if there are any restrictions on passing through Camp Lejeune.

You may see this during exercises! They have the right of way! Note the duck. He crossed right in front of us, we waited…

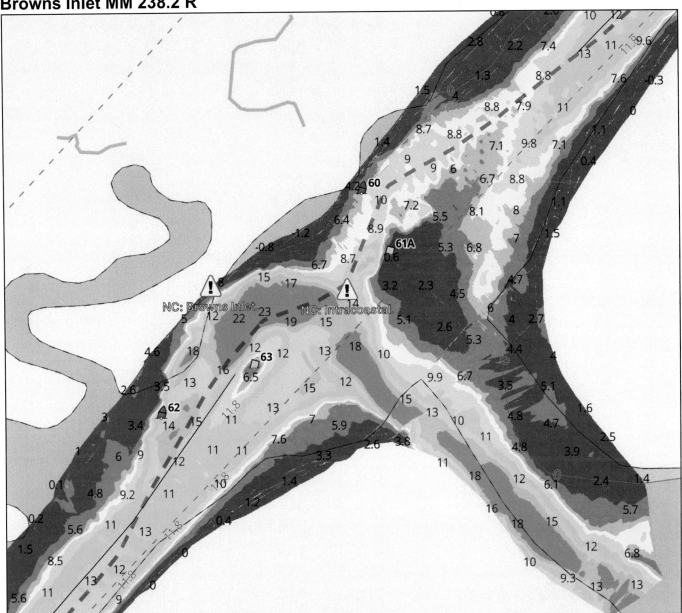

Browns Inlet was dredged in February of 2019, it shoaled in and it's being dredged again in March of 2020. It should be a straight shot for the spring migration. A caution, the buoys may not be moved right away so follow the new USACE survey chart when it comes out. Until then, use tide to get through and follow the dotted blue line, my track of 10/14/2019. The 12/10/2019 USACE survey chart is shown.

Be sure to check on the status of the ATONs and shoaling at the Waterway Guide Alert for the area. The latest routes and tracks for the ICW can always be downloaded at BobICW

New River Approach from North by G65A

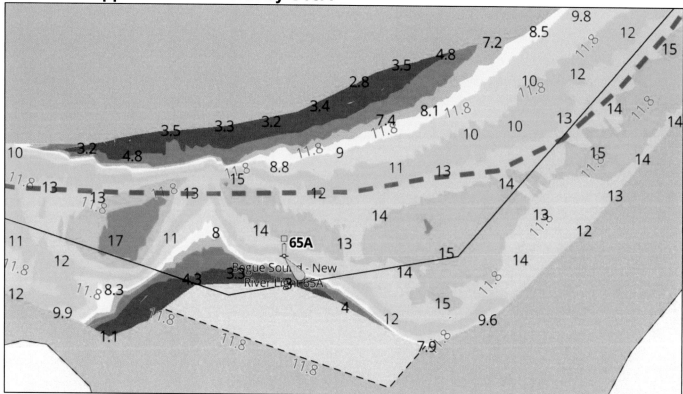

In the last storm, the barrier to the ocean by R65A was breached. Shoaling is progressing next to G65A and you must pass G65A by 80 ft off to avoid the developing shoal just to the west of the buoy. This shoaling is going to get worse with time and it's not scheduled to be dredged this year. Go slow and follow the latest USACE survey. The 9/11/2019 survey is shown above.

At left is a satellite photo from Google Earth that clearly shows the breach to the ocean.

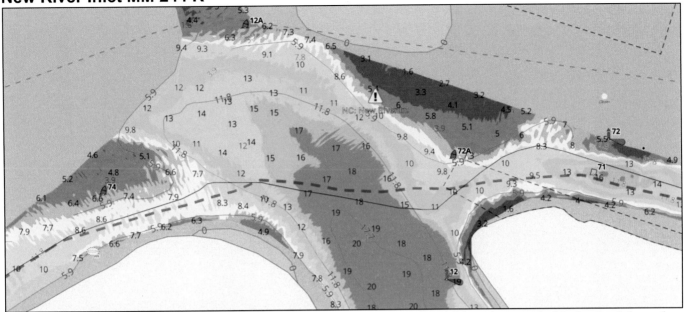

New River Inlet is on the list of areas to be dredged in the spring of 2020 but they are behind schedule and may not get to it until the fall. Check the Waterway Guide Alert icon for the latest status.

The least seen on the blue line was 9.5 MLLW on 10/14/2019. G71 has been moved to the northwest, it's not straight across from R72 as shown on the chart. Note that R72 sits in a shoal, as does R72A and R74! You must pass them about 120 ft off. The only buoy you hug is G71, honor it but pass it close enough to scrape paint off (you want to keep as far away from R72 as you can). As if all this wasn't enough of a challenge, R72A has taken to wandering. It is not well anchored in position and has been seen up on land, down the alleyway between R72 and G71, and even farther up on the shoal.

Few areas have cause boater more headaches than New River Inlet. There's not a day that goes by without a boat going aground or at least touching bottom. The path through is not straight forward, it's a series of "S curves." The most foolproof way of getting through is to load the USACE route at BNR032719. As conditions change at New River, I will load a new route with a more recent timestamp in the name. You can also follow my track of 10/14/2019 shown above as a blue dotted line.

We used to stop at Swans Point Marina but no more. It used to be run by a mother/daughter team and was friendly and helpful with fresh-baked bread in the morning but no more. They left and haven't been replaced. I now skip the place and move on to Top Sail Marina in Surf City which I'll cover next.

The big news is that the Surf City Swing Bridge is no more!! It's been replaced by a 65 ft high bridge. No more waiting for the top of the hour for it to open. Now, if only the Wrightsville Beach bridge would follow suit.

The old Beach House marina was foreclosed but now there's a new marina in the same place that just opened, Topsail Island Marina. It's at the bottom, right of the picture above. Everything we always liked about Surf City is still there: the convenient IGA grocery store, the nearby beach, lots of places to eat, and the local seafood market with fish on ice.

Topsail Inlet MM 270

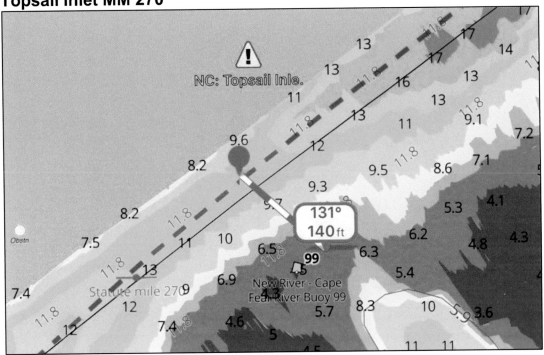

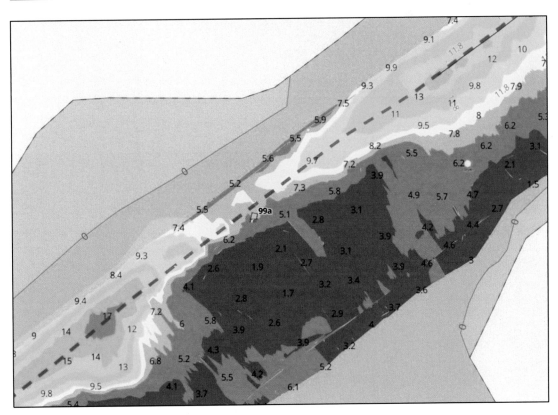

There is plenty of water through here if you stay in the middle of the channel, 12.3 MLLW was the least seen and that was by G99A at the bottom chart. The USACE survey of 2/12/2020 is shown.

Many boaters have hit bottom by G99 and also by G99A by getting too far to the green side, often pushed by a 1 to 2 kt current hitting the boat broadside from the inlet. You can see that both green ATONs sit in shoal water, give both greens a wide berth as shown on the chart. There are no red ATONs to help you stay in the middle, use your charts, especially Aqua Map Master with the USACE surveys loaded. The GPX route BTopS092318 can also help you stay in the middle of the channel.

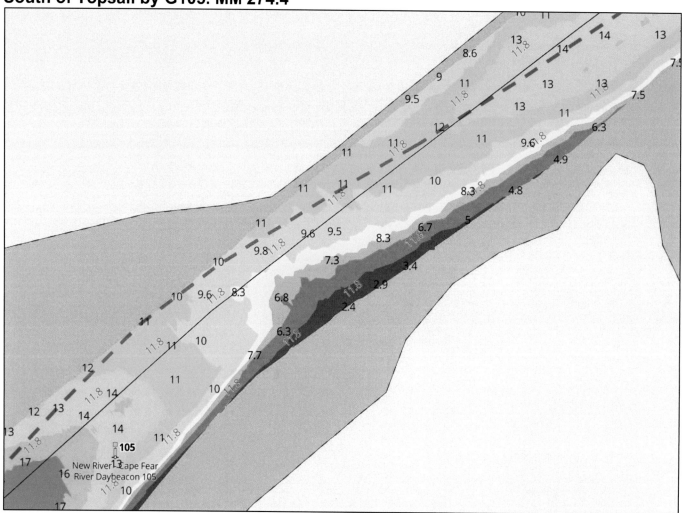

When approaching G105 from either the north or south, shift over to favor the red side to avoid the developing shoal on the green side. The 2/5/2020 USACE survey chart is shown as displayed in Aqua Map Master. The blue dotted line is my track of 10/15/2019.

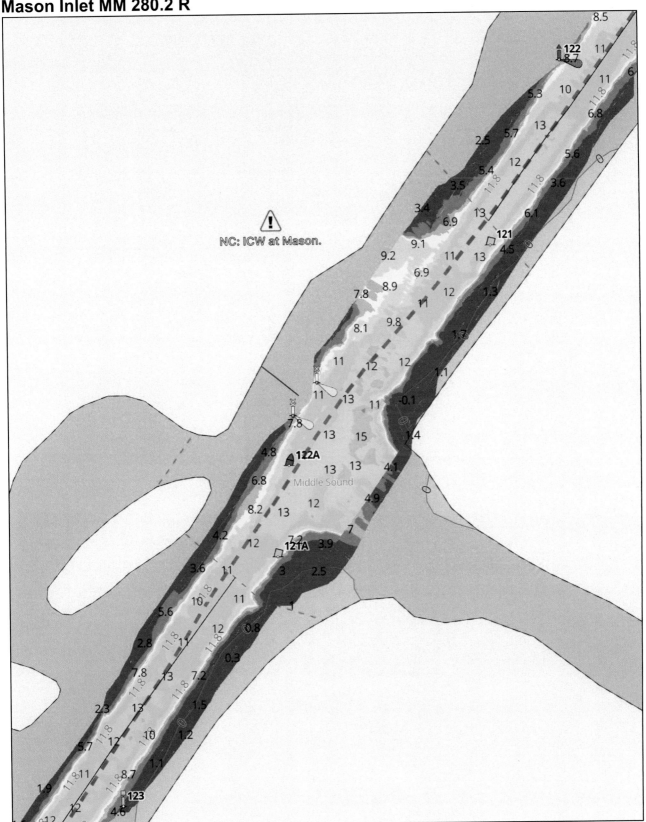

Mason Inlet has been dredged but from experience, I know it will not last. It's been dredged at least three times in the eight years I've been on the ICW. For now, just follow the buoys. Alternatively, you can just follow the blue dotted line, my track of 10/15/2019. For updates, we sure to check the Waterway Guide alert icon displayed in Aqua Map for the area, I maintain all the alerts for the ICW so if conditions change, you'll know it there.

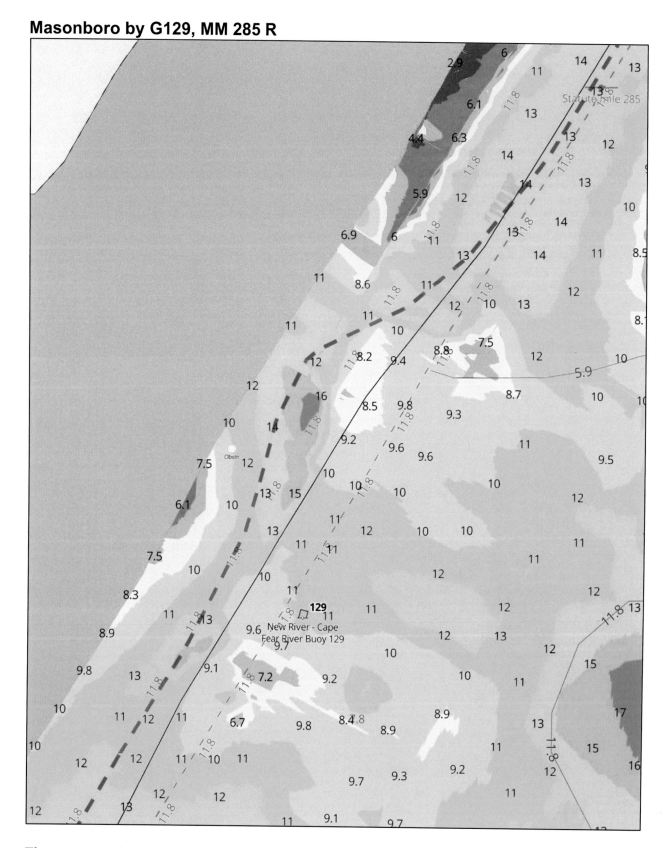

There are two developing shoals:
- One 375 ft north of G129
- One 90 ft south of G129

For the one north of G129, you have to choose which way to pass it, to the west or the east, both paths will work. My 10/15/2019 track is shown. Check the latest Waterway Guide alert for the current status.

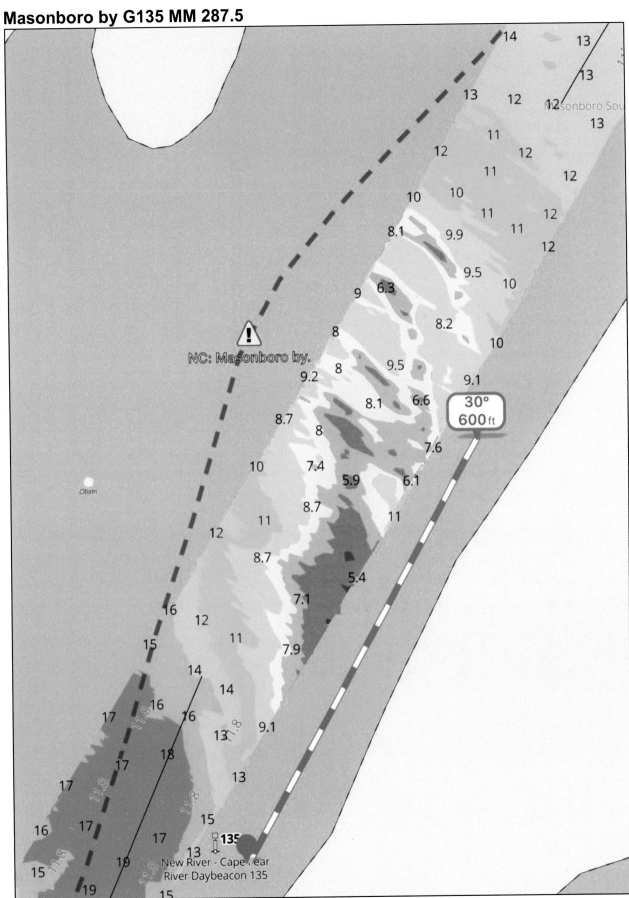

Move over to the red side of the channel at about 600 feet north of G135. There is shoaling on the green side to less than 5 MLLW. Check the Waterway Guide alert for the latest info.

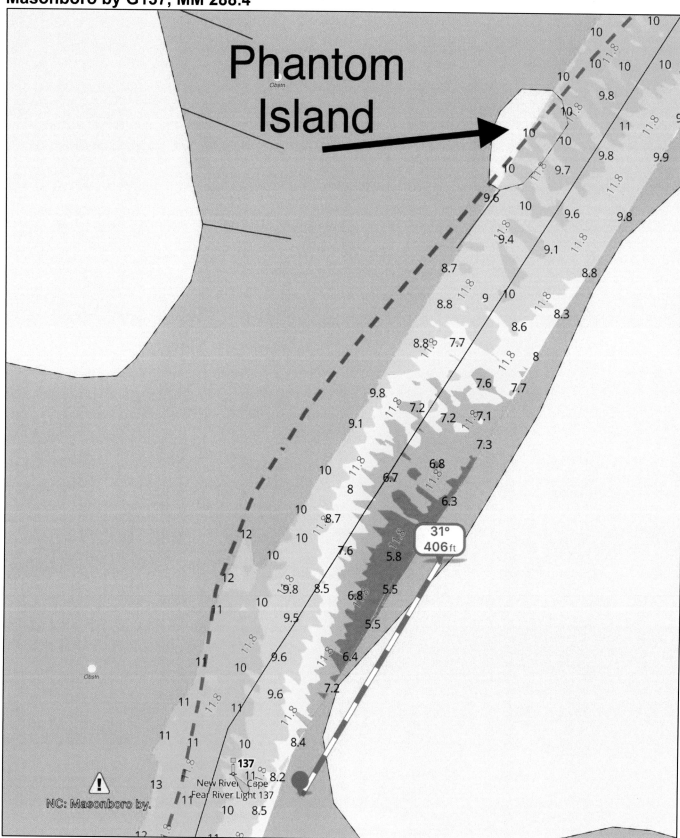

At 450 feet north of G137, favor the red side to avoid shoaling to 5 MLLW on the green side. Check the latest Waterway Guide alert for the latest info. Note the phantom island that is not there. It shows up on both NOAA and SonarCharts. It's a good mark to use on returning to the channel, just go right over it.

Myrtle Grove by R150 MM 292

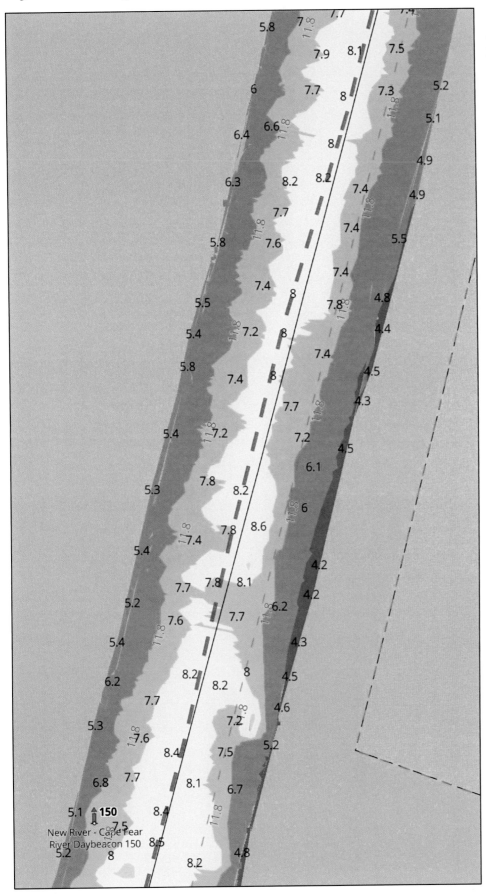

Pass by R150 by 60 feet off but otherwise stay centered in the channel.

There is shoaling on both sides. The 1/30/2020 USACE survey chart is shown as displayed in Aqua Map Master.

My track of 10/15/2019 is shown in the blue dotted line. The least I saw was 8.2 MLLW along the blue line.

Note: do not hug R150, be sure to stay off 60 feet.

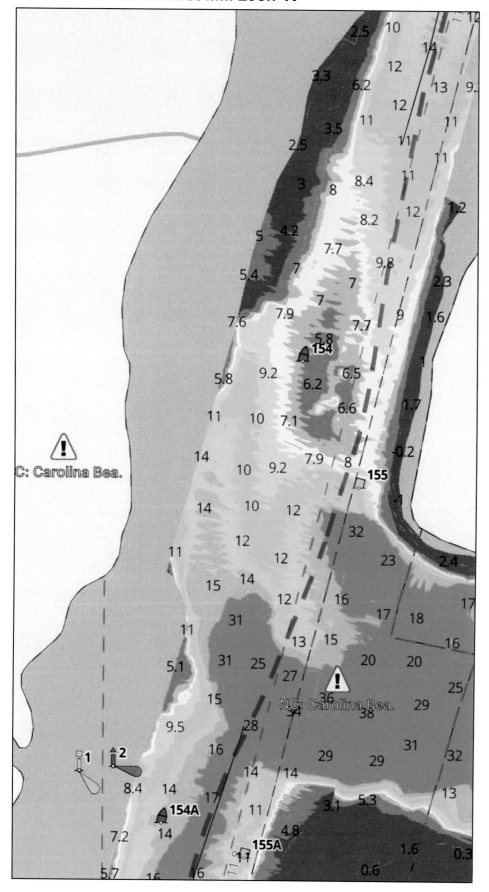

Pass by R154 by 200 feet off.

This area is being dredged 3/2020 but the guidance of passing by R154 by 200 feet is still good. When an area is dredged, the dredged material is never piled up along the edges, it's moved so soundings are only deeper, never shallower nearby.

The 1/30/2020 USACE survey is shown as displayed in Aqua Map Master. Check the nearby Waterway Guide icon for current information.

My 10/15/2019 track is shown in the blue dotted line where the least I saw was 11.5 MLLW.

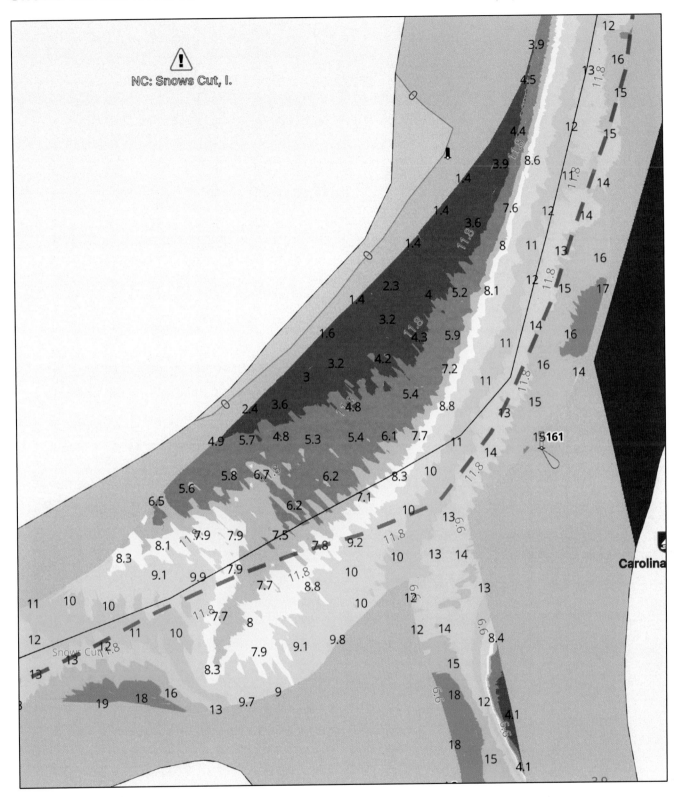

Favor the outside of the turn (green side) for 6.8 MLLW least seen on the blue dotted line track. The 1/30/2020 USACE survey is shown and with this survey, a better track would be to go farther south and follow the deeper water shown in the USACE survey, to 10 MLLW.

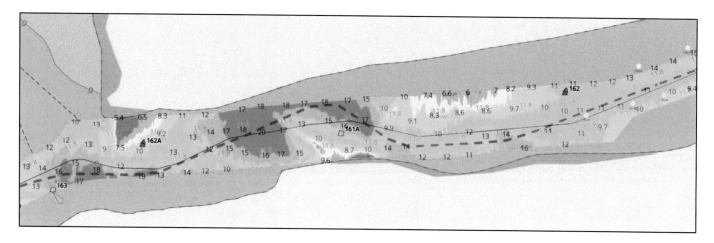

The western end of Snows Cut requires a slalom course around the buoys. Note that you cannot hug R162 and head directly for G161, you will run into a 6 MLLW shoal, you must make the turns shown for the best water. See the latest guidance at the Waterway Guide alert, I will keep it up to date as conditions change. The 1/31/2020 USACE survey chart is shown with my track of 10/15/2019 as a blue dotted line where the least I saw was 14.1 MLLW. This area was due to be dredged 3/2020 but they ran out of time and won't be done until late this fall or next year.

Carolina Beach Moorings MM 295

The town had 9 moorings available when I was there in May 2019. You have to reserve a mooring in advance through DOCKWA for $20/night. When your reservation is accepted by the dockmaster at Carolina Beach, your credit card is charged. You do not have to go into shore to pay, everything is handled over the internet and as far as I know (I tried) there's no way to cancel once you paid for the reservation. There's a nearby dinghy dock with a short walk to the beach.

The moorings are well made with a metal thimble on the end. When not in use, they are stored on top of the mooring ball in a tray which keeps barnacles and slime off the pennant.

Leg 6 Carolina Beach to Charleston 127 NM

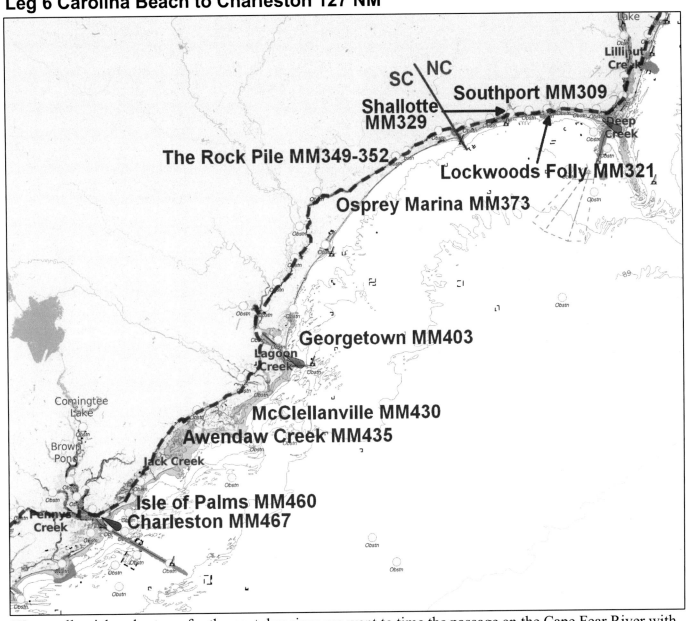

We usually pick a short run for the next day since we want to time the passage on the Cape Fear River with the current behind us (the current can reach 3 kts!) and not against us. You also don't want a wind against current situation either. Good stops are at Southport Marina (12.3 NM) or St James Plantation Marina a little farther. Then it's on to Osprey Marina. (50 NM from St James). We used to stop at Barefoot Landing Marina and tour the outlets but they no longer have docks for overnight stays.

From Osprey Marina, we usually stop at Georgetown (28NM) to time our passage with some tide through the shallows of McClellanville. You can stop halfway to Charleston if you want at the Awendaw anchorage (29 NM from Georgetown) if you don't like the tides for Isle of Palms or just want to take it easy. For 2019, the Isle of Palms has been dredged but not all of McClellanville, only Matthew's Cut is due for dredging there.

Carolina Beach State Park Marina MM 297

Carolina Beach State Park Marina is state-owned and used to be 90% empty during the north and south migrations, but ever since I've been extolling its virtues it seems to be very busy. The cost can't be beat at $36/night flat rate for boats up to 43 ft and with electricity and water included at no extra charge. There has been some shoaling over the last few years with the depth in the channel coming in down to 4.7 MLLW where it used to be 6.7 MLLW. It may be less in the fall.

Nevertheless, the bottom is soft mud and there's still 5.5 MLLW inside at "A" dock. The face dock on "A" only has 50-amp service so you will need an adapter if you have a 30-amp line. The face docks have pilings outside the floating docks so hang a couple of fenders horizontally for the best protection with the rest hung vertically for the floating dock. Tall trees protect the basin so you feel almost no wind, even with it howling outside.

The staff is friendly but they are not used to docking big boats so you're mostly on your own. There are a washer and dryer for marina and RV use. The park setting is great with many nature walks, and you can get a rental car from Enterprise—they will come and pick you up. Bring your boat documentation with you to register because they will ask for it.

Cape Fear River Approach MM 297 R

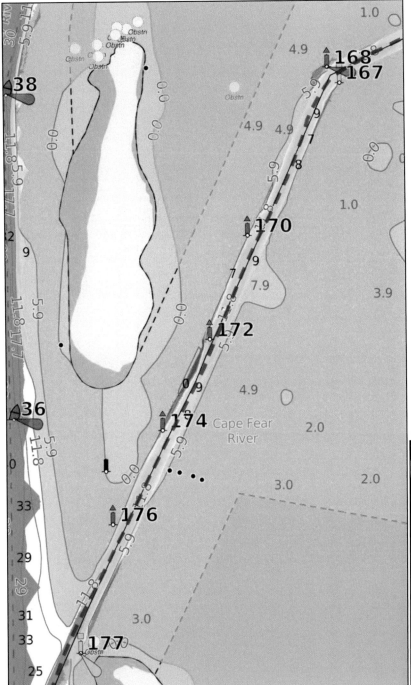

Just stay 100 to 150 ft off the red markers and you're fine for 10.3 MLLW.

Download BCapeFearCut for a GPX route through this passage.

Don't cut the corner at G177; go straight out into the channel. Be sure to time this passage so you have the current with you and without more than a 10 kt on the nose. The current can run 2.5 to 3 kts and wind against current is something you don't want to experience in Cape Fear River.

If you're lucky, you can see a Painted Bunting at a bird feeder set up just for them at Carolina Beach State Park Marina. It's one of the few places you can see the brightly color bird. Venus Fly Traps can be seen on the many nature walks in the park.

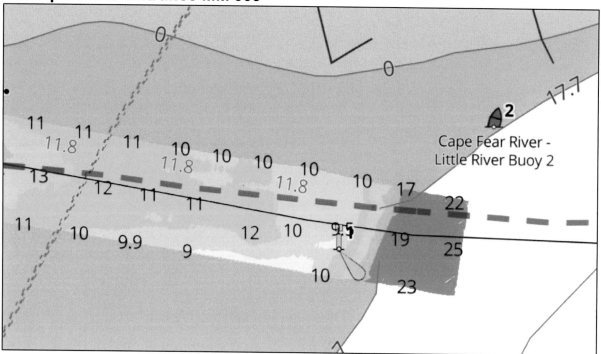

Just follow my 10/15/2019 track (blue line) shown on the 8/26/2019 USACE survey when entering the ICW at the south end of Cape Fear River. There's minor shoaling by G1, so stay about 100 ft off G1 for the deepest water.

We sometimes stay at St James Plantation pictured below just south of the Cape Fear River. It's very nice and they rent out extra slips to transients. It's a great hurricane hole with the three-story homes built on a 12 ft high mound around the marina basin.

Lockwoods Folly Approach by R36, MM 320.2

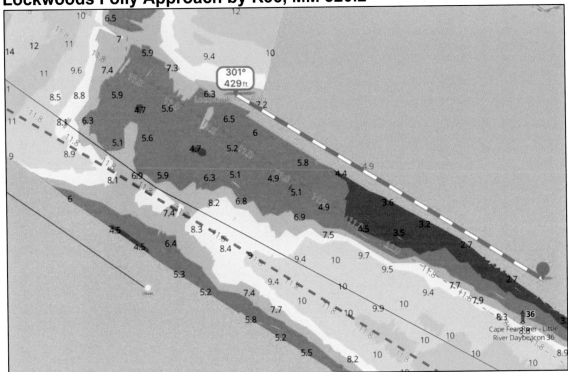

There is a shoal building at 400 feet north of R36. Pass R36 by 100 feet off since the shoal 400 feet ahead (when heading south) is building from the red side. I saw 6.0 MLLW on my 10/17/2019 track. This area is not due to be dredged, proceed with caution.

Lockwoods Folly MM 321

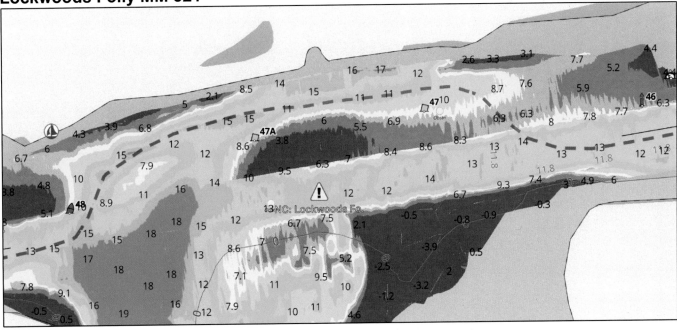

Lockwoods Folly was dredged 2/2020 so it is now a straight shot through. The buoys have been moved to mark the dredged channel. Use the USACE survey as shown in Aqua Map for guidance on how to transit the area. The blue dotted line is was my track of 10/17/2019 which is no longer the deepest water path.

Always check the Waterway Guide alert for this area, it will have the latest status and a link to download an updated GPX route if there's a change.

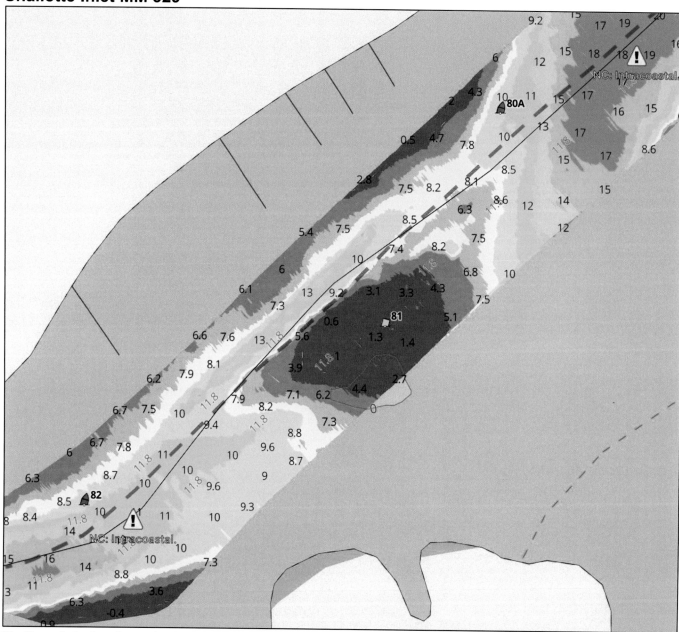

Shallotte inlet has been dredged. It was last surveyed 1/30/2020 by the Wilmington USACE for the above chart. Since this is a traditional shoaling area, check the latest Shallotte Inlet survey. You can see that my blue dotted line track of 10/17/2019 gets too close to the shoaling by G81 (it was centered in the channel on 10/17/2019!) Instead, follow the USACE survey chart for the deepest water. The shoal appears to be very sharp, from 10 ft to 0 ft in only a few feet so stay in the green in the chart.

Also, check the Waterway Guide alert for the area.

Little River Inlet Shoaling MM 341

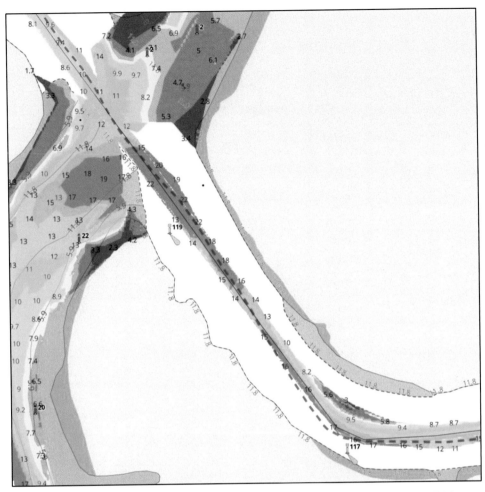

There is a shoal reaching south from the red side opposite G117. The best path is shown by the red dotted line above, my track of 10/17/2019.

Going south, pass R116 by 130 ft off for 17 MLW or better and aim for G117, passing it by 100 ft for 17 MLW, then gradually return to the visual center. This shoal has been here for the last 6 years and is stable. Just stay in the middle of the channel the rest of the way around the turn. The 1/16/2020 USACE survey is shown.

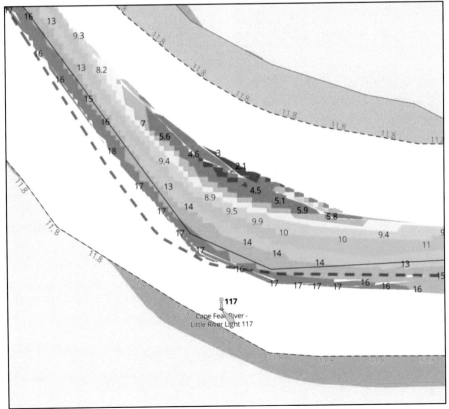

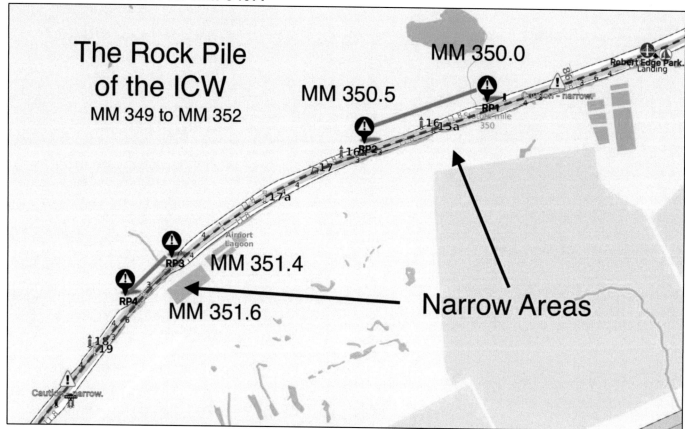

When the ICW was being built, they unexpectedly ran into rock ledge through this area. To keep within budget, the canal was made narrower than normal. It looks intimidating at first; the rock ledges are visible at low tide. There are two narrow sections within the rock pile: at the north end and near the south end with a wider stretch in the middle. **Look at the ledge just outside the channel in the photo!**

It is customary to announce your intention to enter the Rock Pile portion of the ICW with a VHF call on both channels 16 and 13, the commercial traffic channel. If a barge is headed your way, do not enter the Rock Pile; wait until it passes by. You do not want to meet a barge in either of the two narrow sections unless you can back up well! That said, we've never met a barge or any other boat in 18 trips through the Rock Pile. We supplement our VHF call on channel 13 by looking ahead on our AIS display for any on-coming commercial traffic in case he didn't hear our call on channel 13. Needless to say, stay within the marked channel, do not go outside for any reason, or you will find rocks! The channel itself is plenty deep, 12 MLLW at least and it's wide enough for two boats to pass (not barges!); just don't leave any room between the two gunwales, maybe 5 to 10 ft. I'm probably overly cautious, but then I've gone through at low tide and have seen the ledges.

Shoaling by R22A MM 361.4

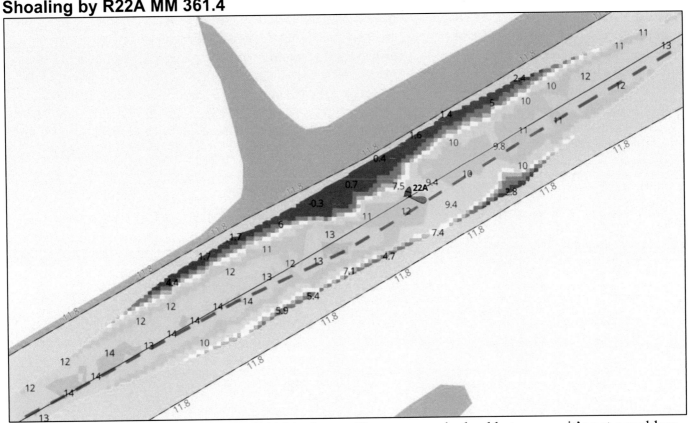

The Charleston USACE survey of 1/16/2020 is shown. The area was dredged last year so it's not a problem anymore unless you hug R22A. I suspect a shoal will rebuild out from R22A eventually so stay in the center or slightly to the green by R22A.

Hague Marina Shoaling MM 369.1

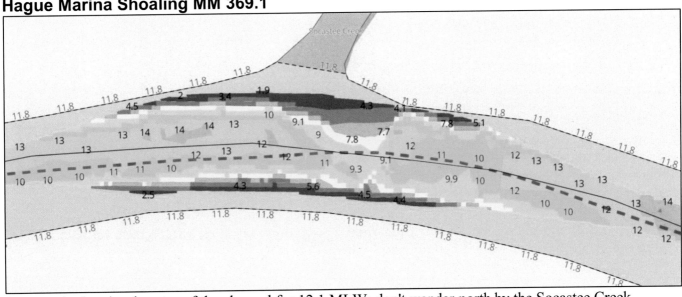

Just stay in the visual center of the channel for 12.1 MLW; don't wander north by the Socastee Creek entrance where a shoal is building up.

The rest of the passage to Georgetown is one of the highlights of the ICW trip south, but you are deep into alligator country. Even with the tides, the water is still fresh, which also breeds alligators. You will see many places to anchor along the route and that's fine as long as you don't have to go ashore.

Socastee Highway Bridge SC544 MM 371.2, Clearance vs Water Level

The Socastee Highway bridge (SC 544) clearance is often reduced due to high water. I compiled a chart of water level vs bridge clearance to estimate when clearance might be enough for your boat. The graph is based on my measurement of the bridge height by using the height board and plotting that against the actual water level as reported by the US Geological Survey (USGS) website. The data is also presented in tabular format for those that don't like graphs. The link for the Socastee Highway SC544 bridge water level is at https://waterdata.usgs.gov/nwisweb/graph...

Note that the chart shows the effects of tide too as well as floodwater. Time your passage for low tide if you need the extra clearance.

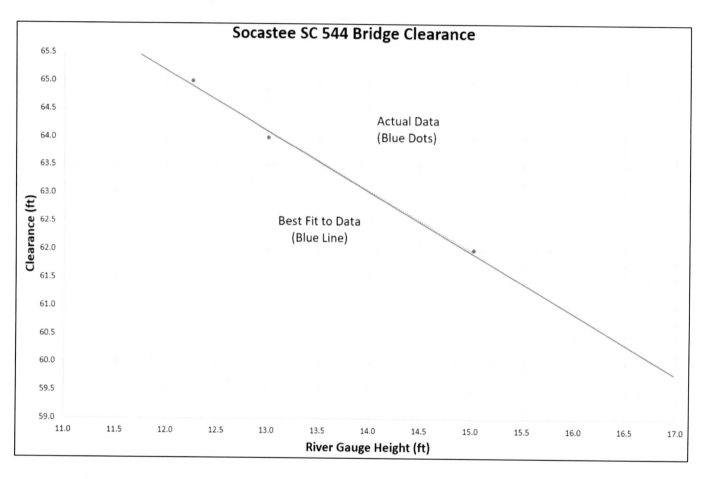

Find the value of the current water level in the graph and see where it intersects the bridge clearance height. Or, find your mast height and find out what the water level has to be for you to pass under. As you proceed through the bridge, please take a photo and post it on the Facebook ICW Cruising Guide page with an exact time. This will allow me to further refine the chart.

Note: this is not an exact science. Water gauges have been known to stick but it's been reliable so far. Check the height board carefully before passing through.

For those who would rather use a table, see below.

The top row is the water level in feet from the link, the bottom row is the bridge clearance in feet.

19.0	18.5	18.0	17.5	17.0	16.5	16.0	15.5	15.0	14.5	14.0	13.5	13.0	12.5
58.4	58.9	59.4	59.9	60.4	60.9	61.4	61.9	62.4	62.9	63.4	63.9	64.4	64.9

Osprey Marina MM 373

Osprey Marina is located between R26A and R26. As you can see from the photo, it's very well protected and there's a long, narrow fairway to enter the marina. There's also dockage on a new bulkhead. The basin inside is a little tight so be careful in maneuvering, and plan ahead.

The dock layout is shown at right. The long face dock on your port as you enter only has electricity along half its length. Osprey plans on adding electrical outlets there by the fall of 2019.

At a daily rate of $1/ft, it's a bargain and they have free pump-outs.

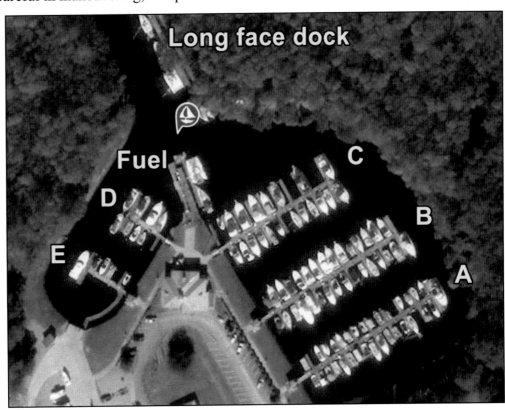

Georgetown Entrance Shoaling MM 403

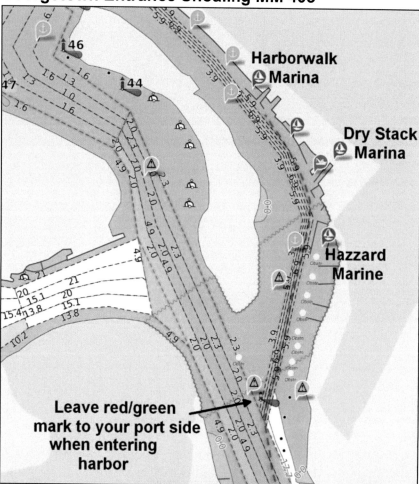

Leave red/green mark to your port side when entering harbor

Georgetown is usually our next stop. The shoaling hazard marks on the way in can be avoided by just favoring the side of the channel next to the docks for 7 MLLW. We usually stay at Dry Stack Marina or Harborwalk Marina and refuel. Be sure to leave the red/green marker at the entrance to your port side as you enter the harbor.

Be sure to visit the Independent Seafood Market (photo at bottom left) several hundred feet northwest of Dry Stack Marina. We always pick up fresh seafood when we're in town. Unfortunately, they are not open on Sunday but they do open at 8:00 am Monday. Take a stroll through town—it's nice.

Harborwalk Marina is shown below.

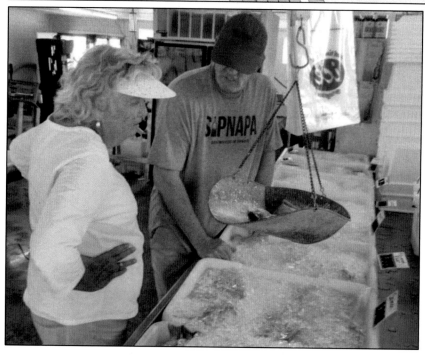

Ann's buys fresh seafood at Independent Seafood, a local market less than a block away. As is the custom along the ICW, all the fish are stored on ice, not in a refrigerated display.

Western Channel ICW Entrance Shoaling MM410

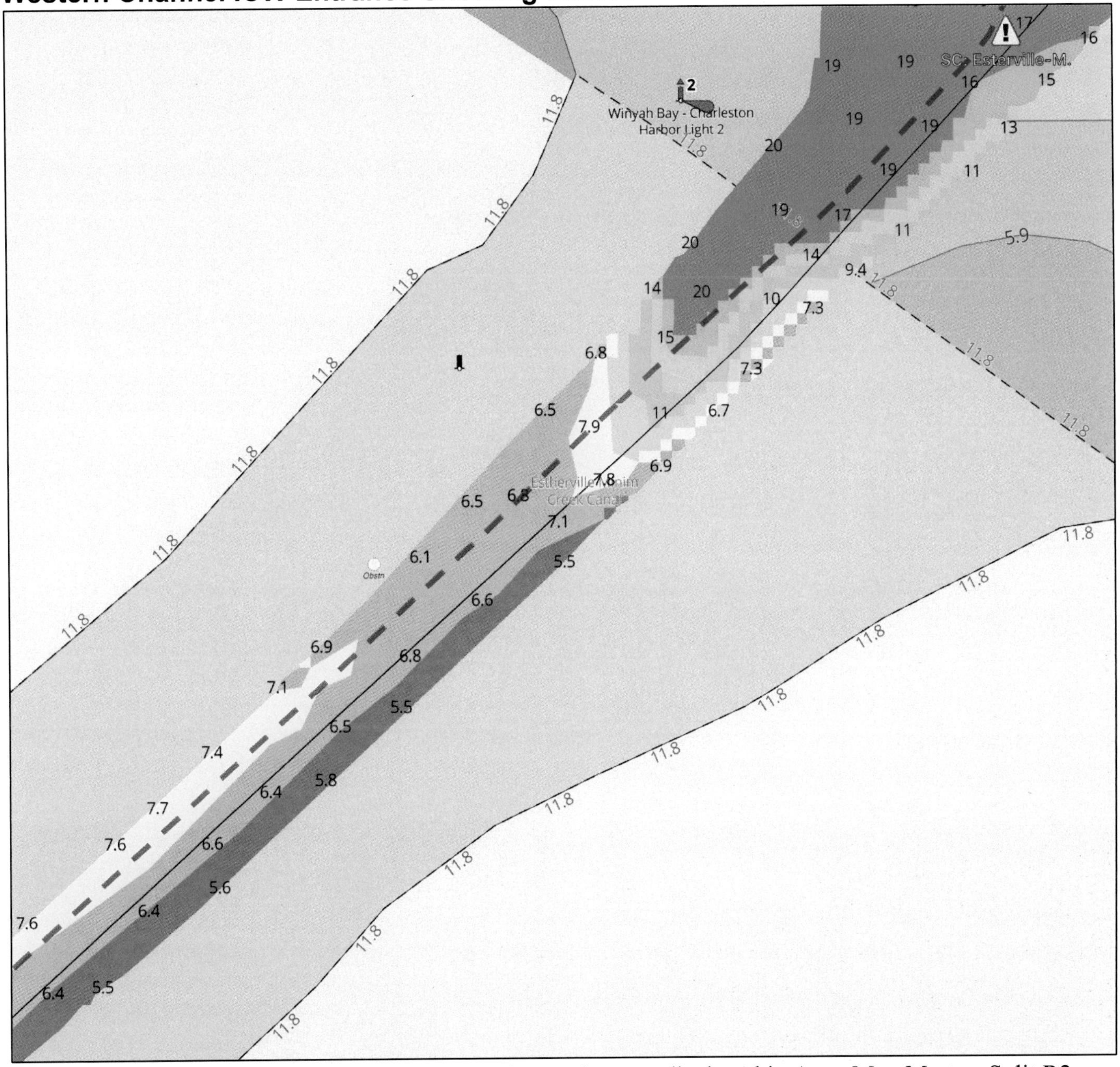

The Charleston USACE survey of 12/4/2019 is shown above as displayed in Aqua Map Master. Split R2 and the south shore for 17 MLLW by R2, 7.0 MLLW farther in as of 10/21/2019. The shallow water will persist for 2000 ft into the ICW. My track of 10/21/2019 is shown as a blue dotted line.

The great news is that Isle of Palms has been dredged, McClellanville has been dredged, and Minum Creek is due to be dredged by 3/30/2020. That makes this passage now easy although there are still some shallow spots to look out for which I will cover. This part by the entrance may or may not be dredged, it's uncertain.

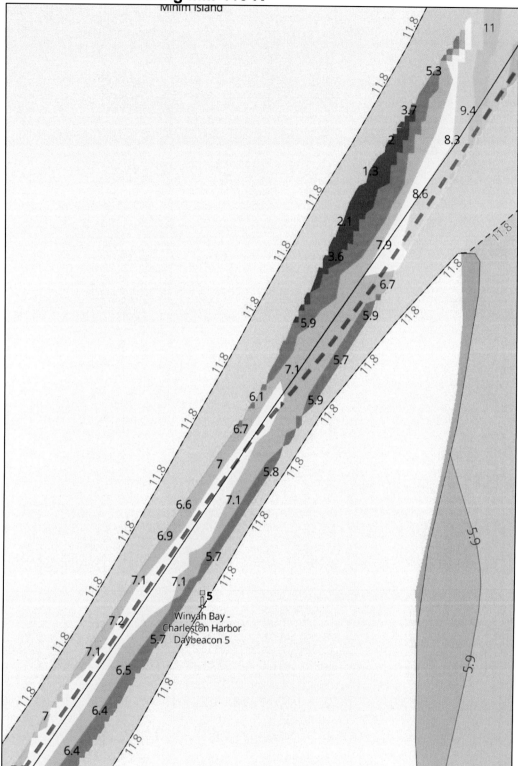

Great News, Minum Creek is due to be dredged 3/2020! Until them, the critical path here at the 7.0 MLLW point is very narrow, less than 20 feet wide for the deepest water. If you stray off the blue line by 10 feet (my track of 10/21/2019), you can find 2 feet less water instantly. Good News, it's due to be dredged 3/2020!

You have several options:
- Pass through at mid to high tide and don't worry about depths (a high tide will add 4 feet)
- Load my track of 10/21/2019 and follow it
- Load the GPX route through Minim Creek (which replicates the track) at BMinim110918.
   - Use Aqua Map Master and load the USACE survey charts and follow the deepest path shown
The 12/4/2019 USACE survey is shown. If you try to eyeball the route, stay off the greens by 100 ft, do not hug!

NOTE: The readings on any part of the ICW close to an inlet as in this case will be affected by winds. A west wind will blow water out; an east wind will blow water in, as much a +/- 1 ft. Go slowly and look at the water when at low tide. Be sure to check the Waterway Guide alert for the area before passing through.

Minim Island by R16 MM 417 R

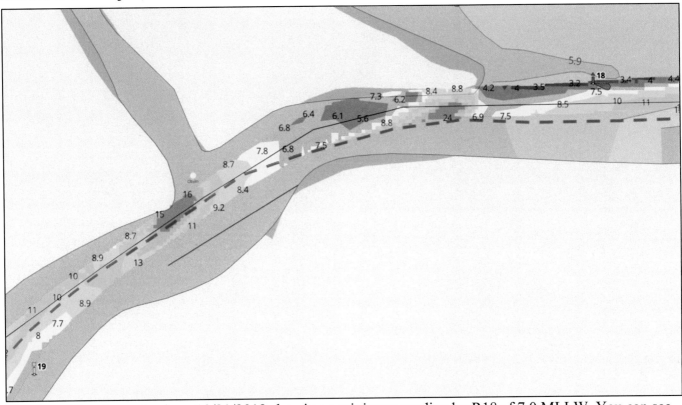

The dotted line is my track on 10/21/2019 showing a minimum reading by R18 of 7.0 MLLW. You can see the importance of following a track, GPX route, or a USACE chart through here!

See the Waterway Guide alerts for the latest info.

South Santee River MM 420

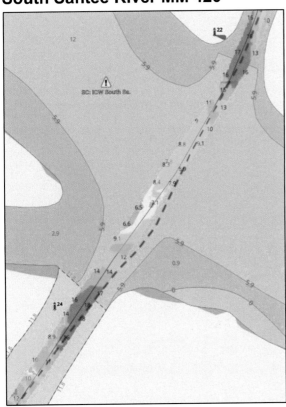

There is strong current as you cross the South Santee River but also beware of minor shoaling on the red side. Favor the green side by R24. The 12/4/2019 USACE chart is shown. Some spend the night here anchored in the river to either side of the ICW. Just remember, you're deep into alligator country now. Generally, you're safe if you're by an inlet, but this location is too far from the nearest saltwater. Of course, you're fine if you stay on the boat, but getting a dog ashore could be more of an adventure than you want.

McClellanville MM 430 by G35 R

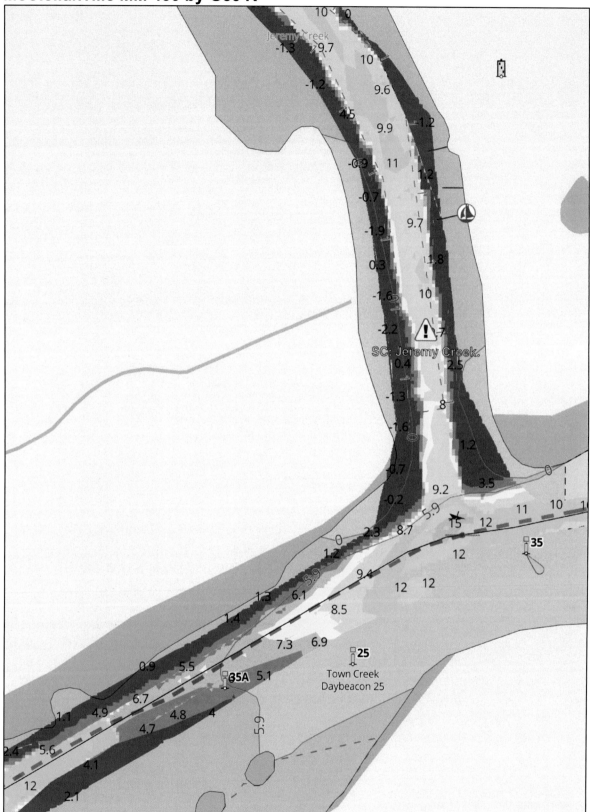

Good News, it's all been dredged to 10 MLLW, Including the channel to McClellanville!

Be sure to check the Waterway Guide alert (the yellow icon above) for the latest status of McClellanville depths and dredging. I maintain those alerts; they will be up to date. They are available in Aqua Map or on the Waterway Guide website.

Awendaw Creek MM 436

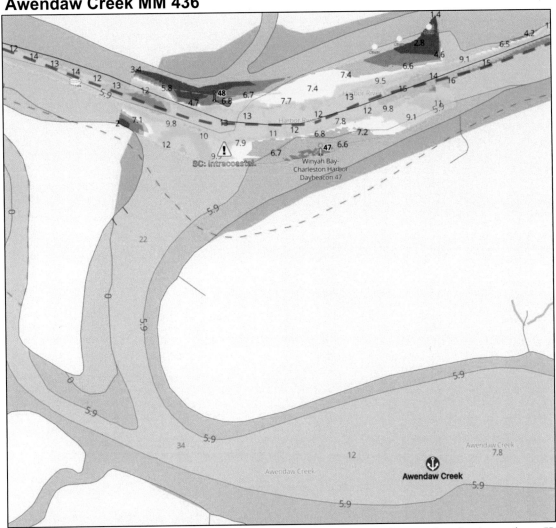

You can either continue onward to Charleston another 27 NM or anchor in Awendaw. We anchor by the Waterway Guide icon to avoid the current around the bend but you can anchor closer to the entrance if you want, no problem. On the way in, don't hug G47; pass 200 to 250 ft off G47. The blue dotted line is my track of 10/21/2019. The 8/19/2019 USACE survey is shown.

There are two options for pet relief:
- There's high ground by R48 at the shore with a gravelly beach that's above all tides.
- There's a public dock in a park setting 0.9 NM down the ICW to the west of R48

The satellite overlay is a feature of Aqua Map. The transparency of the overlap can be varied.

Price Creek Shoaling by R86 MM 448

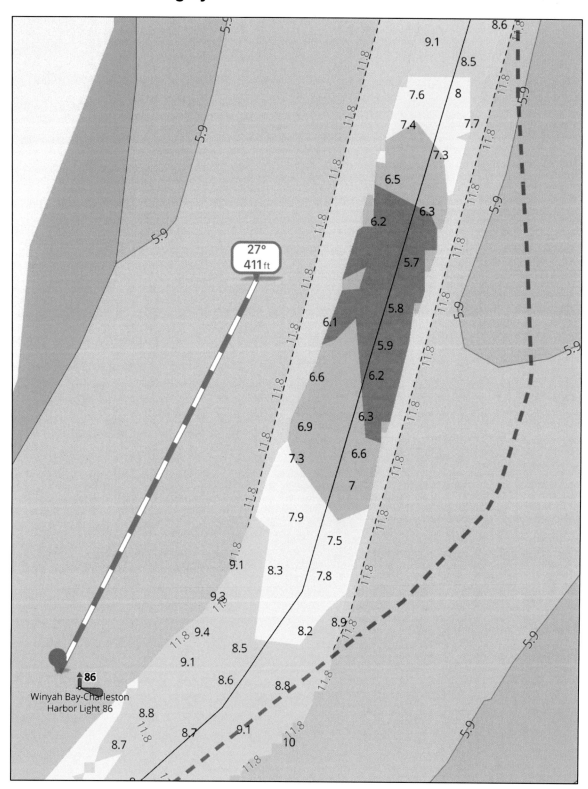

Move outside the channel to the green side to avoid the 5 MLLW shoal in the middle of the channel. You will see 6.3 MLLW on the green side as shown in the chart above. The dotted line is my path of 10/21/2019. The 12/4/2019 USACE survey chart is shown as displayed in Aqua Map Master. Check the Waterway Guide alert for the latest info. This area is not due to be dredged in 2020.

Price Creek Shoaling by G89 MM 449

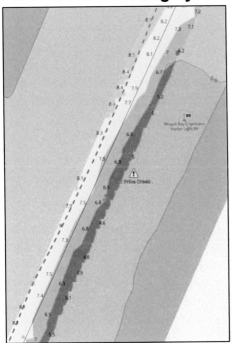

Favor the red side around G89 but stay in the channel. You can see the shoaling on the green side. The dotted line is my path of 10/21/2019. The 12/4/2019 USACE survey chart is shown as displayed in Aqua Map Master.

Toomer Creek MM 452

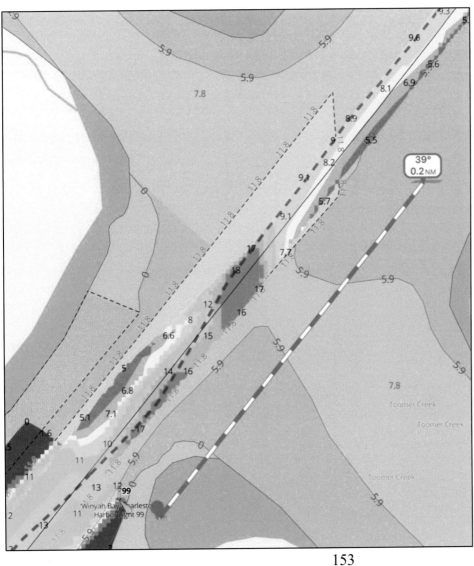

The blue dotted line is my track of 10/21/2019. Favor the red side by the 0.2NM range marker. You can see why in the Charleston USACE survey of 12/4/2019, it's shoal on the green side.

The ICW south of G99, all the way to R104 has been dredged to 11 MLLW, just stay in the middle of the channel per your chartplotter or Aqua Map and you will be fine.

Dewees Creek by G109 and R110 MM 454.8

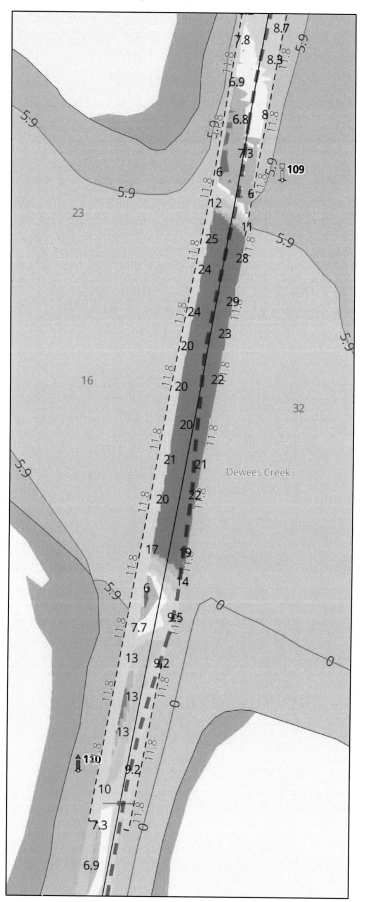

Stay centered in the channel by G109 for 8 MLLW.

Watch the current as you pass over Dewees Creek, it can throw you off course. Use your chartplotter to maintain your bearing.

As you approach the southern shore towards R110, favor the green side of the channel for deeper water to 10 MLLW.

Continuing favoring the green after passing R110 going south for another 1000 feet, then return to the center of the channel.

The blue dotted line is my track of 10/21/2019 and the 12/4/2019 USACE survey chart is shown.

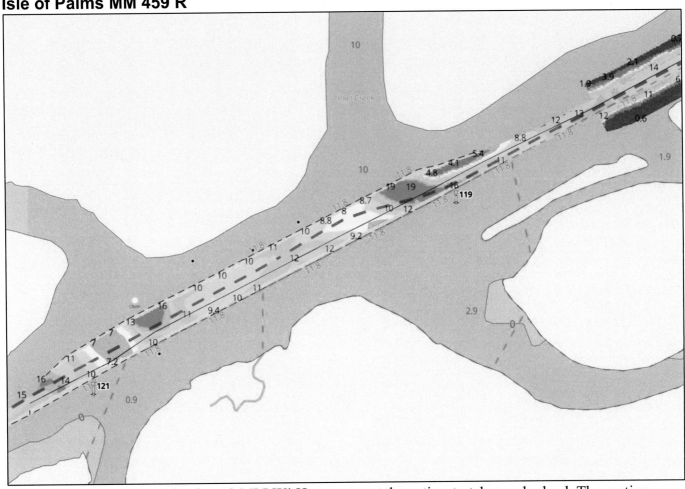

Isle of Palms has been dredged to 12 MLLW! However, not the entire stretch was dredged. The section from just north of G119 to the Ben Sawyer Bridge was not dredged (see chart). Follow my track of 10/21/2019 or the 12/4/2019 USACE survey for safe passage.

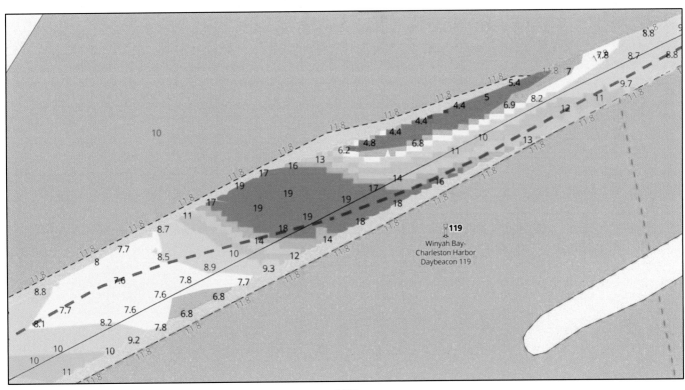

Tolers Cove Marina MM 462

We often stop at Tolers Cove Marina. It's a good staging area if you're not in sync with the tides when going north. You can time your departure so you're at the Ben Sawyer bridge when it's ready to open. The marina also has gas and diesel fuel which we've used on occasion. The marina caters to fishermen so you may be jostled in the early morning hours as they leave to fish off-shore. They will drive you to the nearest supermarket and/or laundromat at no charge. We prefer the nearby Harris Teeter supermarket, a favorite of Ann's. The transient docks are right by the red, Active Captain icon, just off the fuel dock.

Caution: this is not your usual marina, it has little on-site amenities and the fairways and slips are tight. It suits us fine but may not be for everyone.

The above chart uses Aqua Map's feature of a partially transparent overlay of a satellite view that can be adjusted for transparency

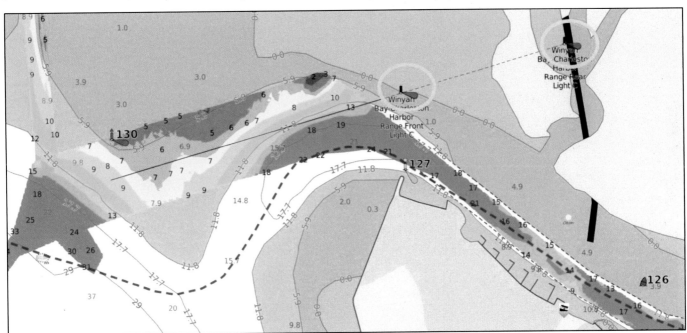

Normally you would follow the range markers (circled in yellow) into Charleston Harbor but there is more depth by avoiding the range and turning more to port when exiting the ICW. Just follow the deepest water per the charts as shown by my 10/21/2019 track

Now it's time to explore Charleston. You will see the Arthur Ravenel Jr. Bridge to the north; the Charleston Maritime Center is nearby, shown above. It is a small marina and not well protected from an east wind or passing boats but it is within walking distance to downtown and a great supermarket, Harris Teeter.

Don't miss Hyman's Seafood, it's been a Charleston institution since 1890! The manager visits every table to be sure you are satisfied, that's him in the photo.

Before making a reservation, ask if they are done hammering the pilings in for the new building next door. We stayed there in October and the noise was too much! They quit at 5:00 but it was brutal until then.

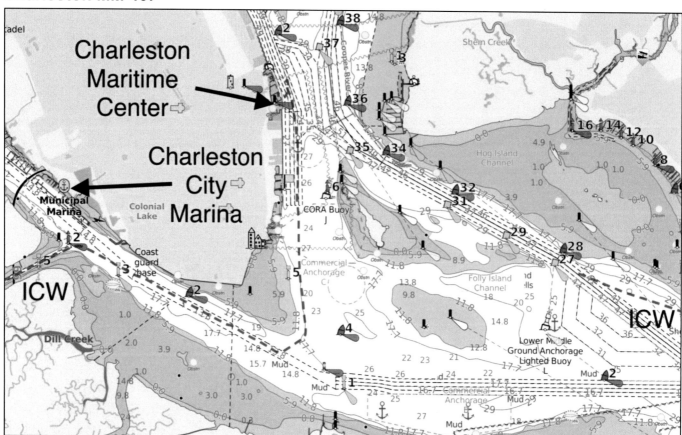

We like to stay at the Charleston Maritime Center because it's within walking distance of downtown Charleston and a Harris Teeter supermarket. I've stayed at St John's Yacht Harbor, which has a courtesy car and good laundry facilities, but it's located past Charleston along the ICW. I've never used the Charleston City Marina, maybe next time. I hear that it's a long walk to shore but they do offer shuttle service to downtown Charleston. I hear that the outside dock can be very rocky with wakes from passing boats. As or next stop, we'll choose either the Steamboat Creek anchorage at 30 NM or B&B Seafood at 43 NM. This is a good staging point for getting in sync with tides at the Ashepoo-Coosaw cutoff, which is always shallow, around 5 MLLW. From Steamboat, it's only a short hop of 36 NM to Beaufort, SC. I'll cover both stops next in sequence in the next pages.

The Charleston Market shown above in downtown is a great place to find local items for sale.

Leg 7 Charleston to Savannah 100 NM

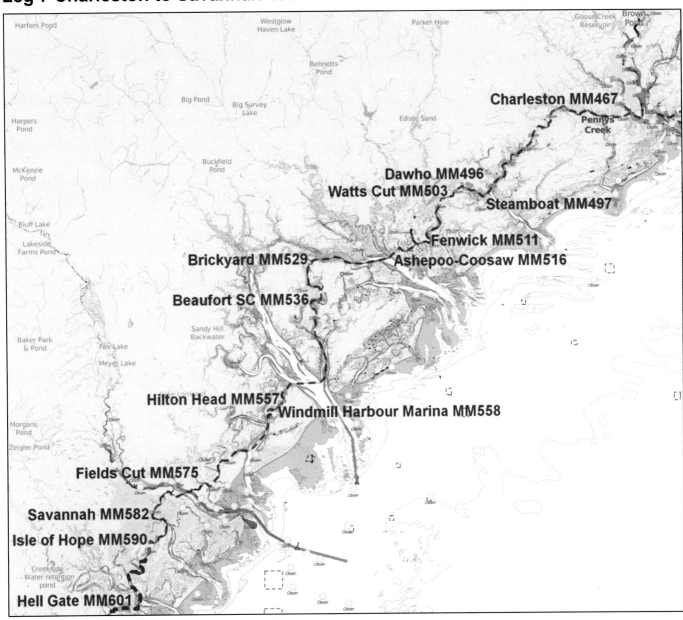

Johns Island, Dawho River, Watts Cut, Fenwick Cut, and Ashepoo-Coosaw Cutoff have all been dredged in the time period from July 2018 to February 2019. However, there has already been shoaling, especially in Ashepoo-Coosaw Cutoff where it's been measured down to 4.9 MLLW where it was initially dredged to 11 MLLW.

On the way, we may stop at Beaufort, either picking up a mooring at the Downtown Marina of Beaufort or by docking or just anchoring out at Lady's Island Marina, where they do not charge for landing your dinghy. Alternatively, we may take a dock at Windmill Harbour Marina which offers outstanding protection from wind and waves. At Savannah, we'll dock at Hinckley Yachts which just installed new showers and a laundromat with a courtesy car available too. Caution, be sure to refuel in Savannah. The fueling stops are few and far between from here south. Field's Cut, just before Savannah, used to be a problem but after the Coast Guard moved buoys to direct boaters to the deep-water route; it became a non-issue and it was dredged anyway (see Chapter 8 notes on Fields Cut). If you need repair work, the best marina for that is Hinckley Yachts in Savannah, GA. They are top-notch and will provide the best repair work available on the ICW.

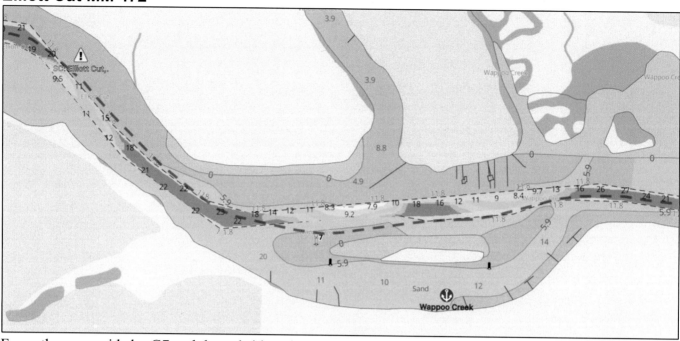

Favor the green side by G7 and the red side going around the bend for 20 MLLW as shone. My track of 10/23/2019 is shown in the blue line. The 8/27/2019 USACE survey is shown.

Of note in this passage is the peculiar schedule of the Wappoo Creek Hwy 171 Bridge. Be sure to study the opening times in Waterway Guide, as they often change.

Here, we're racing through Elliot Cut. The current can run up to 7 kts on a spring tide. We usually see 2 to 4 kts of current on average. It's deep but narrow, so take care.

Dredging Operations MM480 to MM518

Finally, at last, South Carolina has dredged some of the shallowest areas of the ICW. The dredge started from MM 518 by Ashepoo-Coosaw Cutoff and worked its way north to MM 480 at Johns Island, dredging the locations shown below. The dredging started in 2/2018 and continued 24/7 until late 2018.

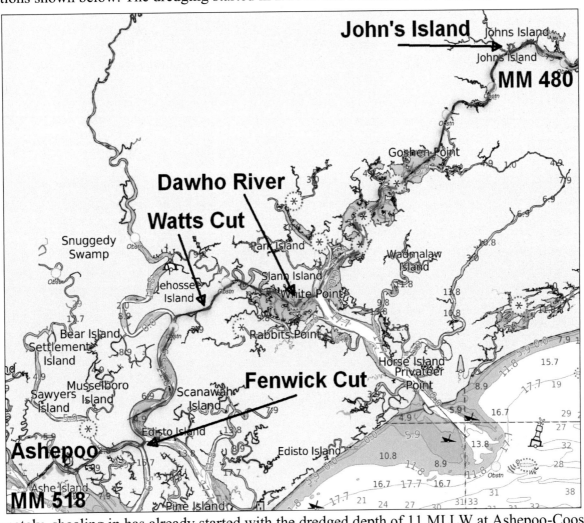

Unfortunately, shoaling in has already started with the dredged depth of 11 MLLW at Ashepoo-Coosaw Cutoff down to 8.7 MLLW as of 10/2019. I suspect that the fluid nature of the South Carolina mud in these areas will cause the same decrease in depth along many of the dredged areas shown above. Be sure to check with the Waterway Guide Alert at each of the shallow areas for the latest info.

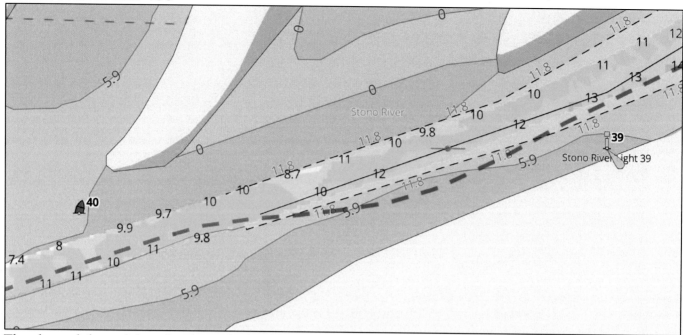

The channel through here has been dredged but there are shoals to 2 to 3 ft on both sides, stay in the middle of the channel. R40 has been relocated to mark the newly dredged channel, just honor the buoys and pass R40 to starboard when going south. My track of 10/23/2019 is shown as a blue dotted line but the better strategy is just to follow the USACE survey of 8/27/2019 which is shown above.

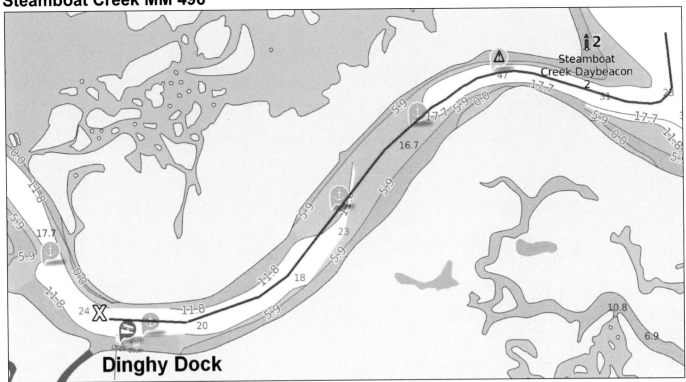

Dinghy Dock

If the tides are not right for Dawho River or the Ashepoo-Coosaw cutoff, we'll sometimes anchor at Steamboat Creek and catch a better tide in the morning. It's well protected and has a public boat ramp for pet relief. We usually anchor at the yellow X to be close to the boat ramp but anywhere is fine. The shoaling mark only applies if you try to hug the south shore on the bend. Just stay in the center or favor the north shore slightly for 13 MLLW at the yellow X. It's deeper in the middle towards the entrance.

What more to want? A dinghy dock for Hoolie, a calm anchorage protected from all directions, and good holding without a lot of current, that's the Steamboat Creek anchorage.

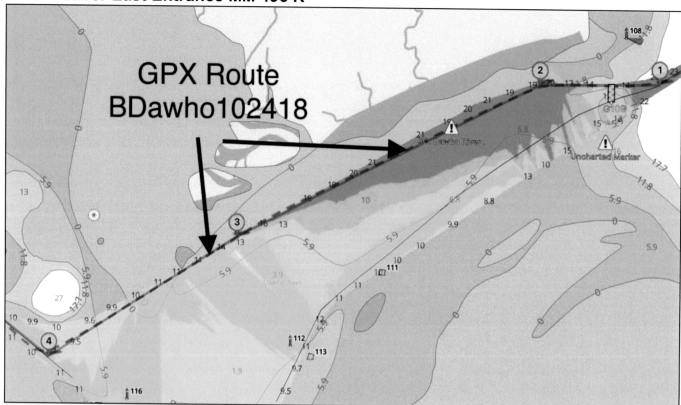

The Dawho River ICW official channel (southern route) has been dredged but it is very narrow, only 90 feet wide. If you throw in some wind and current along with the lack of ATONs at critical turning points, it's very hard to stay in the channel. If you venture outside the channel, you can expect to see an immediate decrease in depth to 4 to 5 MLLW vs 9.6 MLLW or higher in the channel. The 8/27/2019 USACE survey is shown above as displayed in Aqua Map Master.

However, there is a problem in the display due to the way USACE uploaded the file into the eHydro database. Just ignore the blue and green shadings indicating deep water and follow the GPX route shown on the chart. USACE with the Coast Guard is in the process of officially moving the ICW channel to follow the northern route BDawho102418 which is deep to 8 MLLW even without dredging and it's much wider than the southern channel. The GPX route goes from "1" at the northern entrance to "16" at the northern entrance to Watts Cut.

Note that NOAA and SonarChart show the route passing over land, that is not the case, the charts are wrong. You can see the actual soundings taken by USACE along the red route line. The shallowest they found was 9.6 MLLW.

McKinley Washington Jr. Bridge MM 501R

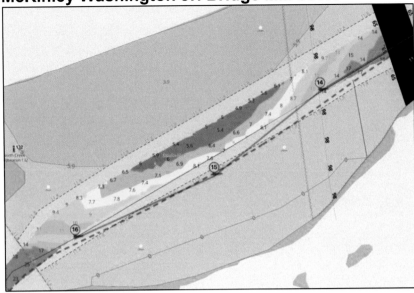

Favor the green side for 7.1 MLLW. The blue dotted line is my track of 10/23/2019. The red line is the southern end of the GPX track for the Dawho passage BDawhoc102418.gpx which extends to the start of Watts Cut at the left of the chart above. You can see that there is a shoal building in from the red side.

Watts Cut MM 503 R

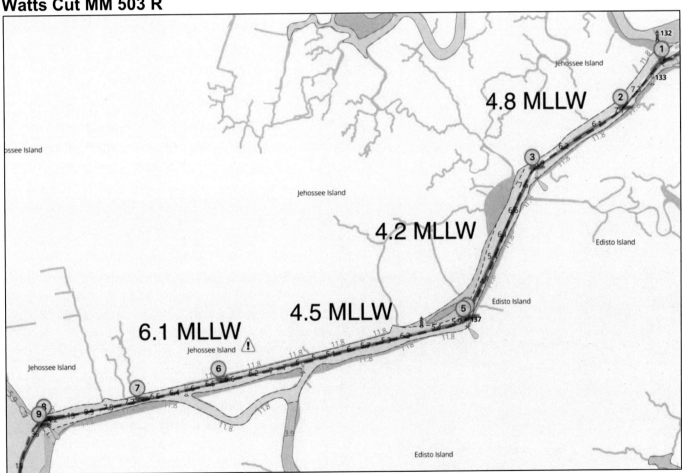

Watts Cut was dredged in the fall of 2018 but shoaling has occurred since then. It's important to either follow my track of 10/23/2019 or the corresponding GPX route of BWatts090318 to stay centered in the dredged channel. Trying to eyeball it by staying in the visual center will not find the deepest water, you need the track or the GPX route for best results but even then, you will need tide. It has shoaled to 4.2 MLLW in spots. The 8/27/2019 USACE survey is shown. Check the Waterway Guide Alert for the latest information.

Fenwick Cut Shoaling MM 511

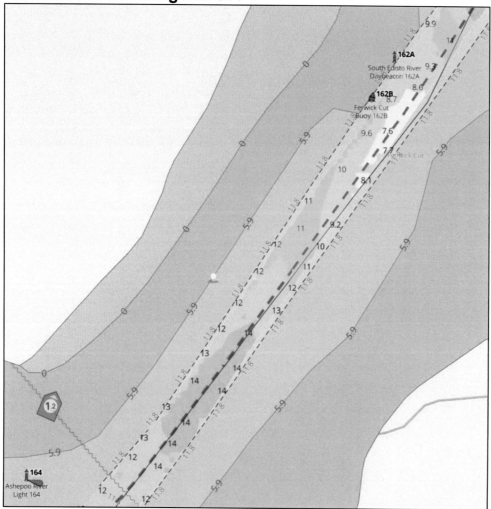

Fenwick Cut was dredged in the fall of 2018 but it too is already shoaling in. The light blue color in the 2/11/2019 USACE survey should be 12 feet MLLW but between R162A and R162B, there is only 8.3 MLLW on my track of 10/23/2019. I would expect the depths to be even less in the spring of 2020. The best you can do is stay in the middle and stay off R162A and R162B by 60 feet. Check with Waterway Guide alerts for the latest info. A GPX route is available at BFenwick062618.

If the tide at the Ashepoo Coosaw Cutoff is not good (e.g., less than 2 ft above low) then you might consider B & B Seafood on the north side of the cut. It

is not a marina, just a face dock used by shrimp boats that you can tie up to for $25/night. They do not have electricity or water. Be sure to check the dock for a plank that may stick out.

It's just before the cutoff on Mosquito Creek. If you get there when they're open, you can buy local shrimp, which is great. The area has ambiance, to say the least. It's not for everyone.

There is also room to anchor around the bend if the docks are full (there is only room for two boats on the face dock). Be sure to call ahead for reservations. In my track of 10/24/2019, I recorded 11.8 MLLW as the lowest spot at the entrance but deviating from that track by as little of 50 ft can quickly find 5 feet less (which I found in my 10/23/2019 track – not as good as my 10/24/2019 track).

Ashepoo-Coosaw Cutoff, North Approach MM 515

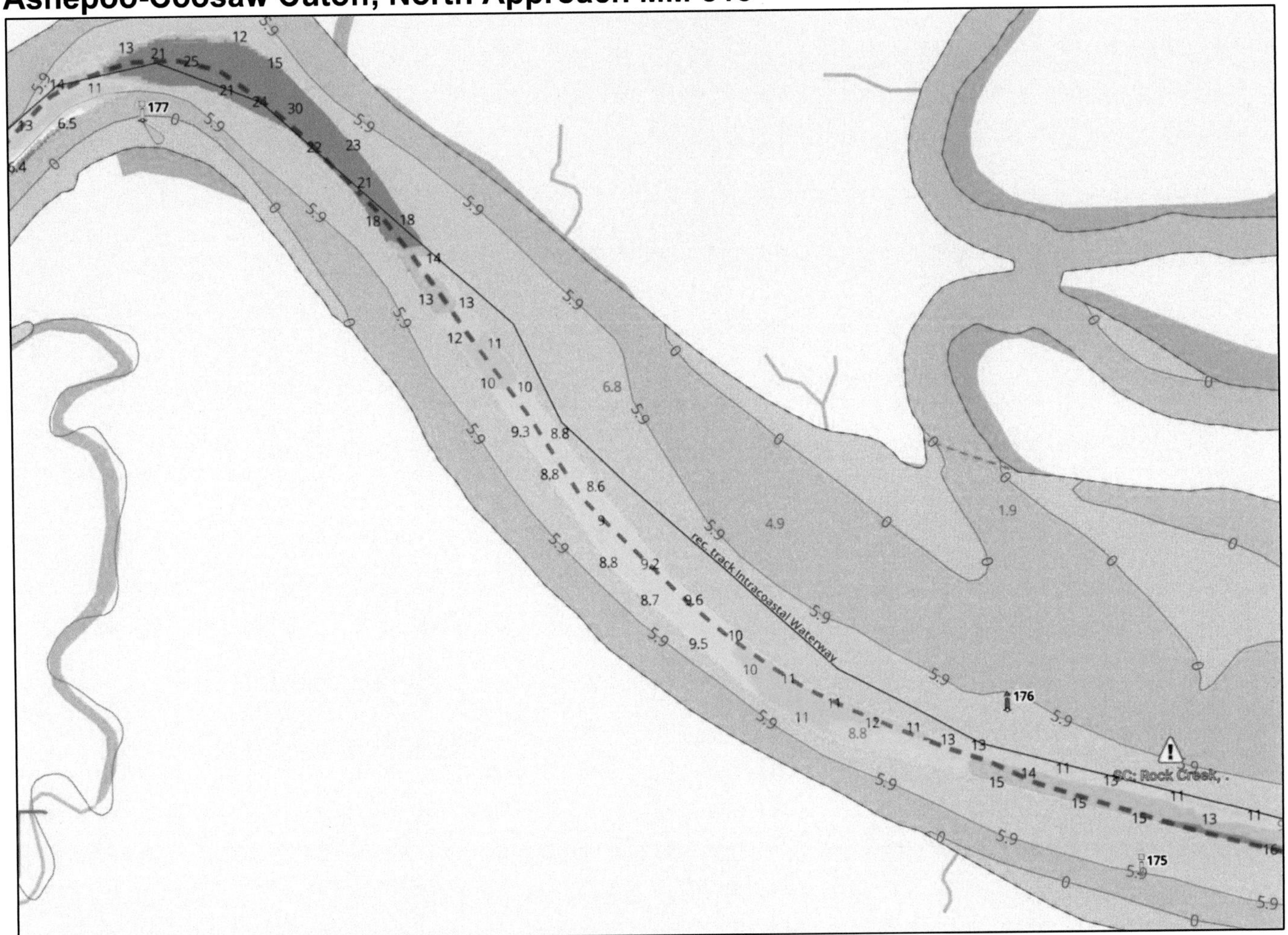

Stay far to the green side as shown in my blue dotted line of 10/24/2019 for the depths shown in the 8/27/2019 USACE survey chart above. The newly dredged channel plowed right through the shoal and is located to the northwest of the blue dotted line. The USACE didn't even survey the dredged channel in their latest chart (shown above). The green side of the channel has been stable for the last five years.

Ashepoo-Coosaw Cutoff MM 516 R

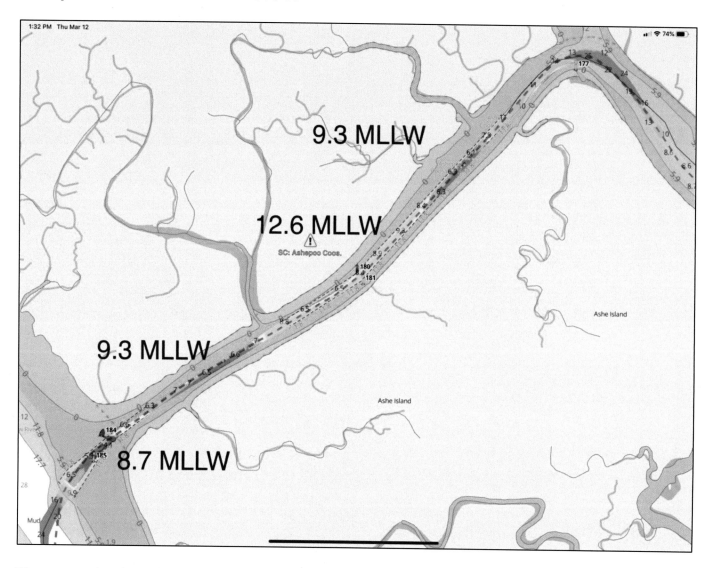

The passage has been dredged over the summer but it has already started to shoal in. You can see there is more shoaling in the southern part, down to only 8.7 MLLW. It is easy to find much less water if you get off the track.

My 10/24/2019 track is shown along with the 8/27/2019 USACE survey. To get the depths shown, you must follow the track which goes down the middle of the dredged channel, it is not the visual center. Download the GPX route at BAshe021119 which follows the middle of the dredged channel (not the visual center!) Check for updates at Waterway Guide alerts.

Brickyard Creek by R210 MM 529 R

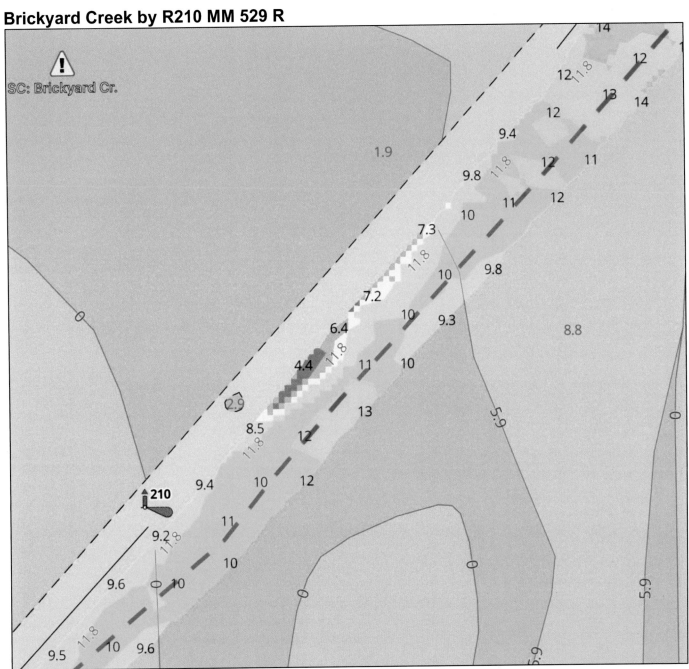

The channel has shoaled to 4 MLLW but there's an easy path around the problem by going outside the channel on the green side. Stay outside the channel from the elbow at the northern end to just past R210 for a minimum of 13.5 MLLW. In addition to my track of 10/24/2019 as shown in the chart, a GPX route can be downloaded at BBrick092617. This area has been stable for the past eight years.

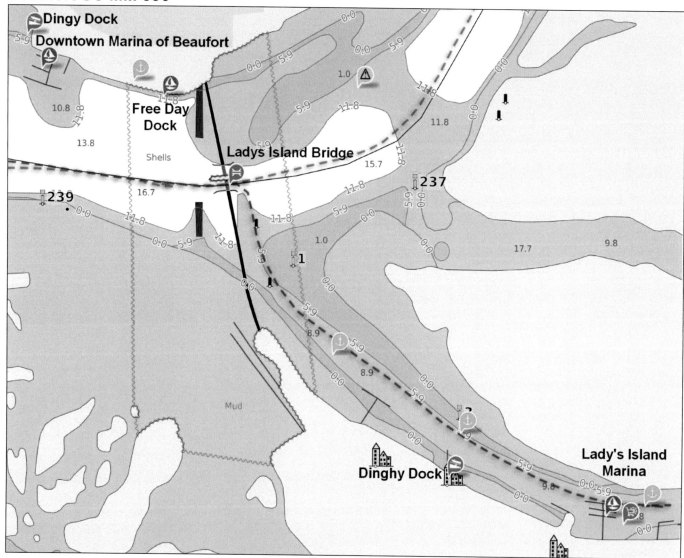

Dingy Dock
Downtown Marina of Beaufort
Free Day Dock
Ladys Island Bridge
Shells
239
237
Mud
Dinghy Dock
Lady's Island Marina

Beaufort is our stop from either B&B Seafood or the Steamboat Creek anchorage. We have stayed at four spots over the years:

- **Lady's Island Marina**. It's a great place with friendly people (pictured at left). You can take a dock or just anchor off the marina. They do not charge for dinghy dockage.
- **Downtown Marina of Beaufort**. This would be my last choice. The marina has ferocious current and they want to put the smaller boats on the inside of the face dock, which presents a challenge in leaving the next day. People have come to grief trying to back out against the current that swirls a bit but it is very convenient to downtown.

- **Moorings** are also available from the Downtown Beaufort Marina.
- **Anchor out**. You can just anchor behind the mooring field and use the free, town dinghy dock or by Lady's Island Marina, which does not charge for dinghy access.

Windmill Harbour Marina MM 558.3

Windmill Harbour Marina is a great hurricane hole. You enter the marina by going through a lock that ensures deep water inside and no current. It's surrounded by three-story houses so you are very well protected from winds in all directions. The approach is somewhat shallow at 4.5 MLLW so we use the tide to help our way in. The South Carolina YC is also located here, a world-class clubhouse with great restaurants and best of all, great people. Be sure to have lunch or dinner, it's a treat.

Daufuskie Island MM 570

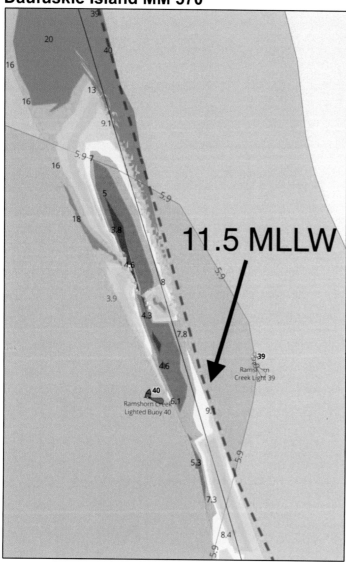

Split R40 and G39 for 11.5 MLLW as of 10/25/2019 which is my track shown as a blue dotted line.

The depth at this spot seems to vary a lot. I've measured as low as 4.5 MLLW in the past and in the spring of 2016, it was 7.7 MLW. The bottom is soft mud if you happen to hit it at super low tide. I think the barges do more to keep this cut deep than anything else. You can see that you do not want to hug R40. The 8/9/2019 USACE survey is shown as displayed in Aqua Map Master.

Walls Cut MM 572

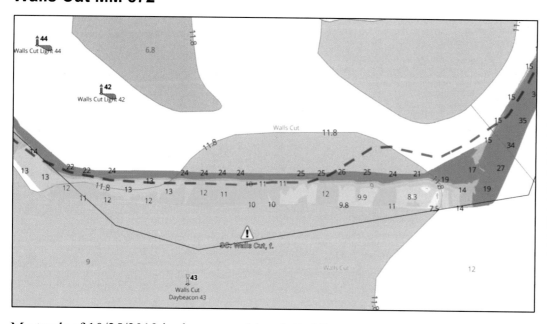

Just keep in the middle of the channel following the deeper water per your chart for 14.3 MLLW. Don't follow the magenta line through here (which is represented in Aqua Map charts as a black line and is called the Recommended Track).

My track of 10/25/2019 is shown as a blue dotted line.

Fields Cut Northern Entrance MM 573 R

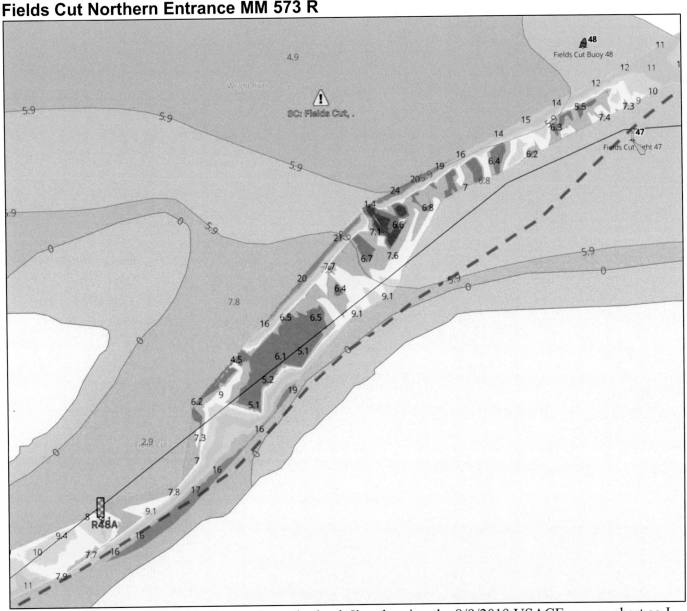

The northern entrance to Fields Cut has been dredged. I'm showing the 8/9/2019 USACE survey chart so I can plot my track of 10/25/2019 which had 10.4 MLLW in the shallowest spot even though the central channel was shoal to less than 2 MLLW. It should be clear sailing in the spring migration of 2020. Hopefully, the buoys will have been moved by then but it's not certain. The blue dotted line should still be good for 10.4 MLLW anyway and the center should have been dredged to 12 MLLW.

Fields Cut MM 573 R

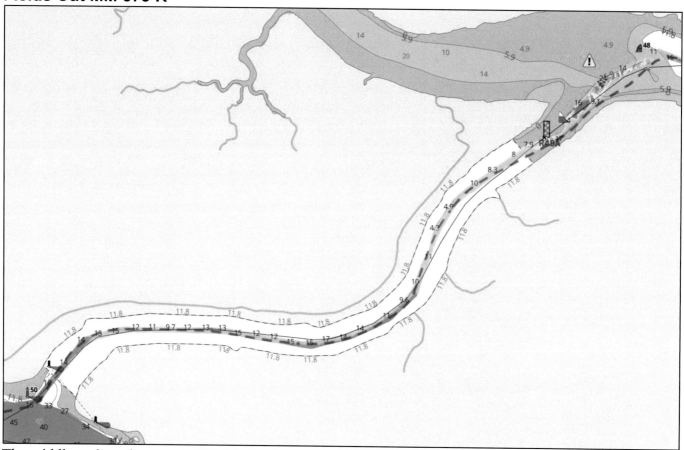

The middle and southern part of Fields Cut is easy, just follow the blue dotted line for a minimum of 14 MLLW as of 10/25/2019, the date of my track.

Elba Island Cut MM 576

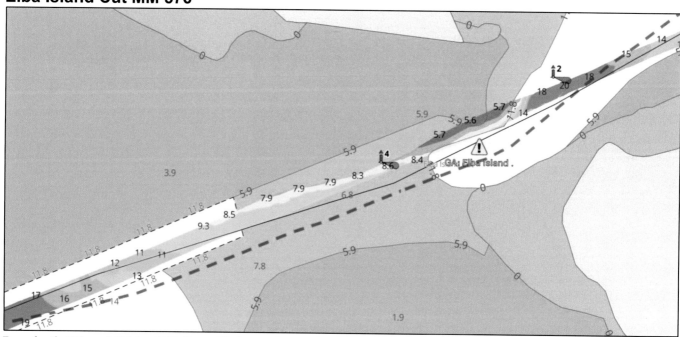

Pass both R2 and R4 by 120 feet off, do not hug – it's shoal by the buoys. Gradually return to the center of the channel south of R4. There is often a very strong current through here, up to 3 kts as you approach R2 from St Johns River, follow your chartplotter course to avoid being set. The 8/7/2019 USACE survey is shown. The minimum seen on by 10/5/2019 track was 14 MLLW.

Wilmington River Shoaling MM 581

When approaching R30 from the north, favor the green side of the channel for 8.9 MLLW.

There is a shoal by R30 so you need to pass R30 by 150 ft for the deepest water (19 MLLW).

Visually, staying on the green edge of the channel splits the marker and shore.

The blue line is my 10/25/2019 track. You will notice that I still favor the green side around the turn for the deepest water.

The shoal here is famous for catching boats that try to cut the turn too close to R30.

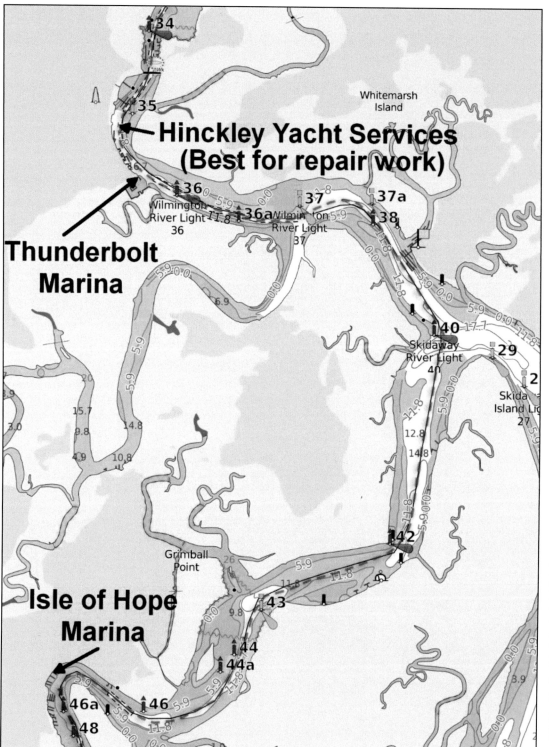

Our next stop is in Savannah at either Thunderbolt Marina if we're making a routine stop or at Hinckley Yacht Services if we need work done on the boat. Be sure to top off your fuel tank at Thunderbolt or Isle of Hope, as the fuel stops are few and far between from here to Jekyll Island.

Hinckley has the best repair services for boats our size; we've stopped there several times for engine work and have been completely satisfied. They take great care to be sure their work is done right! Best of all, if there is ever a problem with a repair, other Hinckley Marinas up and down the East Coast will fix the repair at no cost. At either marina, you can rent a car from Enterprise and explore the area.

The big deal here is to time your passage for at least a 2 ft rising tide at Hell Gate, the shallowest spot on the ICW. It's 16 NM to Hell Gate from either of these two marinas and there may be an opposing tide, so plan ahead if you want to pass through Hell Gate with a favorable tide. If you find the 16 NM too far for the timing to make a good tide, then Isle of Hope Marina is another option since it's only 10 NM to Hell Gate.

Leg 8 Savannah to Fernandina 116 NM

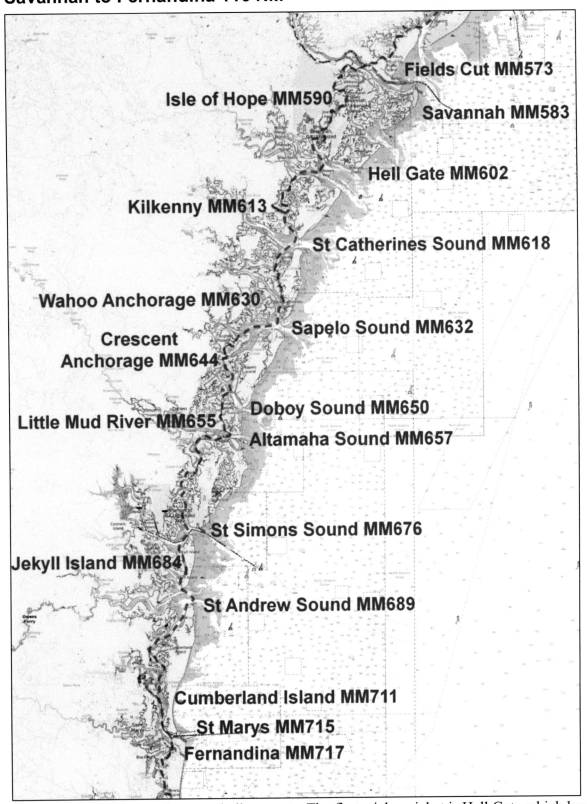

On the next leg, we're getting serious on shallow spots. The first sticky wicket is Hell Gate which has only 5 ft at low tide at best and is 16 NM away from Thunderbolt Marina or only 10 NM from Isle of Hope Marina. You want to hit Hell Gate with at least a 3 ft rising tide to allow room for error.

There are good anchorages along the way at Wahoo and Crescent, both have beaches for dog relief, and we usually wind up at the Jekyll Creek anchorage if the tide is right which has a public dinghy dock.

Hell Gate MM 602 R

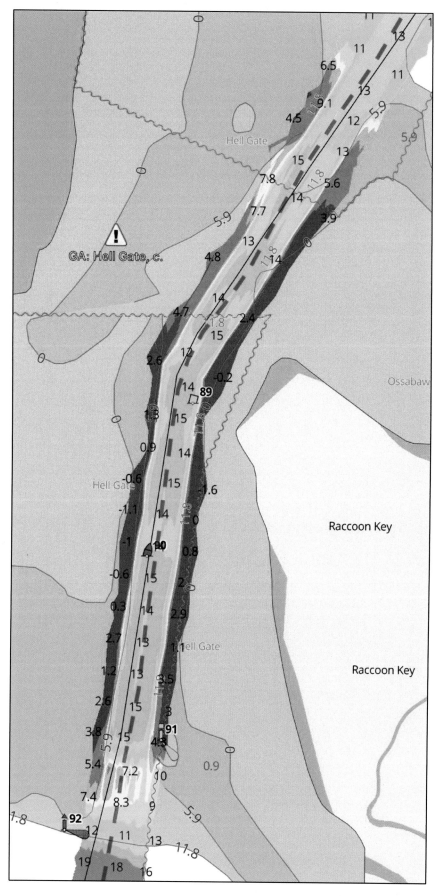

Hell Gate has been dredged to 12 MLLW! There is a short section at the southern entrance that's down to 7 MLLW due to a buried electrical cable they could not move at the time.

See the Waterway Guide alert for the latest guidance.

Hell Gate depths are affected by wind direction (east = deeper, west = shallower). The Savannah tide station can be accessed to see the predicted vs actual tides for the area.

The USACE survey of 10/17/2019 is shown along with my 10/25/19 track as a blue dotted line.

Kilkenny Marina MM 613

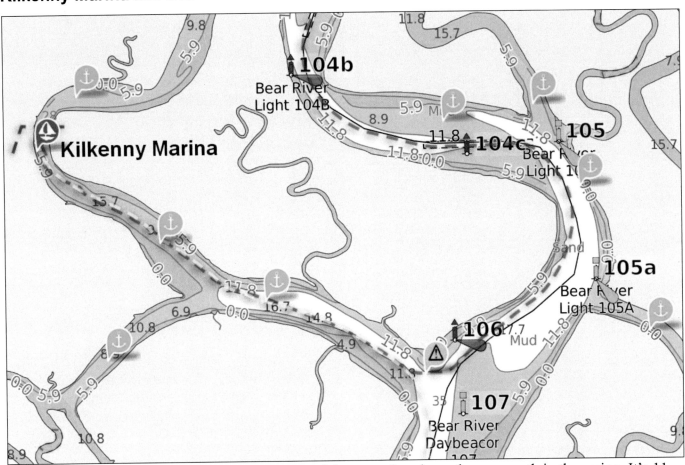

We don't stop at Kilkenny Marina on the way south but we often do on the way north in the spring. It's 11 NM from Hell Gate so it's a convenient place to stage for the tide if needed. As you can see, there are plenty of anchorages in the area if you don't need shore access for a pet. The marina is rustic, to say the least, but the docks are secure and the people are welcoming. The area is surrounded by beautiful, huge live oaks.

When headed south, Kilkenny is the last stop for fuel until the Brunswick or Jekyll Island area. We were caught one time with too little fuel and had to go in on fumes. Check your gauge.

Johnson Creek by R126 MM 624

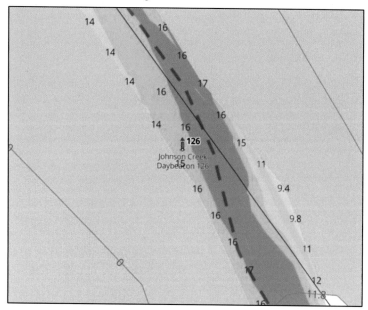

Hug R126 by 30 ft for 18.2 MLLW. There is shoaling to < 7 ft on the green side. This is one of the very few places on the ICW where you hug the inside of a curve for deep water. The 7/13/2019 USACE survey is shown along with my 10/26/2019 track.

Johnson Creek by 131A MM 627

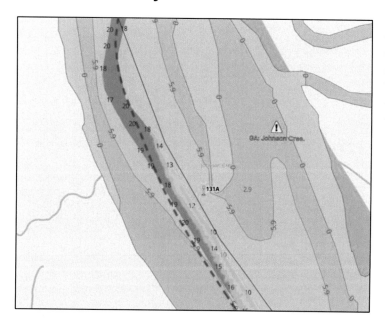

Favor the red edge of the channel for 18 MLW, about 120 ft off G131A. After passing G131A and the second hazard marker going south, cross back over to the green side for deeper water. My track of 10/26/2019 is shown on the 7/13/2019 USACE survey chart.

Wahoo River Anchorage MM 630

The Wahoo River anchorage was a convenient stop for us between Savannah and Jekyll Island. At the present time, it's off-limits for Georgia anchoring due to shellfish harvesting.

Dog Hammock by R150 MM638

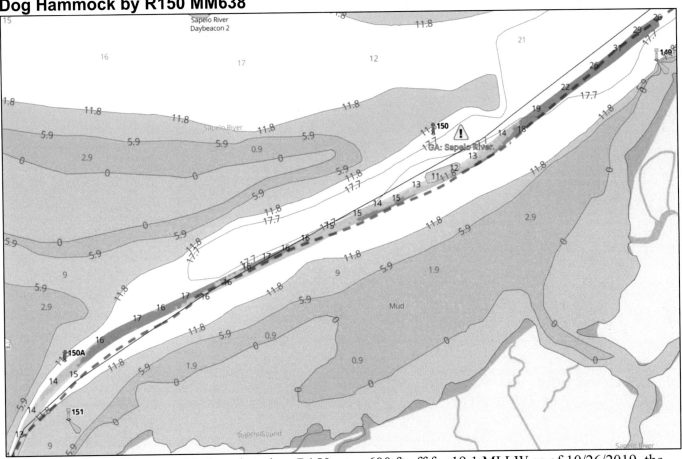

The only way to get into trouble here is to hug R150, stay 600 ft off for 19.1 MLLW as of 10/26/2019, the date of my track. That's pretty much in the middle of the channel anyway. There's only 5 MLW at 20 ft off R150.

Crescent River Anchorage MM 644

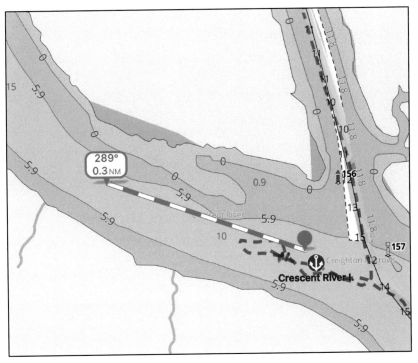

Crescent River is a popular anchorage with cruisers. You will always find a few boats here. The river has good holding in 10 to 15 ft of water. There is a sandy beach good for pet relief that's above water at all tides. We approach the beach from R156. The Georgia anchor law is still fluid but the Crescent River lies outside all restricted areas if you move 0.3 NM farther from the ICW as shown above.

A new anchoring law is in the process of being passed that would greatly mitigate the restrictions and perhaps make the old anchoring spot legal.

Check the Waterway Guide anchor marker Crescent River for the latest information.

Old Teakettle Creek by R160 MM 644a

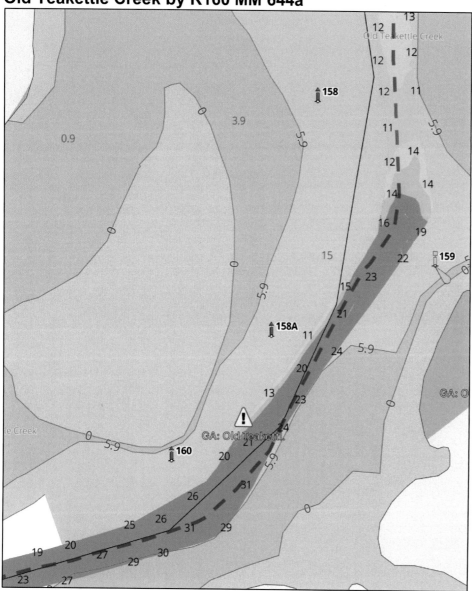

One may ask why is there a shallow marker when there's 28 MLW of depth? The response is that in the past boaters have taken a route close to R160 and have run aground. R160 can be seen sitting on dry land at a spring low tide.

Further complicating the matter is the magenta line, which on many charting programs is shown very close to R160 and if you follow it, you will likely go aground. On Aqua Map, the Recommend Track (otherwise known as the magenta line on Garmin charts) has been redrawn away from R160. With that as a prelude, all you have to do for deep water is follow the outside of the bend for 28 MLW.

In my 10/27/2019 track in blue, I've jogged over away from R158 too, there is a small shoal building out from the red side between R158A and R158.

Doboy Sound by R178 MM 649.5

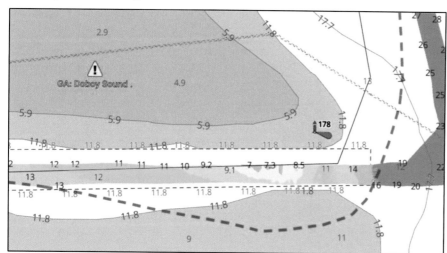

There is shoaling by R178, more so when you hug it. Just to be safe, pass R178 by 500 feet off for 10.9 MLLW.

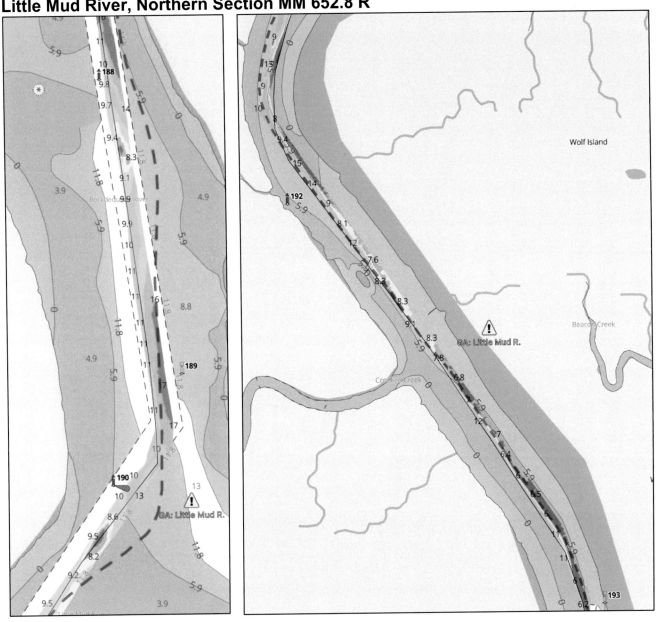

The least water seen in 10/27/2019 was 7.7 MLLW at the southern end of Little Mud River. The northern end has more water. There are twists and turns to find the deepest water, not all are obvious and just being in the middle doesn't work unless you have ½ to full tide, then it doesn't matter.

If you try to eyeball the route, do not hug any of the ATONs. For example, my 10/27/2019 track passes 300 feet off R192 and 180 feet of G193. That's hard to gauge by eye. My 10/27/2019 track is also available as a GPX route at BMud051718 which follows the same track. Now we'll move on to the lower section of Little Mud River where it's shallower. Check the Waterway Guide alert for the latest guidance. The 6/25/2019 USACE survey chart is shown.

Little Mud River, Southern Section MM 655

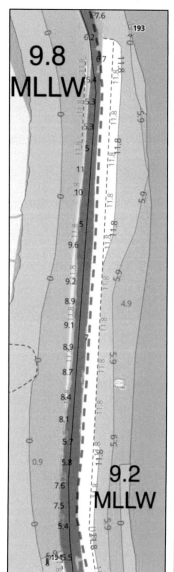

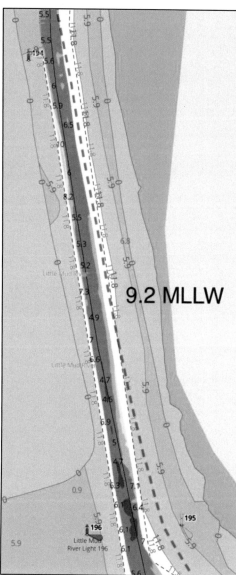

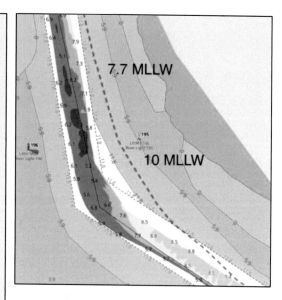

The path through Little Mud River meanders to follow the deepest water but it is still very shallow. On the other hand, it's easy to find water even more shallow than shown in the chart by moving off my 10/27/2019 track.

Once again, it is very hard to eyeball unless you have ½ to a full tide which gives you much more leeway. If you do attempt the passage without a track to follow, just stay off all ATONs by 150 to 200 feet, do not hug them but pass G195 by only 85 feet off.

Altamaha Sound by R206 MM 657.8

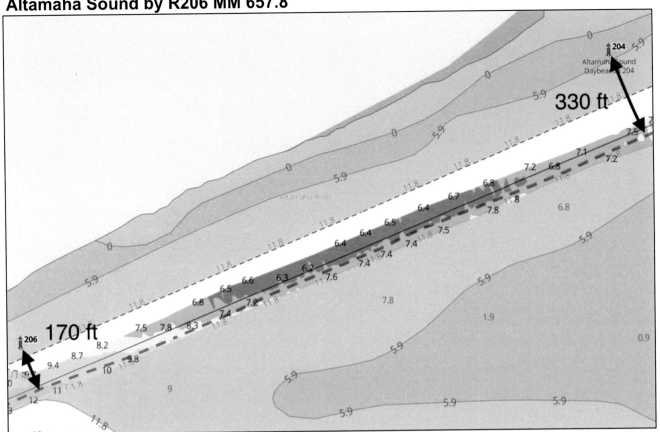

The channel from R204 to R206 is shallow if you get too close to the reds. Take note that R204 and R206 are far away from the channel and many boaters get too close to the reds and find water that's shallower than what I found above. My 10/27/2019 track and the 6/25/2019 USACE survey are shown.

Altamaha Sound by R208 MM 659

This is one of the most famous areas for groundings on the ICW. The track shown on NOAA charts (the magenta line on Garmin) goes right over a shoal area (in red). All you have to do is swing wide for 24 MLLW. Standoff R208 by 330 feet and you will have no problems. My track of 10/27/2019 is shown with the 6/25/2019 USACE survey.

Altamaha Sound by G211 MM 660

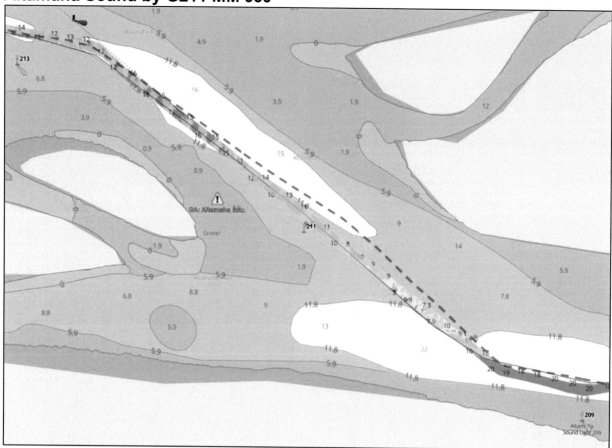

Do not follow the range markers, it is shoaling on the range by G211 and just south. Go outside the channel to the red side for 11 MLLW. My track of 10/27/2019 is shown with the 6/25/2019 USACE survey.

Buttermilk Sound Shoaling by R218 MM 662

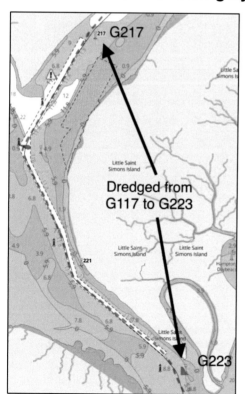

Buttermilk Sound has been dredged to 12 MLLW from G217 to G223.

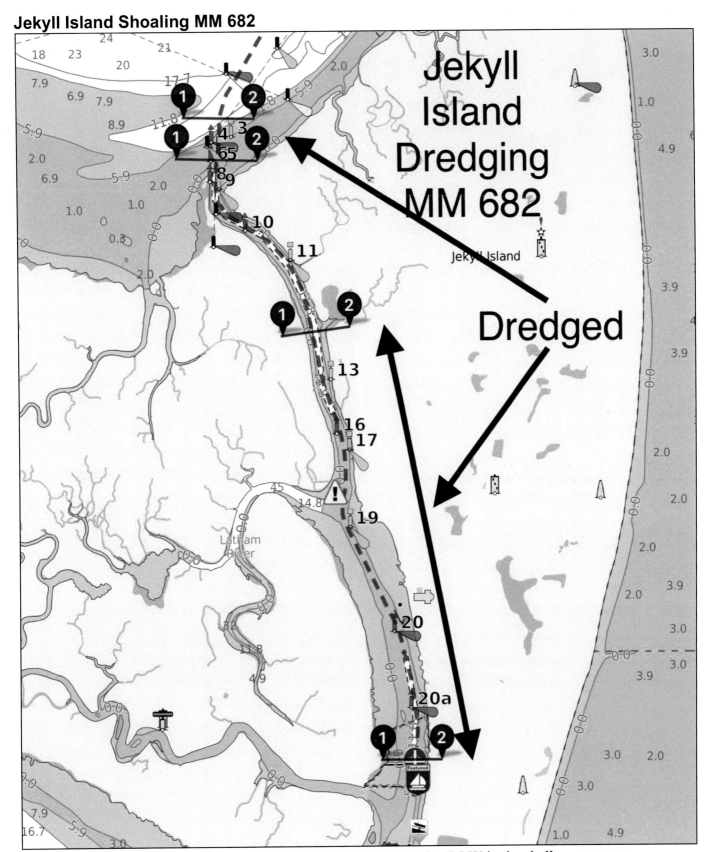

The Jekyll Island passage has been dredged as of June 2019 to 7.2 MLLW in the shallowest spots.

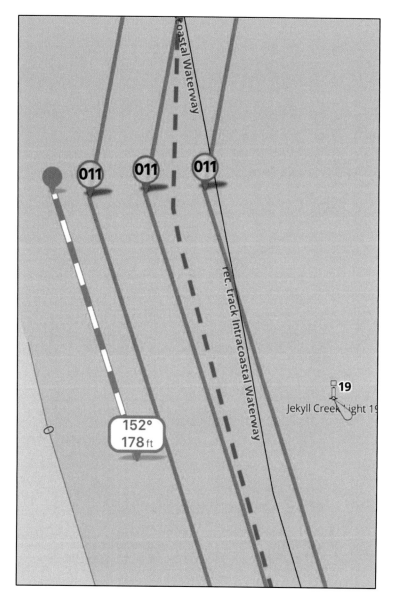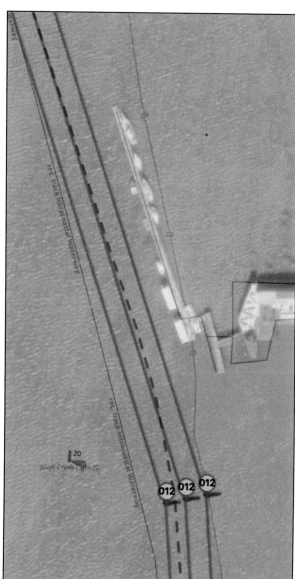

Three red lines are shown in the charts above. The middle red line is the centerline of the dredged channel and the other two lines are the edges. Note that the turns are not located next to an ATON but rather before or after the mark. The channel is only 75 ft wide. The rest of the Jekyll Creek area is undredged. Even when exactly going down the middle (on the middle red line), you only have 37.5 ft to either side before running beyond the dredged channel. Furthermore, the dredged channel does not follow the old channel shown on NOAA charts, it's farther to the east.

The shallowest areas are just north of G19 and just south of R20, both areas have 7.2 MLLW spots.

Given all of the above, it's best to either follow my 10/27/2019 track or download the GPX route represented by the middle red line at BJekCD082719. It is very difficult to eyeball the route at low tide due to the lack of ATONs to mark the way and due to the turns not being located at the ATONs they do have in place.

Please click or tap on the Waterway Guide alert icon for the latest status of this famously shallow passage

Jekyll Island Anchorage MM 685

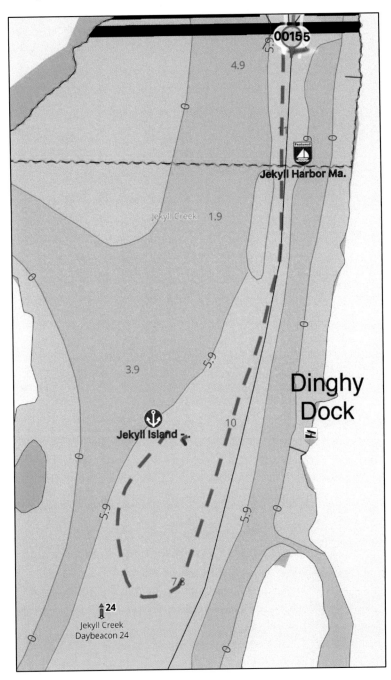

We always anchor at the Jekyll Creek somewhere on the line from R24 to the Waterway Guide anchor marker depending upon the number of boats. The charts for the area are incorrect. The depths range from 8 to 12 feet along a line from R24 to the Jekyll Creek green anchor marker at the top of the chart.

If you anchor on top of the Waterway Guide anchor marker, you will have 11 MLLW there and at least 8 MLLW in a 120 ft radius around the anchor mark (regardless of what the charts say). Navionics SonarChart is accurate here.

The directions are:
Turn in by R24 and maintain a heading for 20 degrees magnetic. You will find 8 MLLW along the way and 11 MLLW at the anchor marker although you can go in farther.

We usually anchor about halfway between R24 and the anchor marker in 8 MLLW. The holding is excellent and there is a public dock across the creek for pet relief or for just exploring the island. When it's time to leave, you must retrace your path back. You cannot go from the anchor marker directly to the creek; there is a 2 ft shoal that will stop you. However, there is no problem if you just leave the same way you came in, lots of water with 8 MLLW.

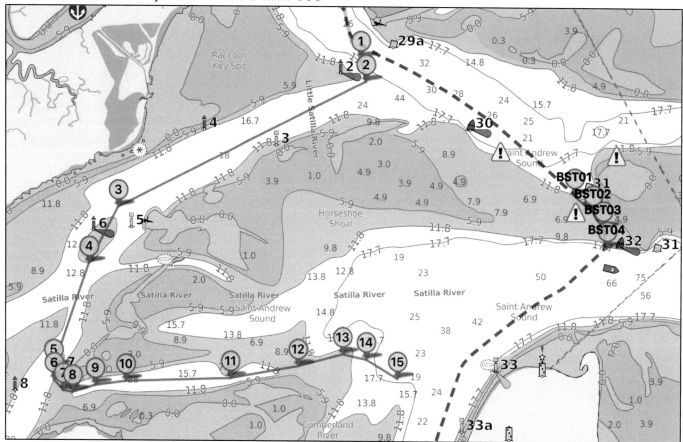

There are two routes through St Andrews Sound. The route on the right (BStAnd) is the usual path at 8.6 MLLW and follows the ICW but it can be very rough with high winds and waves. The route on the left (BStAndAlt) is more protected for 6 MLLW. Chose the outside route in calmer weather, consider the inside route with strong southeast winds and waves.

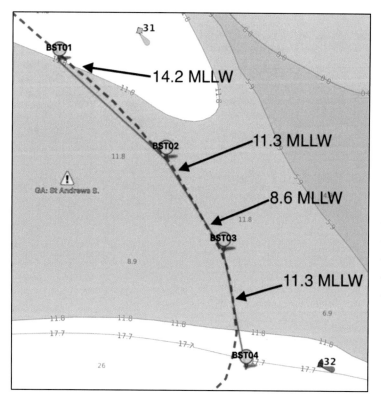

Here's the detail of the route by R32. The buoys here tend to move around and are hard to see in hazy conditions or with a lot of wave action. It is wise to always have a route loaded in case the buoys have drifted (again!) so you'll know where to go. The route does not honor R32, it's too close to the shoal area and in high waves, it becomes very difficult to keep a steady path when close to R32.

I've provided the waypoints for manual entry below:
WP1 N30 59.632 W081 24.562
WP2 N30 59.533 W081 24.431
WP3 N30 59.440 W081 24.359
WP3 N30 59.321 W081 24.331

Cumberland Island MM 714

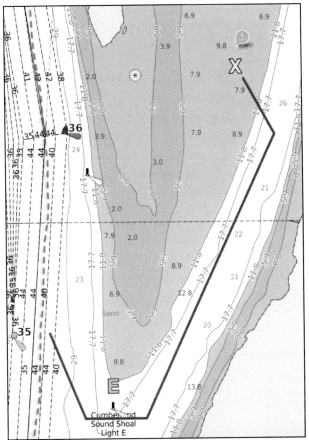

You should always visit <u>Cumberland Island National Park</u> at least once on your trips north or south along the ICW. They have horses that are free to run anywhere on the island. There's lots of wildlife and it's also a national seashore. The nature walks are not to be missed.

We usually anchor by the X but there's lots of room. However, the protection is not so hot and the current runs 2 kts. In settled weather, it's a great stopover and fun to explore the island. In winds of 15 kts or greater, the anchorage can be rocky.

There's a dinghy dock free for use but check the status on Waterway Guide alert to see if it's been repaired from the last storm.

The lodge is the main meeting place on the island. The dinghy dock is close by. There are trails to discover, a beach to relax on, and horses to watch.

Fernandina Anchorage MM 717

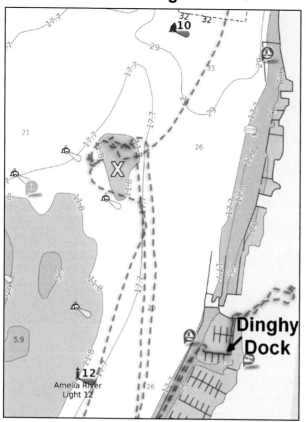

We always stop by Fernandina on the way south but we haven't picked up a mooring or used the marina in years. We just drop the hook at the yellow X, dinghy to their dinghy dock, and pay the $4/day fee. We swing much better on our anchor than on their moorings, which tend to bump against the boat when wind is against tide. There's a Saturday morning farmers' market we try to shop at when possible.

There's an excellent hairstyling shop, Magna's, on Main Street near the marina that Ann uses whenever we're in town. Ann's stylist is at left and the owner, Stacye, is at the right in the photo. The town is great to explore, lots of shops and places to eat. We get our fix of Mexican food at Pepper's on Main Street.

The Fernandina marina has finally opened but call to be sure there are no last-minute problems. See the latest status at the Waterway Guide alert icon. It is supposed to be back in operation by the spring of 2020.

Here's Ann after getting her hair done at Magna's on Main Street. It's a great place for hairstyling.

Leg 9 Fernandina to Jacksonville Free Docks on the ICW 19 NM

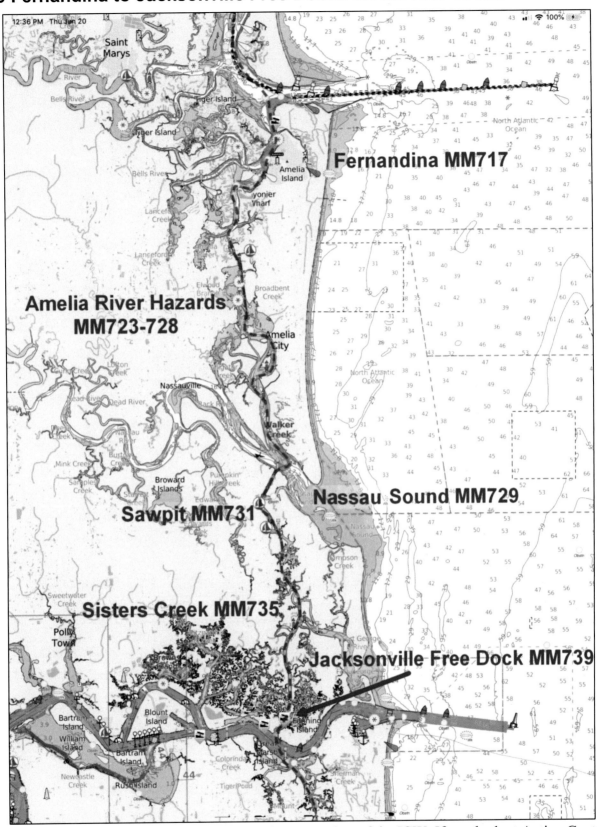

Just south of Fernandina is one of the most notorious stretches of the ICW. If you look at Active Captain you will find conflicting advice on how to pass through, I strongly recommend loading the BFernD091519 GPX route. The passage to Jacksonville has many shallow spots but none are impassable at low tide; just follow the guidance. If you visit downtown Jacksonville, be sure to time your visit with the strong currents in your favor. We usually just use the Jacksonville Free Docks off Sisters Creek for the night.

Fernandina Shallows MM 718

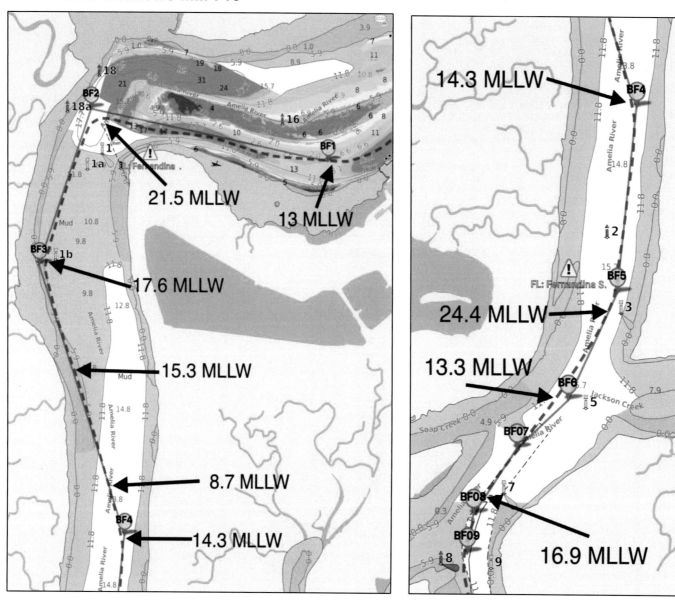

Fernandina was known as the graveyard of boats. There are shoals everywhere and most were not marked. All that changed over the last two years with a new channel being dredged and marked. There are still not enough buoys marking the best path. Just load the BFernD091519 GPX route and you're home free (or follow my 10/28/2019 track, the blue dotted line). Check Waterway Guide alerts for updates.

Note: the BFernD091519 GPX route is an update from BFernD2. I changed the format to include a date and also moved the route farther away from R16 due to shoaling into the channel.

Kingsley Creek Chart Problems MM720

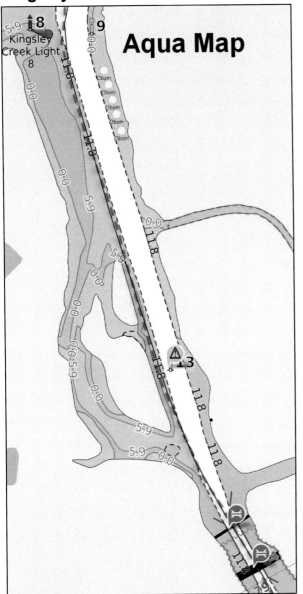

You know something is seriously amiss when you see a green mark near the red side of the channel by the hazard marker (G13)! I looked at the charts by Garmin, NOAA ENC charts, and Navionics. I found all were shifted to the east, showing G13 either in the middle of the depicted channel or even on the western edge. However, there was one exception: Navionics SonarChart.

The Navionics+ chart is shown bottom left. The Navionics SonarChart is shown at bottom right. All three charts show my track of 4/2018 (red in Aqua Map and yellow in Navionics).

In the Navionics+ chart, my track is shown outside the channel like it is on the NOAA ENC charts displayed by Aqua Map. The Navionics SonarChart does show the channel correctly. This example shows the value of having multiple chart sources available.

Regardless of how the channel is displayed, just stay in the visual center, equidistant between the shores and markers, honoring all marks for 12 MLW.

At R14 (off the chart to the south) follow the green edge of the channel for 15 MLW. Whatever you do, don't cut the corner at R14

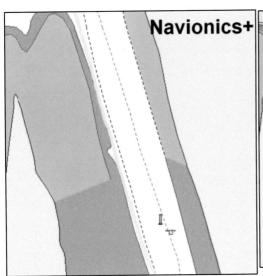

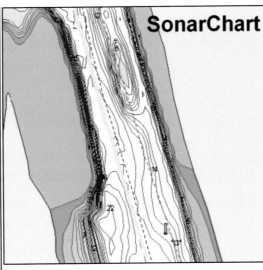

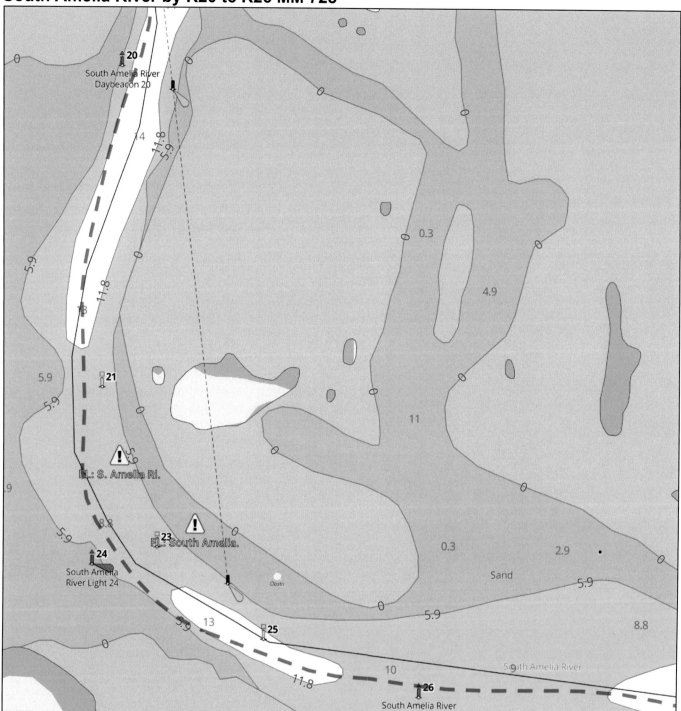

Pass R24 by 140 feet off and otherwise, try to split the ATONs. There is an 8.4 MLLW spot just north of R24. It's less than 100 feet long, then it's deeper both north and south of the shallow spot. When coming from the north, you can line up to aim at R24 before turning to port about 120 feet before the mark. The shallow spot also shows up in SonarChart. All depths have been corrected to MLLW. See the Waterway Guide alert for the latest info. The blue dotted line is my track of 10/28/2019.

South Amelia River Alligator Pass R34/G33 MM 725 R

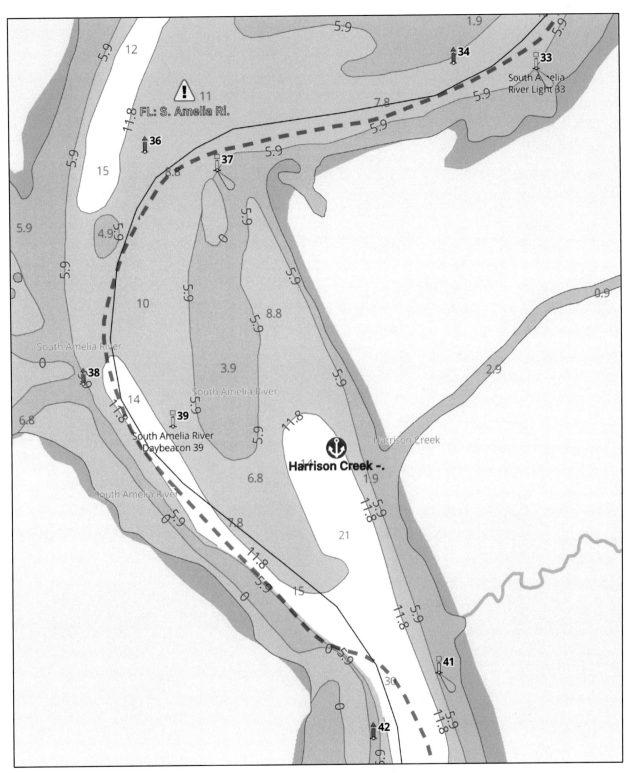

There is plenty of water here but only on the track, there are shoals nearby. My 10/28/2019 track is shown for a minimum of 13.6 MLLW. See the Waterway Guide alert for the latest info.

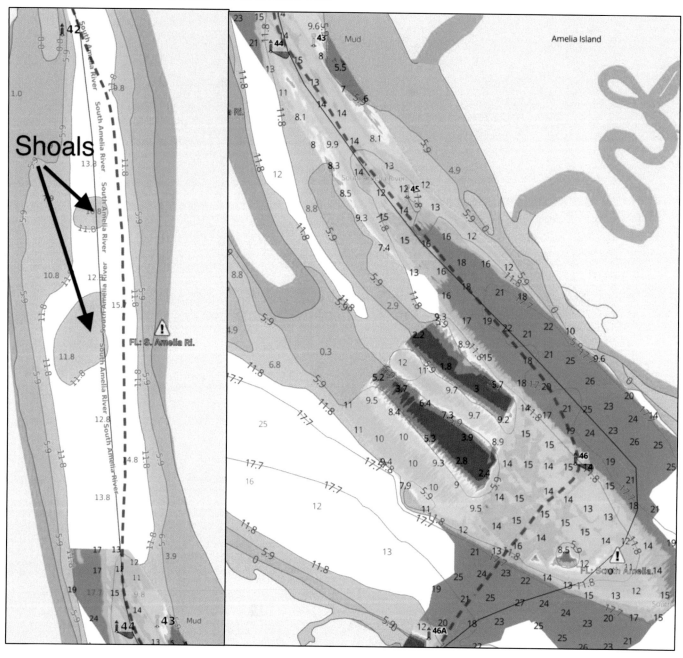

There are two shoals right in the middle of the river between R42 and R44. They are NOT as deep as the chart shows and the Recommended Track (magenta line on Garmin) runs right over them. I seldom pass by without seeing a boat stuck on one of the shoals. They are easy to avoid, just follow the blue dotted line favoring the green side, my 10/28/2019 track.

Split R44/G43 for 16.4 MLLW. The area was dredged in the spring of 2019. My 10/28/2019 track is shown in blue. See the Waterway Guide alert for the latest info.

The area between R46 and R46A was dredged in the spring of 2019. You can now take a direct line between the two ATONs. However, note that, for some reason, the dredge didn't completely clear the shoal (the red in the middle of the chart) It's easy to get set when starting from R46! There is often a strong current in the area and you have to be diligent in paying attention to your chartplotter. If they had cleared that last piece of shoal in the middle, you would have had nothing to worry about – but they didn't. The 4/8/2019 USACE survey is shown.

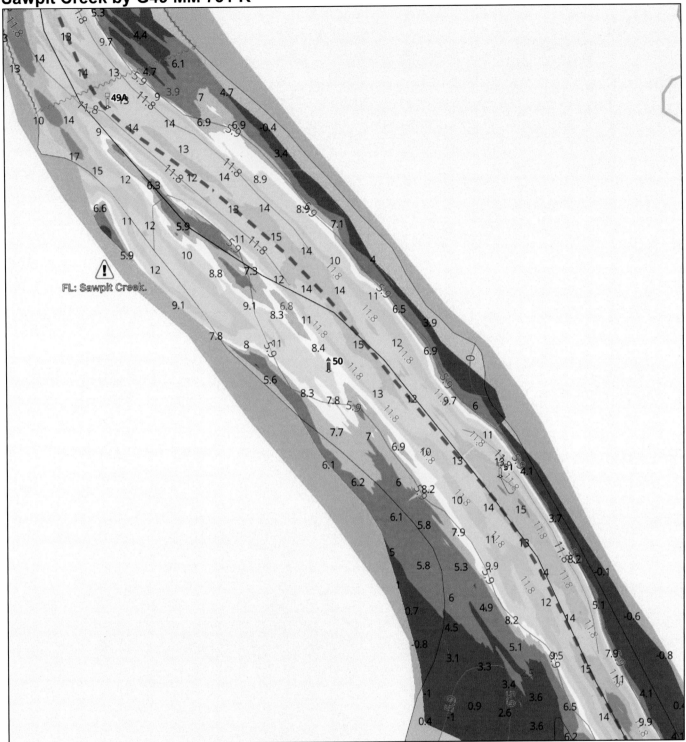

Sawpit Creek has been dredged and the 4/8/2019 USACE survey after the dredging is shown. My 10/28/2019 track is the blue dotted line. Check the Waterway Guide alert for the latest info. This is the area where you used to hug the shore since the middle was all shoal, no more, at least until it shoals in again.

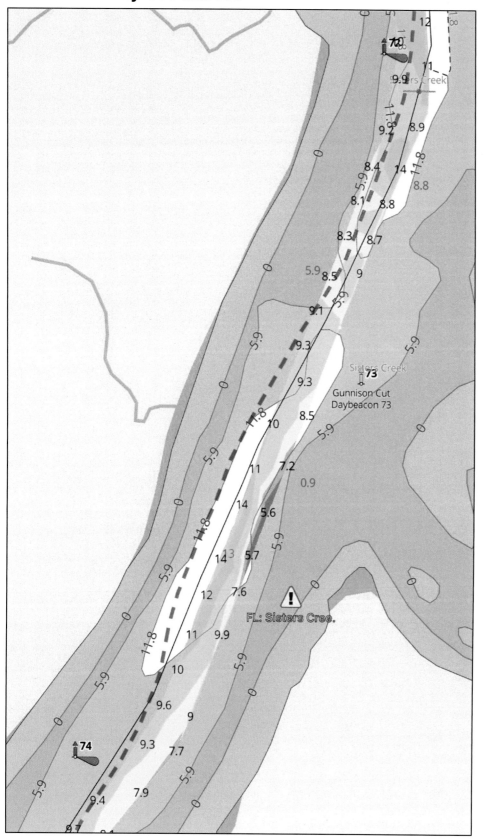

You have to do a bit of an "S" curve through here. Heading south, pass R72 in the middle of the channel, then favor the green side to avoid the shoaling north of G73 (shown in yellow and red on the chart).

Then switch over to the red side by G73 and finally returning to the center of the channel by R74.

The least I saw was 9.8 MLLW along the blue dotted line, my track of 10/28/2019.

This section of the ICW was supposed to be dredged in the spring of 2019 but I've seen no evidence of that so far.

Check the Waterway Guide alert for the latest info.

Jacksonville Free Docks MM733

If you don't feel like continuing the run to St Augustine, which is still 31 NM south, then you have excellent alternatives:

First, there's the new Jacksonville Free City Dock (see photo) that can accommodate four to five boats and more with rafting. The docks are new and in excellent shape. There's a park by the docks for walking and pet relief. There's a friendly crowd around, making it a very nice stop.

The second option is to anchor in Sisters Creek about 0.2 NM south and take advantage of a town dinghy dock. I've used both options and they work well. Alternatively, you can go to the free dock in downtown Jacksonville. Just be sure you have the tide with you when you go.

Leg 10 Jacksonville to Titusville 121 NM

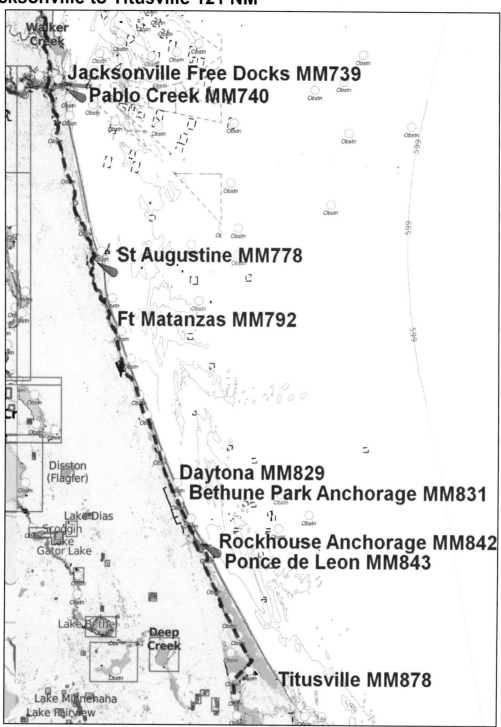

From Jacksonville, we like to anchor out at Ft Matanzas, a National Monument site 41 NM south. On the way, we pass by St Augustine, which is a great place to visit and refuel. We sometimes take a mooring or a slip and the town has many attractions. If you've never been there you ought to go. From Ft Matanzas, we can reach Rockhouse Creek, 44 NM south and anchor out. It has good holding and the prerequisite place to take Hoolie. From Rockhouse Creek, we travel to Titusville 32 NM away, our home for the holidays. We'll take a slip there for two months while we rent a car and go home for Thanksgiving and Christmas. Another option is to take a mooring or dock at St Augustine and then make just one stop at a Daytona anchorage before moving on to Titusville; it's what we've done for the last three years. We like the Bethune Point Park anchorage in Daytona which has a free dinghy dock although it has not been repaired yet from hurricane Irma. You can just use the sandy beach next door for pet relief by the park.

202

Pablo Creek Entrance from St Johns River MM 739.8

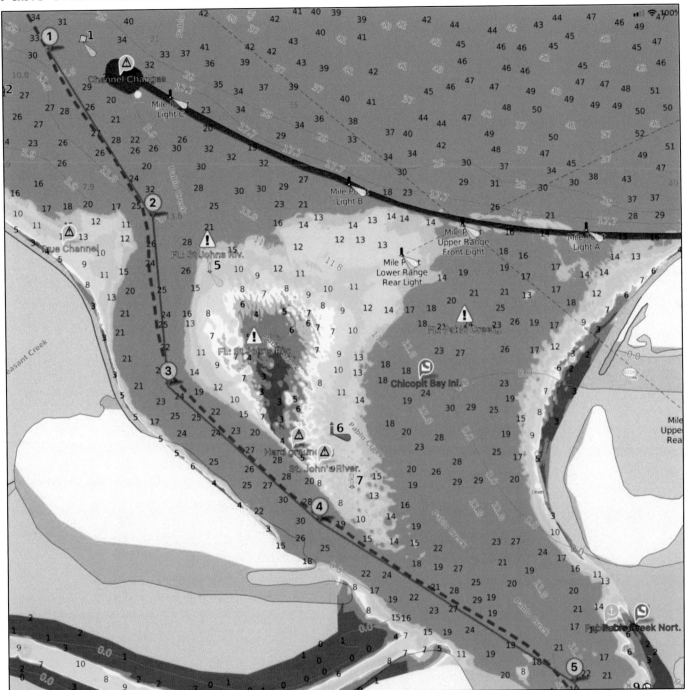

The north entrance to Pablo Creek from the St Johns River gave boaters fits during the 2018 fall migration. A shoal formed out of nowhere in the middle of the channel. All the charts were wrong, including SonarChart which I used for this section and hit bottom in 10 MLLW according to SonarChart.

Once the USACE did a survey, we then knew how to navigate the area. The 4/5/2019 USACE survey is shown in the chart. My 10/29/2019 track is shown in blue and a GPX route is also included in red at BPablo011219. It's handy to have the route or track loaded since it can be hazy in the area with lots of current and the buoys are small and hard to see. It's good to have a reference when you're trying to dodge marine traffic while crossing St Johns River. As you can see, there's plenty of water depth if you just follow the route. See the Waterway Guide alert for the latest info.

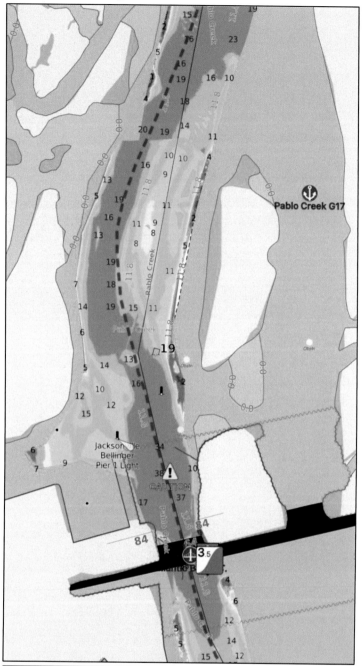

There are three cautions to be considered (from top to bottom):

Top shoaling area:
In the spring of 2016, I saw 7.4 MLW at the shoaling spot but others have reported 6 MLW. After that, I now follow the blue dotted line to the west of the shoal area (in yellow on the chart) for 15 MLW which was my 10/29/2019 track.

Strong currents by alert mark:
The current can run up to 6 knots through here. The bridge and adjacent land can cause the current to funnel through and also swirl; it will push your boat side to side if you hit the bridge at max current. It's not advised to pass through with another boat coming in the opposite direction when the current is flowing so much.

Going under the bridge:
If you encounter wind against tide, there can be a standing wave directly under the bridge, lessening the clearance per the height boards. To add to the confusion, the height board on the north side does not agree with the height board on the southern side:

Reported on one passage:
North Side = 64.5 ft
South Side = 63.5 ft
One boat with a 64 ft mast lost their Windex and static arrester when they proceeded after seeing the north board at 64.5 ft.

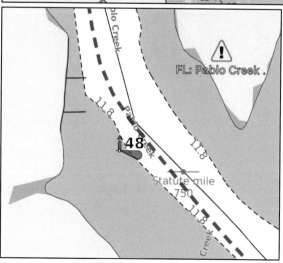

Pass within 100 ft of R48 for 13.3 MLLW. There is shoaling on the green side through here.

Pablo Creek south of here for the next 15 statute miles is narrow and lined with houses on one side. Many of the charts are still off for the area. I used to see my boat icon going overland when I was in the visual middle of the channel. The charts have been cleaned up recently and are much better now unless you have an old chart. Just stay in the visual middle of the channel for 10 or so MLLW.

St Augustine Shoals MM 778

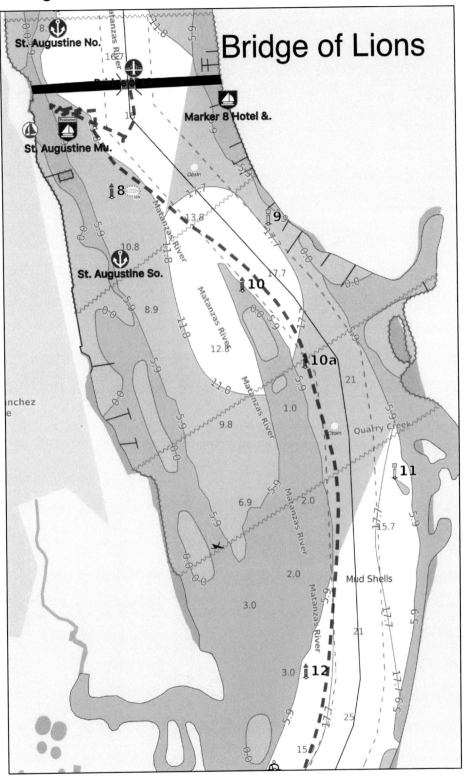

St Augustine is a major stop for us. One year we stayed here four days when the wind was piping up to 20 to 30 kts but we were on a dock, not a mooring. There were reports of people getting seasick on the moorings; it was very rough, worse in the north field.

If you've never been to St Augustine it's a must stop. The town is great to walk through and there's a fort to explore. Unfortunately, there's nothing in the way of provisioning unless the free shuttle is running during migration time.

We only take a mooring if the winds are calm; a long trip for pet relief from the south mooring field in a north wind greater than 10 kts is not a happy time (there are no close-in moorings for transients, they are all taken by long-termers).

On the chart, you can see the recommended route where you'll have no problems. The hazards are on the red side so just favor the green side and you will be fine.

From St Augustine you have several choices:
Matanzas River anchorage 12 NM
Daytona anchorage 47 NM
Or you can choose one of the many marinas along the way. If you take the Matanzas anchorage, then the Rockhouse Creek anchorage is a good hop south. I'll cover both.

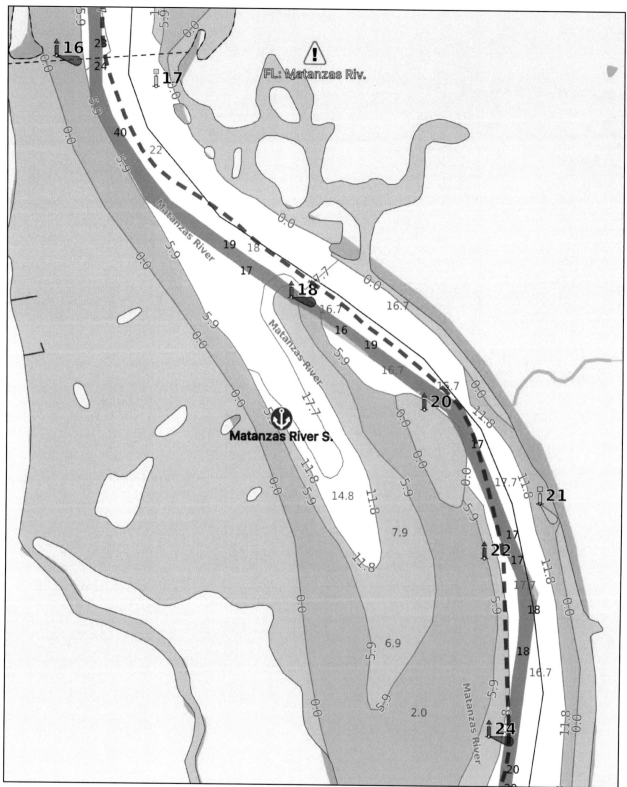

Favor the red side by R16, then center in the channel until R18 where you need to favor the green side around the curve to R24. There are two shoals building: one from G15 to G17 and one around R20.

Matanzas River by R30 MM 783

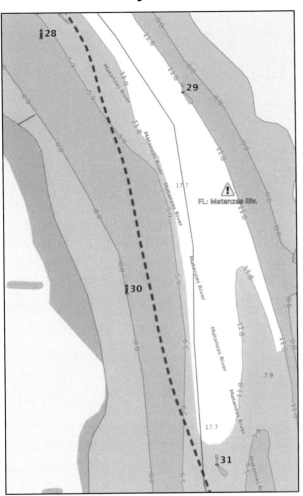

For the last five years, I've taken the track shown by the blue dotted line for 11 to 20 MLW. My 10/31/2019 track is shown.

Going south:
R28 11 MLW 30 ft off
R30 by docks, 30 ft off

Then aim for G31, you will be far outside the channel as shown on charts but with plenty of water. This path avoids a developing shoal at the hazard mark and it's shorter too.

Matanzas River by R38 MM 785

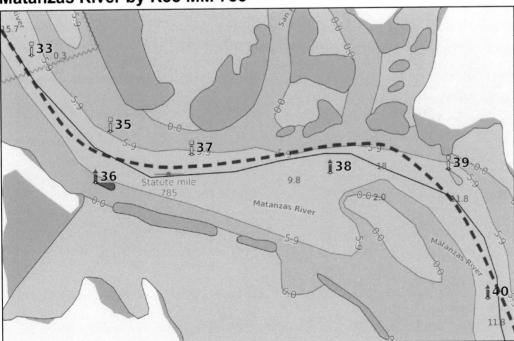

Pass G35, G37, and G39 by 50 ft off for 20 MLW. A shoal is very localized to R38. There is another shoal reaching out from R36, which is the reason to keep close to G35 and G37.

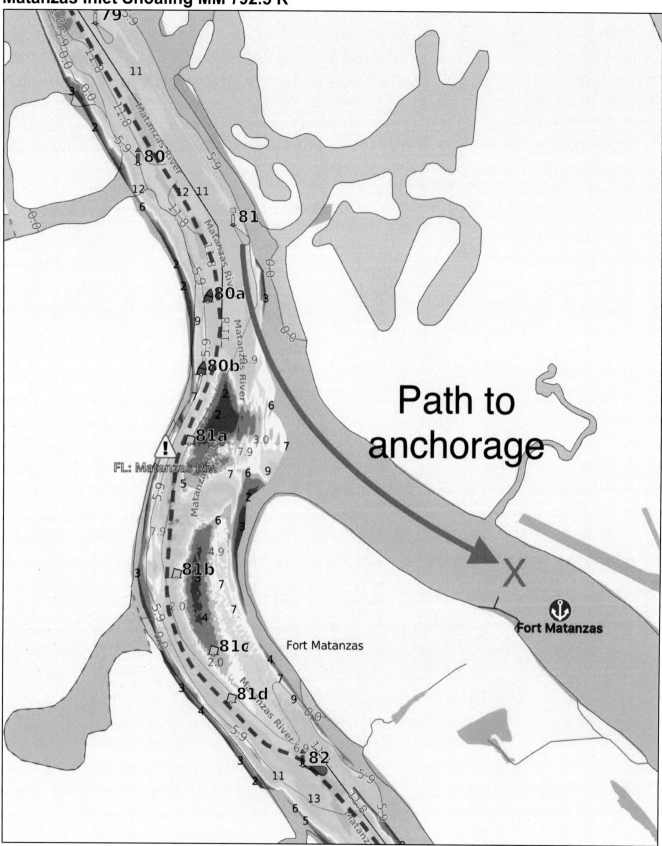

Matanzas has been dredged but there are no green buoys yet and no USACE survey. You can go down the middle for 10 MLLW. See the <u>Waterway Guide alerts</u> for the latest info. The chart shown is before dredging, it does not show the dredged depths. It's there for reference.

Ft Matanzas National Monument MM 792.5

The approach to the Matanzas anchorage is shown on the previous page with an "X" for dropping the hook in front of the fort—good holding and wake good protection. The approach shown has been constant with 8 MLLW for the last eight years, with no problem with depths. Ft Matanzas is a must-see if you've never been there. There is no charge for anything. Even the guided tour of the old Spanish fort which involves a boat ride over is free. Notice the cannons guarding the anchorage!

You can take your dinghy to the ocean side and enjoy the beach!

There are also nature trails to explore and a park house with many exhibits. You can't use their dock but you can beach your dinghy on the sandy beach and walk over to the park house to catch a ride to the fort or to walk along the nature trails. You can also take your dog to the sandy shore on the north side of the anchorage, the south side is off-limits at all times.

Bethune Park Anchorage MM 831

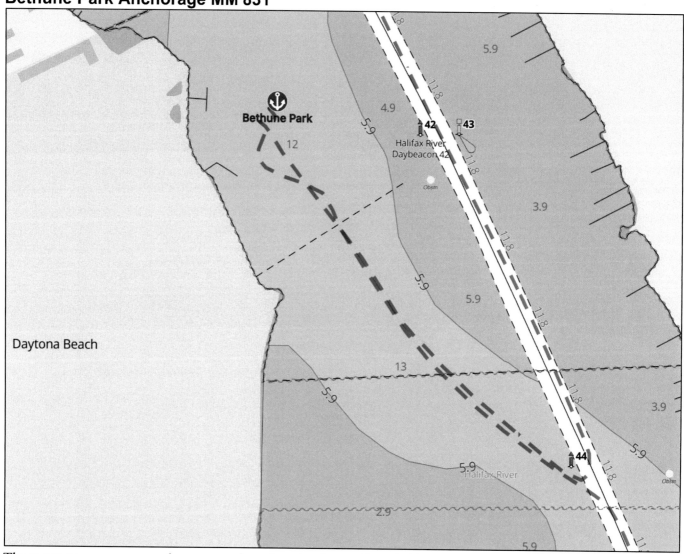

There are many, many anchorages and marinas to choose from in Daytona and we've stayed at several, but our favorite stop is the Bethune Point Park anchorage for 8 to 10 MLLW. It has a sandy beach for landing Hoolie and a park for walking him around. The approach is to round R44 and then head in as shown by the dotted line which was our actual track on 11/1/2019. I suppose if the wind is 20 kts or higher it would not be as good, but it's fine at 20 or less. You can expect some wakes from passing boats during the day but it settles down at night. From Bethune, it's 41 NM to Titusville where we leave the boat over the holidays.

Note: the Navionics SonarChart is grossly wrong on depths in this area, the NOAA chart is correct but don't anchor north of the Waterway Guide anchor icon, it's shallow there.

Halifax River by G69 MM 838.5

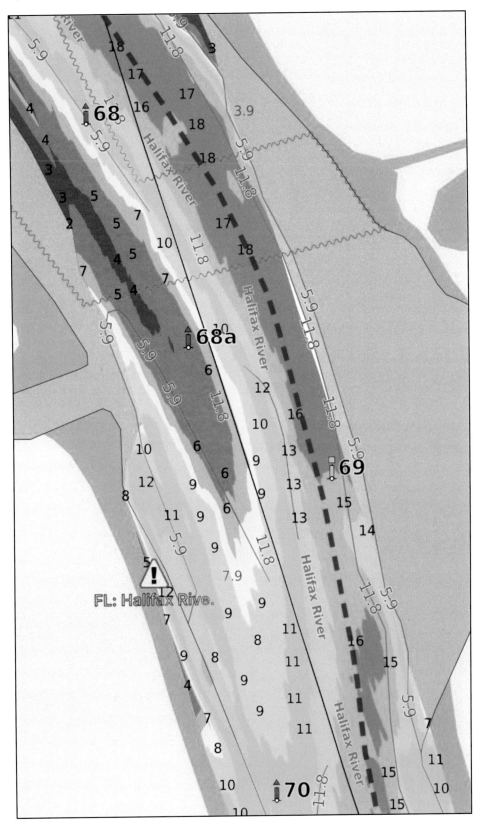

There is shoaling in the channel by R68A. The Coast Guard has rebuoyed it recently so now it's just "follow the buoys" for 16 MLLW. Still, take it easy and pass G69 by no more than 50 ft off. My 11/1/2019 track is shown in a blue dotted line.

Ponce de Leon Inlet by R2 and R2A MM 839.5

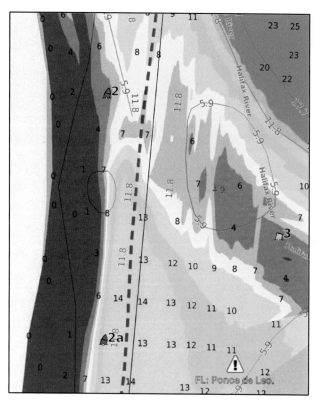

This is a traditional shoaling area. It was just dredged in the spring after the survey was taken in the chart at left but it will shoal up again sometime in the future. Check the Waterway Guide alert for the area for the latest information. On my 11/1/2019 track shown in blue, I recorded 7.1 MLLW as the least seen. Pass the two reds by 80 feet off, don't hug. The survey shown was before the dredging. See the Waterway Guide alert for the latest info.

Rockhouse Creek Anchorage MM 842

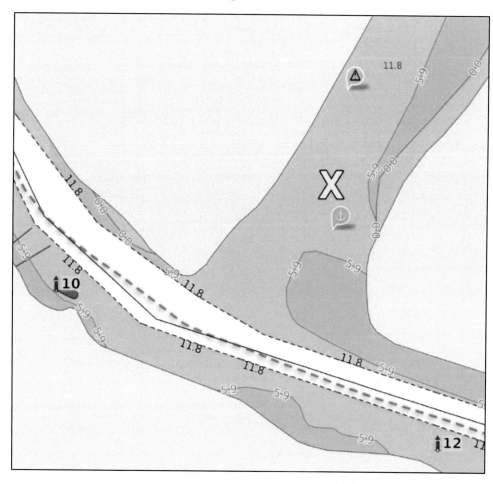

Rockhouse Creek is another of our favorite anchorages. We anchor by the yellow X. There is access to sandy beaches and even to the ocean by dinghy if desired. The holding is good but expect current of 1 to 2 kts. It's 10 MLW right up to the mangroves on the northwest shore but it can get crowded.

There is pet relief by the shore but recently there have been signs to stay off. If so, there are miles of nearby sandy beaches before the bridge by the ocean. It's dead calm on the inside beaches. It is deep right up to the mangroves on the west shore.

From Rockhouse, it's 31 NM to Titusville, our next stop.

Ponce de Leon Inlet MM 843

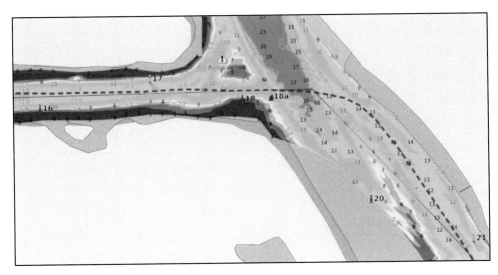

This place was just dredged over the summer of 2018 and it's still holding up. It has to be dredged about every two to three years. For now, just honor the buoys for 10 MLLW. However, notice the exit when going south. You need to swing out and pass R20 by about 400 ft to reach the deep-water channel on the green side going south. See Waterway Guide alert for the latest info, this is an active shoaling area.

New Smyrna Beach MM 845.5

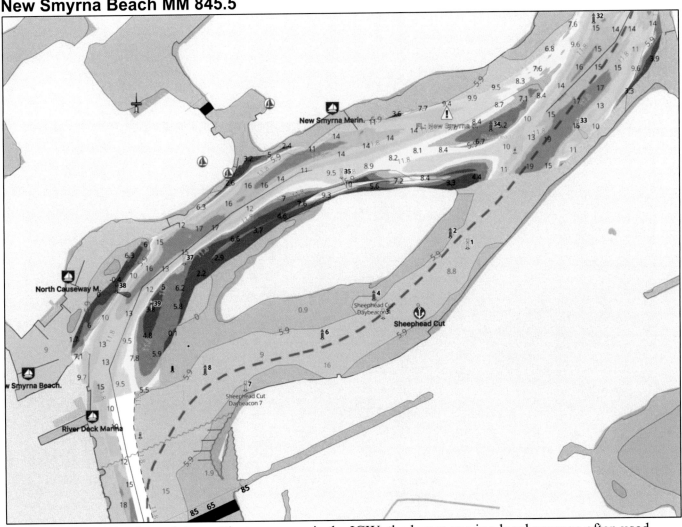

There are two paths through here. The upper one is the ICW, the lower one is a local passage often used instead of the ICW. The ICW route always seems to be shoal by R34. It was dredged over the summer of 2018 but it will undoubtedly shoal in again. I bypass the mess and just take the Sheephead Cut as the locals do for a dependable 12 MLLW. My 11/1/2019 track is shown as a blue dotted line.

Mosquito Lagoon by Haulover Bridge MM 869

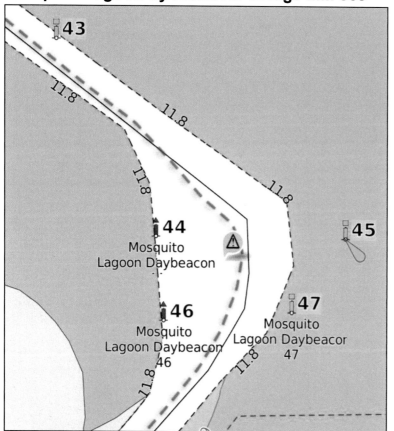

The shoaling mark warns against hugging the two reds. If you follow the Recommended Track (or the dotted line), there's no problem for 12 MLW. Go slow, lots and lots of manatees.

From here south to Titusville, just stay in the channel per your chartplotter. There are no hazards unless you leave the channel.

The SonarCharts from here to Titusville show only 6 to 7 MLLW in the channel. They are wrong, there is 10 MLLW to Titusville and south.

Going south from here we heard a noise alongside the boat. Looking over, we discovered there were three dolphins keeping pace with Fleetwing! They swam alongside the boat for several minutes. Video of dolphins racing Fleetwing. It was a magical moment.

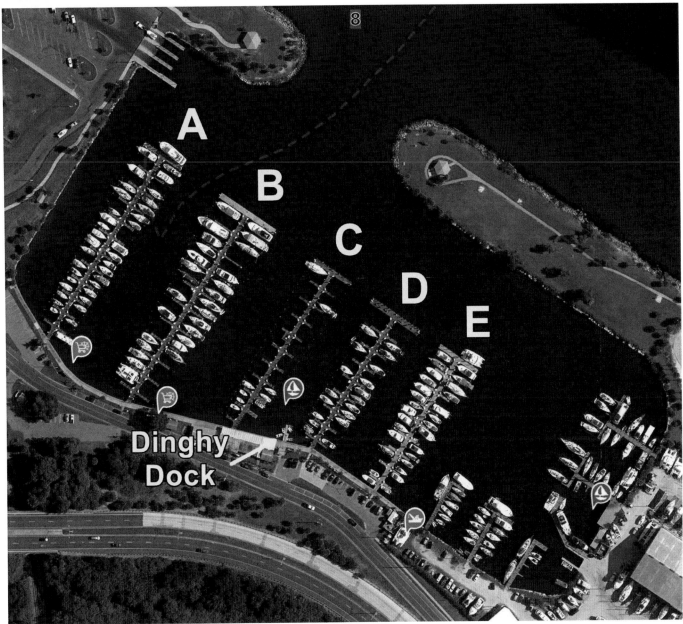

We split our trip south in the winter into two segments: the part north of Titusville and the part south. We leave the boat here while we return north for Thanksgiving, Christmas, and New Year's. That's also just about all the winter we want; a few snow flurries or even a snowfall is fine, one or two. Then in the first week of January, it's time to return to Titusville and summertime to continue our journey to Key West.

The attraction of the Titusville Marina for us is the combination of good folks caring for your boat while you're away and a very reasonable price of $10.50/ft for a month's stay. There are lots of things to see such as the NASA Space Center, Merritt Island Wildlife Refuge, and lots of nature parks. Of course, there's all of Orlando if you like that sort of thing. Hoolie likes it here because of the dog park right next door. He gets to run and run and run, Brittany heaven.

Dock map for Titusville Marina

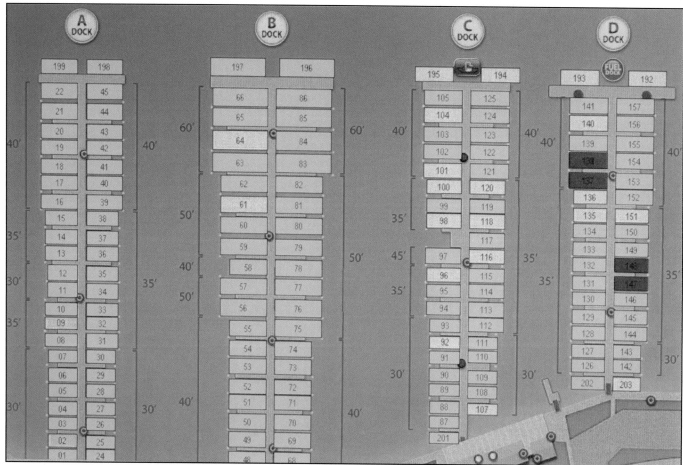

The dock numbers are shown for A through D, the most common docks for transients. The map is handy for finding your dock in such a large marina. The docks are fixed but there's less than a foot change in water level during your stay (driven by wind). The pilings are the most massive I've ever seen in a marina. All the docks have a badge lock for security. Laundry is only $1.50/load and we enjoy the running trails. The marina has many manatees, up to 20 when we're around, and lots of wildlife. For us, it works.

Occasionally you will see an alligator swim by (this is Florida!). We've only seen two in the marina in nine years of docking there.

Our usual next stop is Vero Beach, 64 NM south. There are many alternatives if you do not want to travel that far in a day. The Melbourne anchorage is 35 NM south and we've used both sides of the bridge anchorage, depending upon the wind direction. Pet relief can be had by the bridge roadway.

Leg 11 Titusville to Miami 183 NM

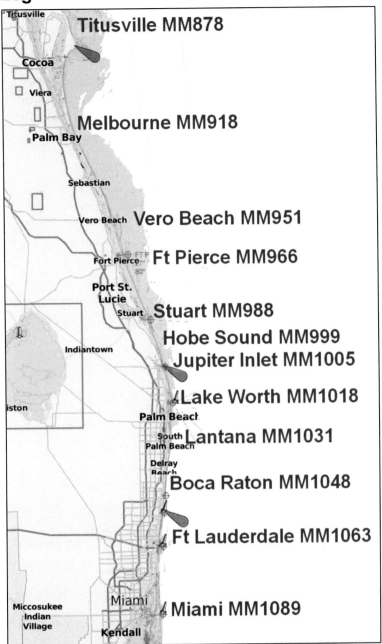

Titusville MM878
Titusville
Cocoa
Viera
Melbourne MM918
Palm Bay
Sebastian
Vero Beach **Vero Beach MM951**
Fort Pierce **Ft Pierce MM966**
Port St. Lucie
Stuart **Stuart MM988**
Hobe Sound MM999
Indiantown
Jupiter Inlet MM1005
Lake Worth MM1018
Palm Beach
iston
South Palm Beach **Lantana MM1031**
Delray Beach
Boca Raton MM1048
Ft Lauderdale MM1063
Miccosukee Indian Village
Miami **Miami MM1089**
Kendall

We usually stop at Vero Beach next but it's a long day at 64 NM. You may want to stop in-between, perhaps at the Melbourne anchorage. Vero Beach is a great place to provision since they offer free buses to anywhere in the county. Since the first stop is the Publix supermarket with West Marine right across the street, that's usually as far as we get. Many cruisers spend the entire winter there but it's too cold for us.

Next, it's on to an anchorage at Hobe Sound by R38 south of St Lucie inlet. There are other fine anchorages, too, but we're partial to Hobe Sound. There's a sandy beach nearby, of course, for Hoolie relief. You will get some wakes during the day but it settles down during the night.

From Hobe Sound, it's on to West Palm Beach about 22 NM south. The attraction for us is the free dinghy dock for Hoolie and the protected anchorage between bridges. Note the bridge opening times and time your passage; you will have a ton of bridges but they are spaced well for a 7 kt cruising speed. An alternative is the Lantana anchorage just south of the bridge with a nice restaurant nearby with a dinghy dock. There's also a public dinghy dock for Hoolie relief.

Our next stop is at Ft Lauderdale at either the Las Olas Marina mooring field at $40/night or on the north side of the bridge for free at the anchorage. We always take a mooring for the easy dinghy ride in for Hoolie and to do laundry at their excellent laundromat. If you do anchor and want shore access via the marina they will charge $20/day for the dinghy dock. You can celebrate passing through 16 bridges today!

From Ft Lauderdale, we look for a calm day for the outside passage to Miami just 28 NM away. Be sure to monitor VHF 16 in case the Coast Guard closes Government Cut. It's the only inlet on the ICW that's ever closed to recreational boaters as far as I know. The reason for a closure is the narrow channel. If two or more large ships come in close together the Coast Guard will announce the closure. You have to do circles or use one of the inlets farther south like Biscayne Channel, but then you would have to pass across the channel that's closed. Eventually, the Coast Guard will open the channel again via another announcement on VHF 16. In nine years of ICW trips, we've never arrived at a closed inlet, but it's been close two times when the inlet was closed shortly after we entered. Once through the inlet, we head for the Marine Stadium anchorage, completely protected with an amazing view of Miami at night. Pet relief is nearby as well as running tracks on the north side. We'll wait for good weather to go down the Keys from here. If you go in February, check to be sure it's open for anchoring. It's closed during the Miami Boat Show.

Vero Beach City Marina MM 951

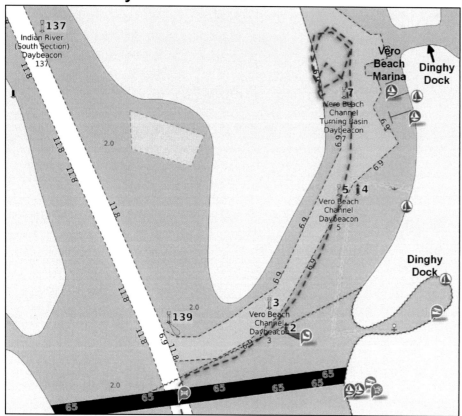

Vero Beach is a great stop. It's good for provisioning with their free bus service directly to a large Publix supermarket with a West Marine across the street. You can take a longer free ride to reach a shopping center complex with a Walmart adjacent.

They offer both moorings and docks. There is always room since the policy of the marina is to double or even triple up on moorings if the demand is there. So, the standard practice when you take a mooring is to put out fenders for additional boats.

The Vero Beach Marina is the only place on the ICW that I'm aware of that requires the sharing of a mooring. It's their way of never turning away a boater, which is good. Some may find it inconvenient, but we don't. Note: All boaters on a mooring still pay full rate each. If you choose to anchor north of the mooring field, you still have to pay the full mooring fee if you want to land your dinghy at their dinghy dock, even if you don't use their facilities otherwise.

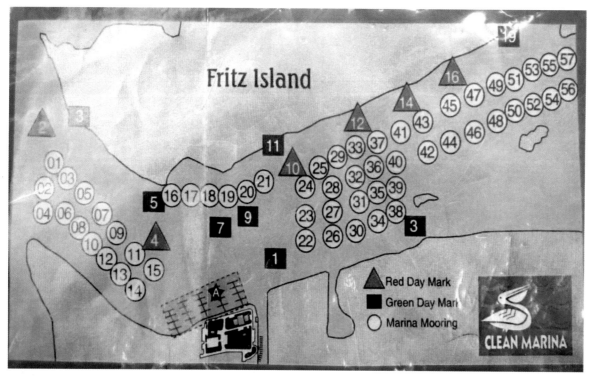

At left is the Vero Beach mooring field layout. You will be given a mooring number to find.

From Vero Beach, our next stop is the Hobe Sound anchorage, 41 NM south. There are lots of other choices along the way but we've found Hobe Sound to our liking. It has pet relief on a sandy shore, it's usually not crowded, and there's room for a dozen boats.

Vero Beach Anchorage Area

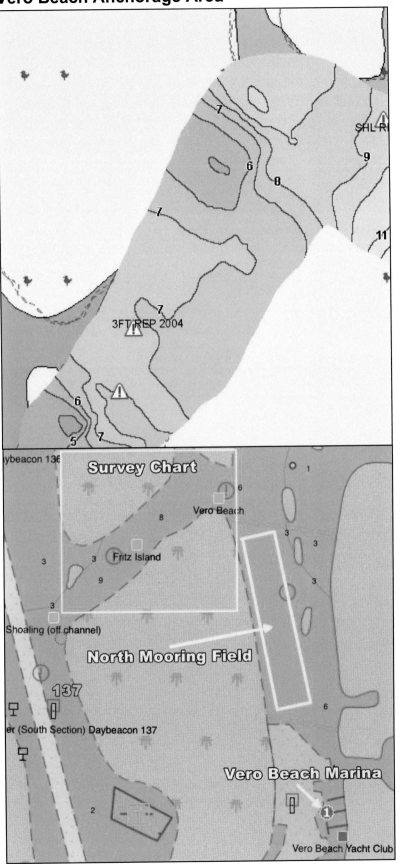

The chart is a survey I made of the Vero Beach anchoring area north of the mooring field. I sounded the anchoring area using Navionics' SonarChart Live app. The app draws a chart on your iPad in real-time and corrects it automatically for MLW per the nearest tide station you specify. I have this chart on my iPad and my boat position shows up in real-time right on the chart.

There's room for about six boats to anchor comfortably in the slot between the upper mooring field and the ICW channel to the southwest. I've seen as many as a dozen boats there. Unfortunately, you can't enter the anchorage area directly from the ICW; it's too shallow by the channel. You have to motor through the mooring field and bend around to port after passing all the moored boats. There is certainly enough depth but it's a long ride to the Vero Beach dinghy dock. Oh yes, if you want to use the dinghy dock, they will charge you $20/day even if all you want to do it tie up and not use the facilities.

I've included a larger view chart of the area so you can see where the survey chart fits in relative to the north mooring field, the ICW, and the Vero Beach Marina.

219

Fort Pierce Shoaling MM 966

The shoal by R188 has been dredged. Stay in the channel for 8 MLLW minimum. You can see that you do not want to wander over to the red side. The 6/19/2019 USACE survey is shown at left with my 1/13/2019 track.

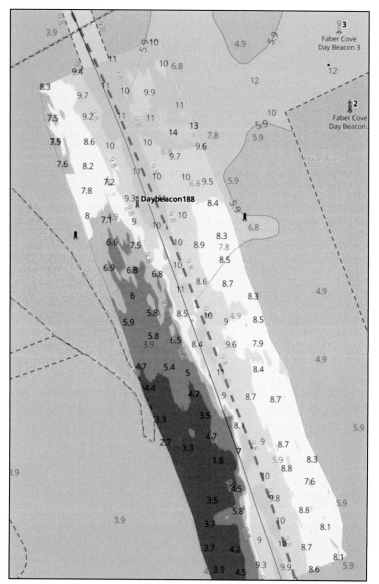

Many boaters we know love to stay at Ft Pierce shown at left with its new seawall protecting the expanded marina. It's located right in town with many restaurants, galleries, shops, theaters, parks, and lots of things to do. I can understand the attraction for those staying long term and for waiting for weather for the Bahamas crossing.

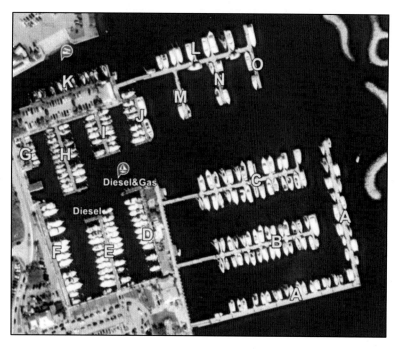

Indian River by R228 MM 985

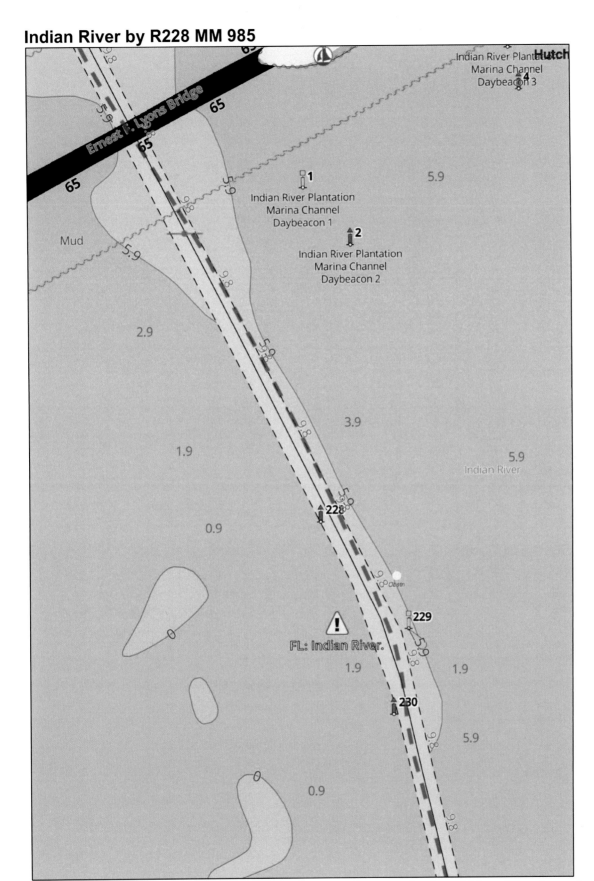

This shoal has not changed for the past eight years. Just stay in the middle of the channel as seen on NOAA ENC based charts (Aqua Map and most others). The least I saw on my 1/13/2020 track (blue dotted line) was 7.3 MLLW by R230.

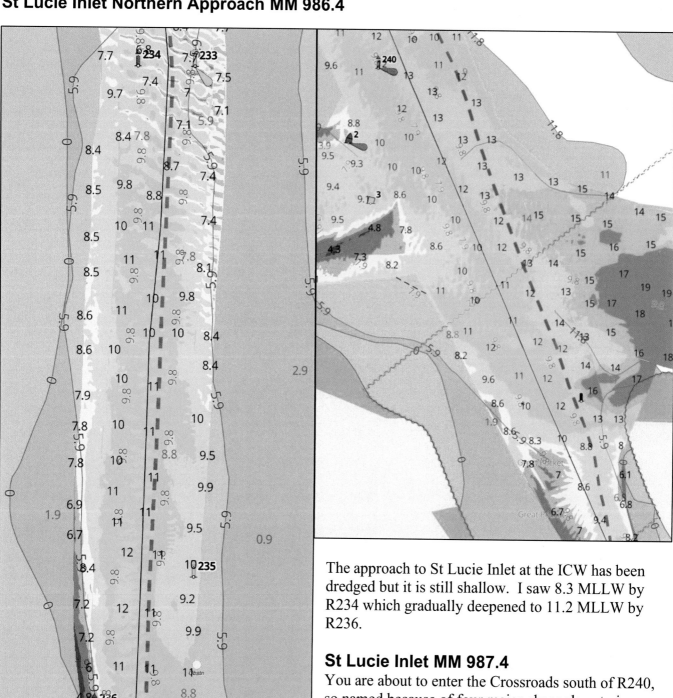

The approach to St Lucie Inlet at the ICW has been dredged but it is still shallow. I saw 8.3 MLLW by R234 which gradually deepened to 11.2 MLLW by R236.

St Lucie Inlet MM 987.4

You are about to enter the Crossroads south of R240, so named because of four major channels entering one area. Fishing boats using the St Lucie inlet are going east-west (they do not slow down), snowbirds are going north-south, traffic to and from St Lucie River is coming and going from the west and usually turn north or south at the Crossroads. In short, expect anything.

South of the crossroads, follow the USACE survey to enter Hobe Sound, it's relatively narrow. My 1/13/2020 track is shown on the 1/16/2020 USACE survey which was before dredging

Hobe Sound to Ft Lauderdale Bridges – a GPX Route to Follow with Bridge Info

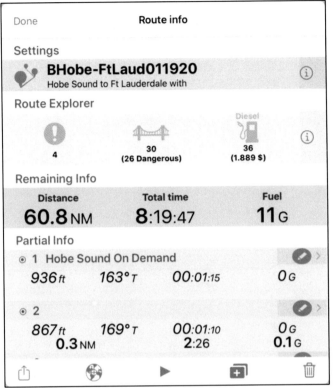

I've transited the ICW from Hobe Sound to Ft Lauderdale and return a dozen times at least. It has lots and lots of bridges and some people avoid the trip at all costs – but we don't mind. As a private aid, I've put a GPX route together with a waypoint at every bridge that shows the name of the bridge (so the bridge tender will answer your call for an opening) and the opening schedule. See the first example for the Hobe Sound bridge, "On Demand". If you can do 7 kts, you can make all the bridges, they are timed just right for that speed without waiting.

If you have Aqua Map Master, you can view the summary showing 28 bridges, 5 of which are fixed, the cheapest fuel and that there are 10 alerts to pay attention to. But wait, there's more – Aqua Map has been busy with a feature called, "Route Explorer". See below.

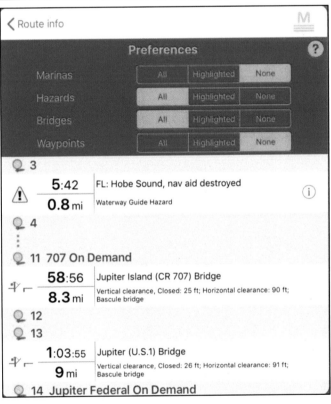

Tapping the "i" in the Route Explorer box brings up this display. I'm interested in Hazards and Bridges so I chose to highlight all of them. I was not interested in Marinas or Waypoints so I chose "None".

The display condenses to just bridges and hazards with an ETA to each bridge. That's kinds of handy in knowing whether you're doing to make that next bridge and what the official name is of the bridge so you can give them a call.

For now, the opening schedule is summarized in the top display but if you tap on the bridge as shown in the bottom display, you will get more bridge information.

Best of all, I've modified the GPX route for the deepest water as shown by the most recent USACE surveys and I will be applying further changes as the bottom conditions change.

The GPX route can be downloaded at BHobe-FtLaud011920. The last 6 digits of the route name represent the date of the route. The date may change in the future as I update the route due to shoaling. Be sure to load the latest version from GPX Routes.

Hobe Sound Anchorage MM 998

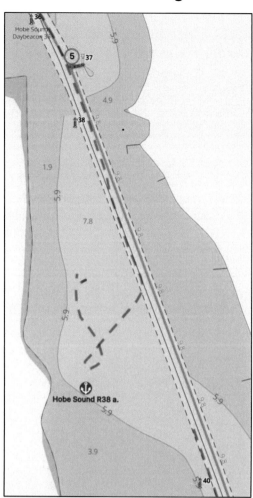

The anchorage at Hobe Sound between R38 and R40 is one of our favorites. It has pet relief on a sandy beach right off the back of the boat and there's room for a dozen boats without feeling crowded. The holding is excellent in 8 to 10 MLW.

There's some boat traffic during the day but it's calm at night. The sunrises are something to get up for, just spectacular with the clouds abundant over the gulf stream.

The anchorage is just south of waypoint 5 in the Hobe to Ft Lauderdale route.

From here we aim for the Lantana anchorage 29 NM south.

There is also an anchorage at Peck Lake that we've never taken. It always seemed to be too crowded and pets were not allowed on the beach, a no-go for us. If you don't have a pet, I understand that the beach is nearby for exploring.

The beach on the western shore is ideal for Hoolie relief.

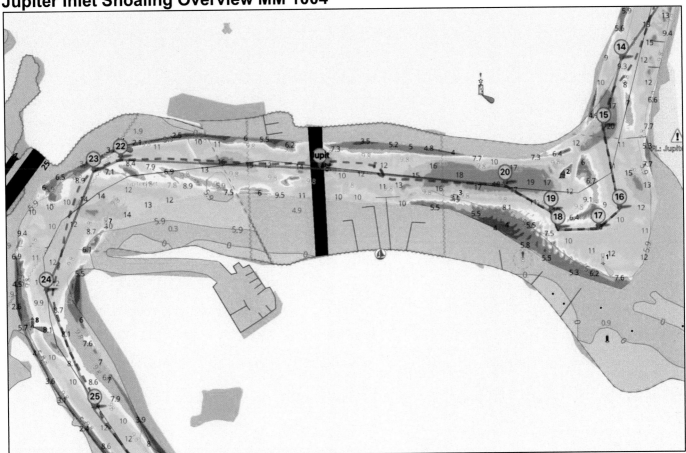

There always seems to be shoaling in this area. See the detail on the next page for more information on what to expect by R2. For the rest of the path through here, I've threaded the route to avoid the worst of the shoaling per the 10/3/2019 USACE survey which I followed in my 1/14/2020 track (blue dotted line). Just going down the middle will pass over 5.5 MLLW in spots.

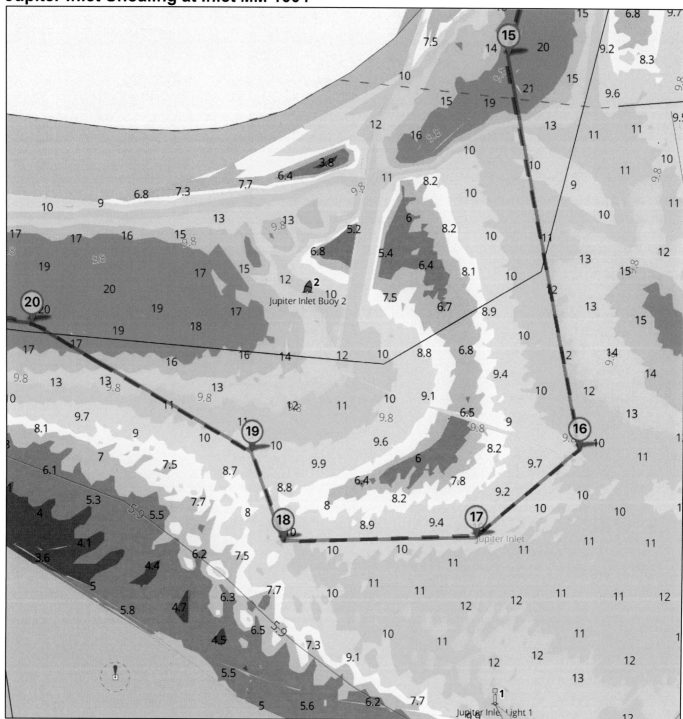

I've shown a detail of the area by the Jupiter Inlet. The area is prone to shoaling and during the boating season, buoys will be moved to direct boaters to avoid the shoals, we hope.

Meanwhile, R2 directs boaters directly into a shoal of 5.2 MLLW. When I came down in January, I chose to pass R2 on the wrong side, taking faith in the USACE survey that showed a deep-water path. I was rewarded with 17 MLLW. However, two other boaters grounded trying to follow my track, backed out, and proceeded around R2, honoring it although with less water than 17 MLLW. Based on that feedback, I have modified my track to go around R2 at about 300 ft distant as shown in the chart for 9 MLLW.

My modified track is shown (T_1_14_20V2.gpx) along with the BHobe-FtLaud031720 GPX route (red line with numbered waypoints 15-20).

Lantana Anchorage MM 1031

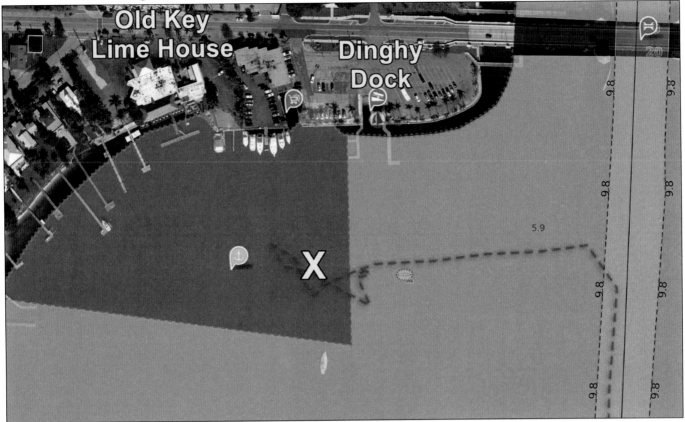

We've stayed at various marinas in the area but the anchorage just south of the Lantana Bridge offers good protection from the north and east and adequate protection from other directions.

We anchor off the park boat ramps in 7.1 MLLW. There is not a formal dinghy dock but you can tie up to the ramp for pet relief. I've gone directly over the mark for the wreck and didn't see a bump on the depth sounder. It deepens to 12 MLLW farther out, away from the boat ramp and shallows somewhat closer in.

If you go, be sure to eat at the Old Key Lime House restaurant. They have a dinghy dock, a good atmosphere, and good food. Eat-in the bar half, not the formal restaurant. They have specials in the bar during happy hour that are not featured in the formal restaurant. Pets are not allowed, even at their dinghy dock. From here south 13 bridges have to be raised for us to get under. If you can do 7 kts then you can make them without waiting but check on the Flagler Memorial Bridge to see if the construction is completed. Otherwise, it only opens on 15 minutes past the hour.

Boynton Inlet MM 1034

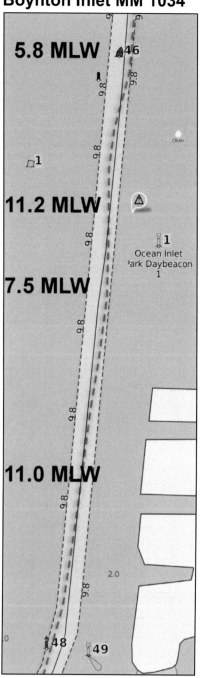

Note that buoy R46 is shown in the middle of the charted channel so you have to favor the green side as charted to honor the red buoy. Also, note that both G1's are not ICW buoys; the G1 on the right is part of the inlet marks, so just stay in the channel. If you wander over towards G1 you'll find shallow water. There are reports that this area has since been dredged to 8 MLLW.

Ft Lauderdale, spring break!!

A real French bakery is only two blocks from the Las Olas mooring field. The owners are from France; the pastries and bread are fantastic.

Ft Lauderdale Mooring Field MM 1064

We like to stop at the Las Olas Marina mooring field when in Ft Lauderdale. It's within walking distance of the beach which is always fun to see, especially on the return trip north when the spring breakers are in town. The marina office has been moved to trailers while a parking garage is being built, so call ahead for details. The moorings are first come, first served and they have a short loop. Be prepared to reach down and have a line ready to thread through the loop.

You can pick up some groceries at the nearby CVS store. There is a great French bakery two blocks towards the beach. The marina has an excellent array of washers and dryers in an air-conditioned room. We always do laundry here.

The downside is the cost, $40/night and there are only 9 or so moorings. But then I've always been able to find a mooring for the past eight years. Since it's right by the bridge, the mooring field is in a no-wake zone. If you don't want to use the mooring field or if it's full, you can always anchor north of the bridge in the marked anchorage area. If you still want to use the facilities of the marina for laundry or showers, they charge $20/day for the dinghy dock and facility use. If you use the dinghy dock at night, be sure to put lights on your dinghy. There are patrol boats ready to ticket you if you don't.

From here we either aim for Marine Stadium in Miami 28 NM south or if the weather is good, we'll anchor at Caesar's Creek 49 NM south. In extreme cases of good weather or predicted bad weather for the next day, we have gone 70 NM to Rodriguez Key.

229

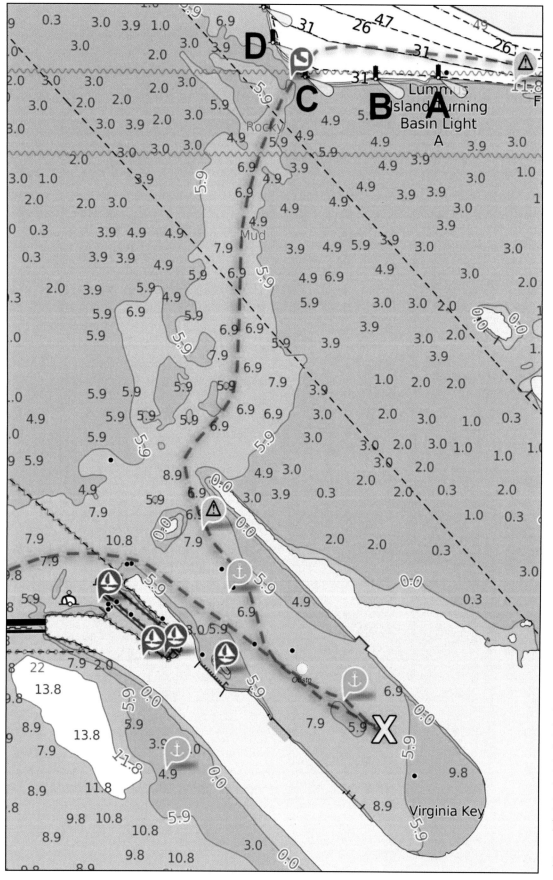

We have to go outside from Ft Lauderdale to Miami. There is a bridge with only a 55 ft clearance, the Julia Tuttle Causeway Bridge, that we cannot clear with our 55.2 ft mast. So we usually run down the coast and come in Government Cut at Miami. However, the Cut is sometimes closed to recreational traffic when large cruise ships or container ships come in. The closure is announced over VHF 16 and you cannot enter; you circle until it's over, maybe several hours or longer! Or else, you go farther down the coast to another inlet, perhaps the Biscayne Bay channel.

If we can get in Government Cut, we anchor at Marine Stadium via the dotted line (7.5 MLLW along the way) and yellow X. It's completely protected and 9 to 10 ft deep with good holding.

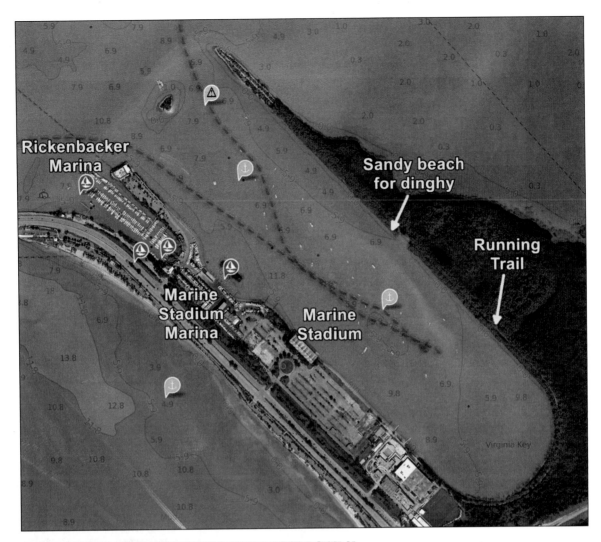

There is a sandy beach for pet relief and a running trail on the northeast shore. It's also the training grounds for Olympic sailing and you'll see many racing sailboats practicing along with racing shells and war canoes. You will have a stunning view of Miami at night. The marina stadium anchorage is used by the Miami Boat Show during February and is closed to anchoring. By the end of March, all the temporary docks are gone and the anchorage is reopened. If you plan on using the anchorage during February be sure to check the dates for the Miami Boat Show.

Marine Stadium is our staging area for good weather going down the keys. If the tides are right, we'll anchor at Caesar Creek 23 NM south, which has a dinghy dock for Hoolie. If the weather is good, we'll go down Hawk Channel to Rodriguez Key 51 NM south. In the area there are several options; one is Rodriguez Key itself if it's a calm night since it's open to any wind with an easterly component. A wind under 10 kts is fine and 10 to 15 if it's out of the north, but higher than that and it can get bumpy, especially for the ride to the boat ramp for Hoolie.

Leg 12 Miami to Key West 136 NM

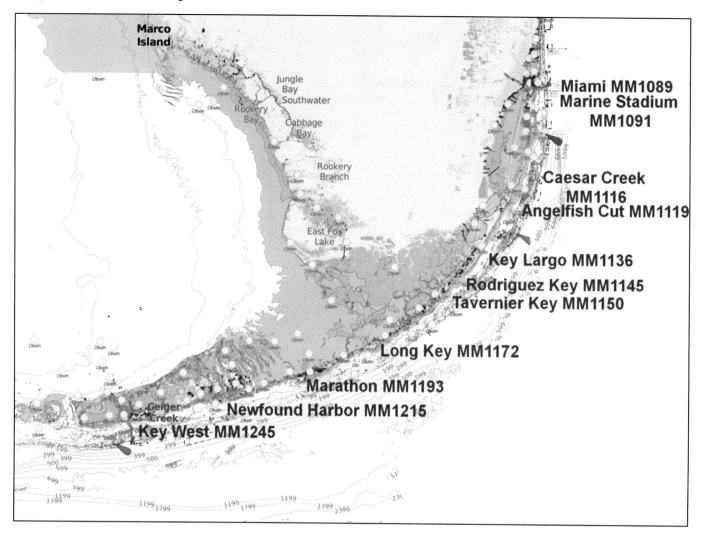

There are three choices on the way to Marathon:
1. Sail down Biscayne Bay and anchor in Caesar's Creek, 23 NM away.
2. Sail out Biscayne Channel and down Hawk Channel and anchor at Rodriguez Key, 50 NM distant. For a shorter run, you could also anchor at Caesar's Creek and enter and leave from the ocean side which has more depth, 5 ft at low tide.
3. It is possible to stay on the inside and continue down the ICW but check for the latest depths, it's shallow. Boats with 5 ft or less draft have made it to Marathon on the inside, we have not.

You have two choices to Key West from Marathon:
1. Stop on the way at Newfound Harbor and anchor at Picnic Island, 22 NM distant.
2. Go directly to Key West at Key West Bight, a run of 44 NM.

Once we're in Key West we take a dock at Key West Bight Marina at $53/ft for a month's stay. The dock we take has no fingers, so you exit off the bow to the fixed dock, which is at the same height as the bow. You can pay more at other marinas for more convenient access from your boat but we've grown fond of the city marina.

Now it's time to sit back and relax for two months and explore Schooner Wharf's music, Duval Street, the sunsets at Mallory Square, and all the things going on. Oh yes, if you installed webcams at home you can watch the snow in New York! It's one of my favorite pastimes. In two months, we'll reverse our course and head back north.

Caesar Creek Anchorage MM 1115

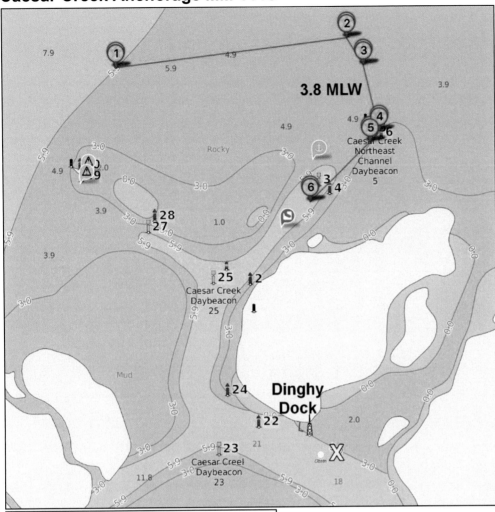

3.8 MLW

Rocky

Caesar Creek Northeast Channel Daybeacon 5

Caesar Creek Daybeacon 25

Mud

Dinghy Dock

Caesar Creek Daybeacon 23

Somewhere you have to get out to the ocean side of the Keys. You can go out the Biscayne Channel and we've done that or if your draft is less than 5 ft, take the Caesar Creek passage at peak high tide via the red line. It's not for the faint of heart. I typically see 5.1 to 5.3 ft of water with a high tide of 1.3 ft at the Billy's Point tide station; it's doable, but just barely. I've never touched bottom with my 4 ft 9-inch draft, but I heard it's rocky.

Once inside (whew!) we anchor at the yellow X. There is a dock at the ranger station with a ladder that we use to take Hoolie ashore. You will have current so back your anchor down. The next morning you have a little more leeway on your exit time out to the ocean. It's about 4.5 MLW so you can exit with just a foot of tide, no need to wait for high tide depending upon your draft.

WP1	N25. 24.209	WP4.	N25. 24.466
	W80. 14.019		W80. 13.911
WP2.	N25. 24.312	WP5.	N25. 24.493
	W80. 13.899		W80. 13.944
WP3.	N25. 24.331	WP6.	N25. 24.444
	W80. 13.881		W80. 14.400

We've used this anchorage for years, and like it for the location in going to Key West. The route we use for reaching the Caesar Creek anchorage from Biscayne Bay is shown in red with waypoints for manual entry but only attempt at high tide if you have a 5 ft draft. The bottom is hard rock. The GPX route is BCaesar. Honor the buoys.

Rodriguez Key Anchorage MM 1145

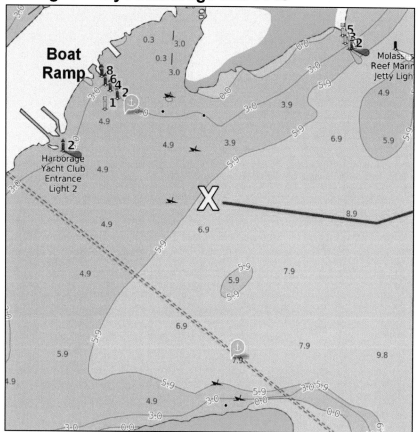

This anchorage is wide open to the east and south. It's only good in very light winds (<10 kts) or winds out of the west or northwest. If a swell is running, the waves will work their way around anywhere you try to hide. When we use the anchorage, we drop the hook by the yellow X to be close to a public boat ramp for pet relief. The restaurant by the boat ramp was wiped out by Hurricane Irma.

This is the first place going down the Keys where you can see the bottom in 10 ft of water. It's fascinating to sit on the side of the boat and watch the marine life below. You can also anchor much closer to Rodriguez Key if you don't need to use the boat ramp. Our next stop is Marathon 49 NM south.

That's our chain lying on the bottom in 10 ft of water!

If the winds are not right, there are two other choices:
- Blue Waters Marina is located in Tavernier, about 8 NM farther towards Marathon. They do not always have dockage available. The approach is only about 4.5 MLLW, tide helps. It's usually $2/ft.
- Pilot House Marina is in Key Largo and has about 4.5 MLLW on the approach if you carefully follow the directions. Rates vary widely from $3/ft to $4/ft, call ahead.

Marathon was devastated by Hurricane Irma but they have made a comeback. The mooring field is in full operation but the dinghy dock that was in front of the Tiki Hut is no more, at least at the time I was there in 4/2018. Never fear, they have plenty of dinghy dock space, which now uses the fairway by the marina office so it's better protected than ever (they added more docks for dinghies there).

Many snowbirds spend the winter at Marathon City Marina on one of the 220 moorings. There is a whole subculture of boating present with activities planned, etc. For us, it's a stopping over place on our trip down to Key West. In the winter months, it's usually impossible to get a mooring without waiting for weeks. They do not take reservations; it's first come, first served, and even then you have to dinghy to the marina to apply in person for a spot on the waiting list. At the end of March, the waiting list shrinks less than a dozen.

We either get a mooring or set the hook by the yellow X. It is always crowded so be prepared for close quarters when anchoring and maybe a conversation with your neighbor at night if the wind changes. If you want to go ashore, the marina wants $22/day just to land a dinghy, the same price you would pay for a mooring! There are other places to land a dinghy such as down by the beach at the southern entrance but it's a hike. We don't spend a lot of time here, just waiting for good weather to move on to Key West.

There is a Publix a mile north via a sidewalk or a $5 cab ride. There's a West Marine in the opposite direction. If you're here long term you can always buy a bike from somebody leaving. Enterprise will bring a car to the marina and they have a $12.50/day rental special on most weekends. For fresh fish, be sure to visit Key Fisheries across the street. They both sell and serve fresh fish caught locally. We often buy whatever looks the freshest and cook dinner on the boat.

After passing by the bridge, you can officially ask for a mooring and if one's available, you will be assigned a row and a number. A row has a letter and a mooring has a number. The row designations and numbering are not consistent so a map helps locate your assigned mooring. Transients are usually assigned in rows from J through U.

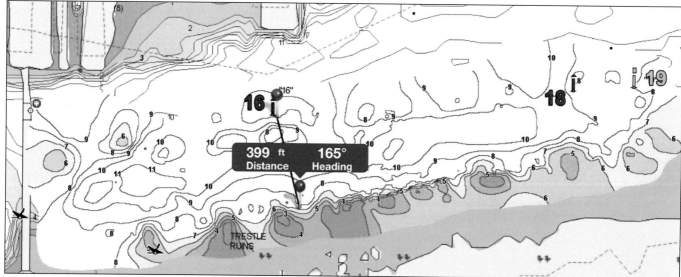

Above is a survey that I took in my dinghy. There's more room to the south of the markers than what's shown on the charts, especially south of R18 and G19. The line of shallows on the chart (dark blue) roughly corresponds to the zero-depth line on the nautical chart. Be sure to take advantage of the extra room when the anchorage is crowded. You need lights at night for traveling to the docks in your dinghy and it's enforced by the FWC; they have a training facility here. I have a red/green bow light and a white light at the aft. The FWC boating requirements are in addition to the Coast Guard list. Note that three flares are required when operating a dinghy at night. The marine organisms that foul your hull are extremely active in the harbor. If you stay more than a few days, you'll need a bottom scrub for maximum speed.

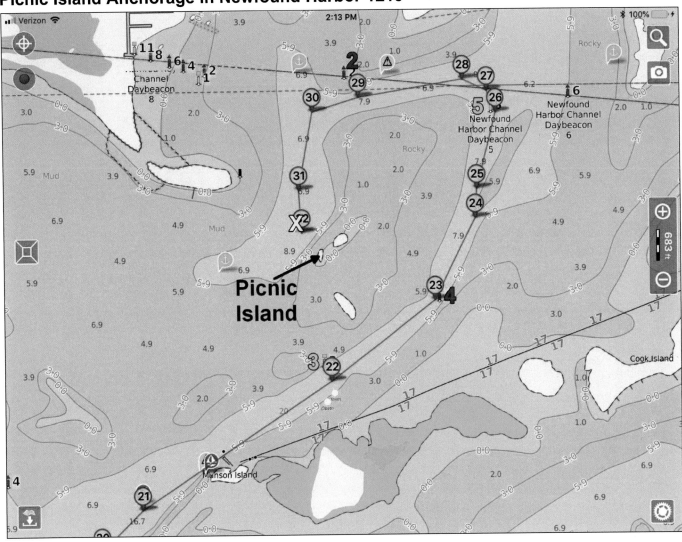

Picnic Island

We sometimes come from Caesar Creek to Newfound Harbor if Marathon is crowded and the weather allows the 90 NM trip. From Rodriguez Key, it's 66 NM and we've done that trip several times. The approach can be a little disturbing. Watch your depth carefully, as you have to take a large turn around the entrance. The chartplotter will be a big help but you may go over 7 MLLW spots along the way.

Once past the entrance, it deepens to 15 to 20 MLLW, but past R4 it gradually shallows up again. Take G5 by about 30 ft off for 5.2 MLLW. A little tide helps but I've come in on a dead low with my 4 ft 9 in keel without touching. Once past R2 at the top turn, it deepens again to 8 to 9 MLLW. The holding is good and the wave protection is better than you would expect due to nearby shallows. I've been here in 20 to 30 kt winds and felt comfortable. However, you will get wakes from passing fishing boats about half the time during the day, some will slow down, others will not. There are not many lights here, so the stars come out in force.

I haven't been here since Hurricane Irma hit the Keys. It went right over this area. I looked at Google Earth and Picnic Island is still there but I can see a lot of bare sand where there used to be vegetation.
The island is very pleasant for watching the sunset and many people will be around during the day to enjoy the island. It's a famous place for letting dogs run free.

Key West Bight Marina - Our Home Away from Home MM 1245

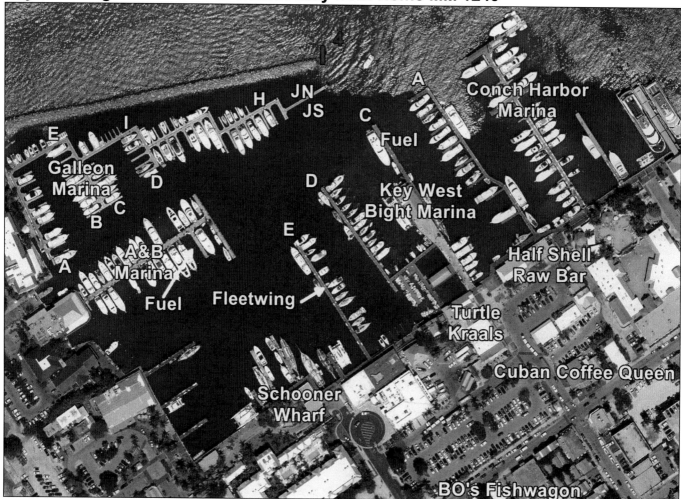

Key West is where we spend February and March each year, at a dock in the heart of Key West, 200 ft from Schooner Wharf, three blocks from Duval Street and Mallory. We have always stayed at <u>Key West Bight Marina</u>. It's run by the city of Key West and they have the lowest rates in the harbor. I have to caution you

that it's not for everyone. Where we dock, there are no fingers; you have to get off over the bow since we dock bow in. The docks are fixed at five feet high, the same height as our bow, so that's no problem for the two-footed crew members. However, Hoolie has to be carried off since he can't negotiate the bow with the jib in the way. I build a strong right arm (again) after about two weeks.

January of 2020 will be our ninth year arriving in Key West via Fleetwing and now everyone knows us. We wave, they wave, it's a friendly town. Key West has a dog park nearby for Hoolie. It's a great place for morning and afternoon walks with all the flowers and things to see. For the past few years, our kids have visited us on the boat with all the grandkids for a week at a time. What fun!

We leave at the end of March for the return trip up the ICW. It's great fun. You ought to try it sometime.

Watch that step

238

Key West Fun

To say there's a lot of things to do in Key West is an understatement. It's the end of the road for many wanderers. Every bar has live music and the number one dream seems to be to retire to Key West and support yourself with your music. It's much harder than it appears, I'm told. The list below is woefully inadequate, it's just the things we do more often than the rest.

My favorite restaurants:
- BO's Fishwagon is a food truck that moved to a corner near the marina and took root. A tree grew up around it and it has an atmosphere all its own but they have the best, pure fish sandwiches around (not smothered in so much in sauce that you can't taste the fish!)
- Cuban Coffee Queen has the best coffee in town. It's another food wagon that took root. Their Cuban sandwiches are the standard of Key West.
- Schooner Wharf and Bar. What other place has happy hour that starts at 7:00 am!! It only lasts until noon but then it starts up again from 5 to 7 pm. Having a meal while it's raining will result in a wet meal, there's no roof – as is the standard in many Key West restaurants. They always have live music and we'll watch the schedule so we don't miss our favorites.
- El Siboney offers authentic Cuban food at very reasonable prices.
- Café Sole is good if you want a sit-down meal with a French flair, nicely served. I would only recommend the fixed price menu served earlier than the normal dinner hour, call for details.
- Bien serves Caribbean and Latin food to eat outside or take back to the boat. It's excellent.

My favorite fish market for when you want to cook on the boat.
- Half Shell Fish Market. There is no competition, it's fresh and fairly priced. It's the same source that supplies all the local restaurants. The Key West pink shrimp can't be beat!

My favorite things to do:
- Walk the alleys. Key West is tropical, no frost ever. It's home to a beautiful array of flowers and trees. Just walking some of the less-traveled streets and alleys provides stunning views.
- Sunday Jazz at the Green Parrot. Sunday afternoons would not be the same without listening to jazz at the Green Parrot. There's no charge, just drop in and find something to lean against (no sniveling!)
- Listen to piano playing at the Gardens Hotel. The hotel hosts live piano playing from Wednesday through Saturday from 5 to 7 pm. There's no charge for listening but they do offer an outstanding, automated wine bar. Buy a card and chose the wine of your choice: a sip, ½ glass or a full glass.
- Fort Zachary Taylor beach. You can wander around the fort too but we go for the beach. We've spent many an afternoon there. During February, they stage a civil war encampment, fun.
- Visit Mallory Square at sunset. Of course, you have to do this, it's the archetypal Key West experience. It's great fun for people watching and, of course, the sunset!
- Just walk down Duval Street and see the sights. Key West now has a free bus that circles Duval Street so it's easy to hop the bus and get off at any place of interest, like the Green Parrot. It runs every 15 minutes until the late hours. Ann likes to visit the art galleries.
- Florida Keys Eco-Discovery Center. It's a great exhibit of local marine life and it's free.
- Key West Aquarium. It's better than it appears from looking in the front door. They have a lot of touchy-feely animals for kids. Well worth a visit.
- Nancy Forrester's Secret Garden. She rescues parrots and a visit there will amaze you with their variety and intelligence along with a commentary on their background. Our grandkids loved it!
- Old Island Days Art Festival. We never miss this. Art from all over the country is on display, free.
- Old Town Bakery. It's the place to get donuts, bread or any type of pastry, all cooked on the premises.
- Key West Tropical Forest & Botanical Garden. It's the only frost-free natural habitat on the continent. This is NOT a complete list – just what we like the most and keep coming back to.

Index

242

Made in the USA
Columbia, SC
18 May 2020